A CERTAIN IDEA OF FRANCE

PRINCETON STUDIES IN

INTERNATIONAL HISTORY AND POLITICS

Series Editors
John Lewis Gaddis
Jack L. Snyder
Richard H. Ullman

A CERTAIN IDEA OF FRANCE

FRENCH SECURITY POLICY AND
THE GAULLIST LEGACY

Philip H. Gordon

PRINCETON UNIVERSITY PRESS   PRINCETON, NEW JERSEY

Library of Congress Cataloging-in-Publication Data
Gordon, Philip H., 1962–
A certain idea of France : French security policy and the Gaullist
legacy / Philip H. Gordon
P.   cm.
Includes bibliographical references and index.
ISBN 0-691-08647-8
1. Gaulle, Charles de, 1890–1970—Influence. 2. Gaulle, Charles de,
1890–1970—Military leadership. 3. France—Foreign
relations—1945– 4. France—Military policy. 5. France—Relations—
Europe. 6. Europe—Relations—France. 7. Cold War.   I. Title
DC4420.G67   1993   92-23532
944.083'6—dc20   CIP

This book has been composed in Linotron Sabon

Princeton University Press books are printed
on acid-free paper and meet the guidelines for
permanence and durability of the Committee on
Production Guidelines for Book Longevity
of the Council on Library Resources

Printed in the United States of America

1   3   5   7   9   10   8   6   4   2

For Rachel

Toute ma vie, je me suis fait une certaine idée de la France.
—Charles de Gaulle, *Mémoires de guerre*, vol. 1, *l'Appel*

Contents

List of Tables

THE AIM in this book is much more than to analyze French national security policies in the 1970s, 1980s, and early 1990s, although it is an attempt to do that. Rather, my primary objective has been to try to place French security policies in the overall philosophical and political framework—the Gaullist framework—that has guided them for more than thirty years. I have sought to understand how, why, and to what extent Gaullist thinking influenced French policy since General de Gaulle left power in 1969, and I have attempted to assess the positive and negative consequences of that influence for France, for Europe, and for the United States. With the Cold War now over and with France at a crossroads where its foreign and security policies are concerned, it seems more important than ever to understand the roots of those policies and, thereby, the prospects for their continuity or change.

When I completed my initial research and a first draft of this study in late 1989, a number of conclusions about Gaullist influences on French security policy had emerged. De Gaulle's ideas, it seemed clear, had heavily influenced French national security decisions, and despite some fundamental changes—including multiple army reorganizations, an Atlantic rapprochement, changes in military doctrine, and the development of a more autonomous European defense—French security policy at the end of the 1980s could still fairly be described as "Gaullist." French leaders throughout the 1970s and the 1980s continued to maintain the ideal of autonomy of decision, defend the theoretical independence of the *force de frappe,* avoid any new or explicit commitments to third-country security, refuse participation in any sort of integrated military command structure, manufacture and procure the vast majority of French weapons in France, and claim for France an exceptional status and special global role. The "Gaullist model," initially questioned by military experts and berated by the political opposition, had become accepted across the entire political spectrum, was being implemented by de Gaulle's former opponents on the Left, and had become the basis for a relative "national defense consensus" in France. One need only compare the main elements of French security policy in the late 1980s to those of France's neighbors to see just how particular, indeed just how "Gaullist," French policy had remained.

It was also clear by the end of the 1980s, however, that Gaullist policies were becoming increasingly difficult for France to maintain. Not only did Gaullist ambitions leave France with a wide range of security commitments, including an expensive nuclear force, the most diversified armed forces in Europe, and military bases around the world, but a changing military balance in Europe made it more important than ever that France increase its commitment on the Continent itself. As the Soviet Union pursued a massive military buildup during the 1970s and 1980s, and as the credibility of the U.S. nuclear guarantee (which had facilitated Gaullist policies in the first place) continued to decline, a greater French military contribution to European defense became increasingly imperative. With the political and economic integration of the European Community proceeding apace, American fiscal problems raising questions about the United States' military role in Europe, and France's own military budgets strained under the burdens of its grandiose ambitions, the Gaullist model was clearly under strain. By the end of 1988, the political, diplomatic, military, and fiscal tensions always inherent in French security policy had reached a peak, and it was legitimate to wonder how long the continuities of the past could last.

The answer to that question, of course, will now never be known. The geopolitical earthquakes that shook Europe between 1989 and 1992 have dramatically changed the longstanding security situation of all European countries, and many of the old questions and dilemmas have changed along with them; France need no longer worry, for example, about the adequacy of its contribution on the "central front." But although the revolutions of 1989 have certainly altered the environment in which French security policy is made, they have by no means absolved the French of the dilemma over what to think about and how to adapt the defense structures they inherited from de Gaulle. On the contrary, the interaction of traditional Gaullist practices with present French security policy seems as interesting and important as ever, and the lessons of the past are still highly relevant. Rather than toss aside my 1989 manuscript as yet another research project undermined by international change or simply conclude it as a piece of historical research, it has seemed all the more important to bring it up-to-date.

Part 3 of this book is an attempt to do so. In it, I address some of the new questions now facing France and ask whether the continuities discerned from the Gaullist years through the end of the Cold War are still present today. To what extent have French security policies remained "Gaullist" during the first few years of the post–Cold War era? What are the prospects that Gaullist influences will endure? Is the new Europe very much like the one de Gaulle foresaw (and for which he tried to prepare France), or has the Cold War been replaced by a cold shower, one that will shock the French into realizing their Gaullist policies have become hopelessly out-of-date? As analysts consider possible European security arrangements for the twenty-first century, the question of whether French security policy goals and practices will remain "Gaullist" or not seems far from academic.

How does this book fit into the existing literature about Charles de Gaulle, about France, and about French security policy? The scholarly and analytical work of my predecessors can be divided into two relatively neat types. On one hand, scholarship is extensive scholarship on de Gaulle himself and on the background, ideas, and guiding principles of this compelling twentieth-century figure. De Gaulle embodied a rare combination of intellect and action and left his mark on an era; the study of his general ideas has been prolific. The second type comprises studies of evolving French military policies and doctrines. These works generally focus on military means, organization, and doctrine and assess their implications for European security or for the Atlantic Alliance. This book is an attempt to integrate the two classes of study, to use the product of the former to provide background and insight into the questions posed by the latter.

Studies of Gaullism and de Gaulle himself are not only extremely numerous but also exceptionally rich.[1] Their conclusions vary greatly, and I have drawn much from them for my own interpretation of Gaullist ideas. I have obviously used many of these works—of which the most fundamental for me have been those by Raymond Aron, Alfred Grosser, Stanley Hoffmann, Edward Kolodziej, Jean Lacouture, and Jean Touchard—as a basis for my own.[2] I do not pretend to have broken new ground in Gaullist scholarship or even to have made a significant contribution to it. Instead, I have relied on this earlier scholarship to reach some of my own conclusions about the sources, meaning, and consequences of Gaullist ideas.

Another group of analysts have focused less on de Gaulle and more on French military policies themselves. These observers have, of course, not overlooked the rather obvious Gaullist influence on French security policy, but they have placed less emphasis on its intellectual roots. The purpose of this second type of study is usually not to interpret de Gaulle but to analyze French policy in various security-related areas such as arms control, nuclear deterrence policy, and conventional military doctrine. Excellent analyses of this sort can be found from writers such as François Heisbourg, Robbin Laird, Pierre Lellouche, Diego Ruiz-Palmer, and David Yost.[3] More easily outdated than broader interpretations of Gaullist ideas, these analyses are complemented by frequent assessments of French military posture, often by French military officials themselves, in *Défense nationale, Politique étrangère, Politique internationale, Survival,* and other such publications.

Because of de Gaulle's obvious importance and influence on French security policy, the fusion of these two types of study seems to suggest itself naturally. Indeed, the relationship between Gaullist ideas and later policy is *implicit* in nearly all analyses of the French military picture. Yet, despite the topic's significance and the surfeit of rhetoric and debate it has spawned, few have looked directly at the implications of Gaullist thinking for French strategy and at the specific limits and constraints it has set on French policy.

Of those who have addressed these questions, Michael Harrison—for whom I had the privilege of working as a research assistant in the mid-1980s—was one of the first to study the logic and influence of Gaullist policies in a changing international context, and his own synthetic study remains one of the best to date. In *The Reluctant Ally*, Harrison accurately identified trends that have proven to be lasting ones, and his observations about the viability of France's flexible alliance membership have only been reinforced over the years. But Harrison's study of "France and Atlantic Security" was written before the three experiences that have provided the greatest and most interesting tests of the Gaullist legacy: the coming to power of a Socialist government from 1981–1986; the "cohabitation" experiment from 1986–1988; and, of course, the European revolutions that have taken place since 1989. Primarily a study of France's alliance relations during the Gaullist years, Harrison's book devotes only 32 of its 304 pages to the years since 1974. It seems natural and important to undertake a complementary study that includes the pivotal subsequent years.

This book, therefore, is both an analysis of French military policies, doctrines, organizations, and budgets from the 1960s to the 1990s and an inquiry into how and why Gaullist ideas influenced French security policy during those years. Underlying this analysis, however, is a third and final objective of this study that may be the most important of all: to ask whether the Gaullist security legacy can serve as an opportunity for the future or whether it is instead destined to be a constraint. Does the Gaullist legacy imply clinging to narrowly defined national sovereignty or can it be a source of self-confidence for the future? Should the French understand it as a call to maximize French independence for its own sake or as a means to ensure French interests in an interdependent world? In the end, will the French emphasize those elements of the Gaullist legacy that have led to jealousies, resentment, and division or those that have helped create a capable and ambitious military power interested in a leading European role? Can the Gaullist legacy be divided into such positive and negative elements or is it, like the French Revolution for Clemenceau, an indivisible "bloc?"

The issue of de Gaulle's national security legacy has now become one of those great intellectual debates for which the French have a passion. Patrick McCarthy has likened this debate to that of medieval philosophers over angels and pins and has suggested that whether French policies have been "Gaullist" or not may not matter much at all.[4] But the question of continuity and change since de Gaulle is, in fact, far from insignificant. Knowing the degree to which French policymakers really accept the basic principles of Gaullist defense doctrine can probably help analysts understand better the most likely evolution of security policy in France. De Gaulle's own Gaullism was a complex and very forceful set of ideas, encompassed in a worldview whose concepts of humanity, society, states, and history carried heavy implications for policy. That French leaders should share that worldview would obviously have different consequences for French policy than if they should not. More than twenty years after de Gaulle's death, and in a world that has changed dramatically from the one in which the General made policy, the French are faced with the challenge of deciding what to do with, and how best to use, their Gaullist legacy. Studying how they have used it until now may help us understand how they might do so in the future.

Acknowledgments

I HAVE accumulated many debts during the preparation of this book and would like to acquit some of them here. First, I would like to thank my professor, adviser, colleague, and friend, David Calleo, who not only taught me more than I can adequately acknowledge in this space but who showed unwavering confidence in my ability to tackle such a challenging subject. Without his advice, time, and example, this project would be incomplete.

Three other scholars also deserve particular mention. Patrick McCarthy not only knows more about France than perhaps anyone I know but seems to know an equal amount about just about everything else—from interest rate differentials to Gramsci. The late Michael Harrison, one of the first to help me get this project underway, was another obvious inspiration: I can only hope my study is a worthy attempt to follow up on his. And Alfred Grosser, my research supervisor at the Institut d'Etudes Politiques in Paris, was willing not only to share with me his insights on France, Germany, and Europe but taught me to be sensitive to the way politics and policies are perceived across borders and cultures.

I would also like to thank Hugh Aller, Dana Allin, Jörg Boche, Frédéric Bozo, Anton DePorte, Julius Friend, John Lewis Gaddis, Gabriele Haasen, Pierre Hassner, Erik Jones, Edward Kolodziej, Jocelyn Mason, Simon Serfaty, Steven Szabo, and Richard Ullman, who have all read, commented on, or otherwise contributed to this work. (I alone, of course, am entirely responsible for its content.) Numerous French officials past and present took time out of their busy schedules for me and deserve gratitude and recognition even if not by name. A generous grant from the Bosch Foundation allowed me to study French-German relations and to revise my manuscript while a fellow at the American Institute for Contemporary German Studies in Washington, D.C., and a travel grant from the Nuclear History Program (for a different project) facilitated a final research trip to Paris. I researched much of chapter 7 during the summer of 1991 while I was at the RAND Corporation, and I would like to thank RAND for allowing me draw on that work here. Portions of chapter 7 are from my RAND report, *French Security Policy after the Cold War*, which is cited in the bibliography.

Anyone who has undertaken a major research project knows that the support of family and friends is as important as intellectual and administrative support. My parents gave me the opportunity to study and travel in Europe in the first place and deserve an expression of great appreciation for that and for the countless other ways in which they have helped along the way. A number of good friends, some of whom I have known since long before I even heard of de Gaulle, have also provided necessary backing and diversion. Most importantly, I surely could not have completed this project without my wife, Rachel. She is much more interested in French cooking than in French defense policy and would not want any long, sentimental dedication. But her support, patience, and affection throughout this whole experience have been unfailing, and so I dedicate it to her anyway.

List of Abbreviations

ACDA	United States Arms Control and Disarmament Agency
ACE	Allied Command Europe
AFCENT	Allied Forces Central Europe
ASLP	Air-sol Longue Portée (Long-range air-launched missile)
ASMP	Air-sol Moyenne Portée (Medium-range air-launched missile)
AWACS	Airborne Warning And Control System
CDU	Christlich-Demokratische Union (Christian Democratic Union, Germany)
CERES	Centre d'Etudes, de Recherches, et d'Education Socialiste
CIR	Convention des Institutions Républicaines (Convention of Republican Institutions, center-Left French political group until merger with *PS* in 1971)
CSA	Conseils-Sondages-Analyses (French polling organization)
CSCE	Conference on Security and Cooperation in Europe
CSU	Christlich-Soziale Union (Christian Social Union, Germany)
DOT	Défense Opérationelle du Territoire (Territorial Defense Operations, for defense of French homeland)
EC	European Communities
EDC	European Defense Community
EEC	European Economic Community
EMS	European Monetary System
EPC	European Political Cooperation
FAR	Force d'Action Rapide (Rapid Action Force)
FATAC	Force Aérienne Tactique (Tactical Air Force)
FNS	Force Nucléaire Stratégique (Strategic Nuclear Force)
FOST	Force Océanique Stratégique (France's nuclear submarine fleet)
FRG	Federal Republic of Germany
GDP	Gross Domestic Product (total value of goods and services produced within national borders)
GNP	Gross National Product (total value of goods and services produced by citizens of the country, regardless of where value is added)
HOT	Haut subsonique, guidage optique, lancement par tube (French anti-tank missile)

ICBM	Intercontinental Ballistic Missile
IFOP	Institut Français d'Opinion Publique
IHEDN	Institut des Hautes Etudes de Défense Nationale (Institute of Advanced Studies of National Defense, French national war college)
IISS	International Institute for Strategic Studies
INF	Intermediate-Range Nuclear Forces
IRBM	Intermediate-Range Ballistic Missile
LDP	Landing Platform Dock
MIRV	Multiple Independently Targetable Reentry Vehicle
MLF	Multilateral Force
MRP	Mouvement Républicain Populaire (Popular Republican Movement, French Christian Democratic party)
NACC	North Atlantic Cooperation Council
NATO	North Atlantic Treaty Organization
NORTHAG	Northern Army Group (NATO)
NPS	Nouveau Parti Socialiste
OECD	Organization of Economic Cooperation and Development
PCF	Parti Communiste Français
PIBm	Produit intérieur brut marchand (market gross domestic product, total gross value of goods and services including value added tax)
PS	Parti Socialiste (France's Socialist party)
RPF	Rassemblement pour la France (Rally for France, Gaullist political movement of 1947–1952)
RPR	Rassemblement pour la République (Rally for the Republic, French political party descendent of de Gaulle)
RRC	Rapid Reaction Corps (NATO)
SACEUR	Supreme Allied Commander Europe
SAM	Surface-to-air Missile
SDI	Strategic Defense Initiative
SFIO	Section Française de l'Internationale Ouvrière (French Section of the Workers' International, name of French Socialist party until 1971)
SHAPE	Supreme Headquarters Allied Powers Europe
SIRPA	Service d'Information et de Relations Publiques des Armées (French Army Public Relations Service)
SLBM	Submarine-Launched Ballistic Missile
SNF	Short-Range Nuclear Forces
SOFRES	Société Française d'Enquêtes et de Sondages (French Polling Organization)
SPD	Sozialdemokratische Partei Deutschlands (Social Democratic party, Germany)

SSBN	Nuclear-Fuelled Ballistic Missile Submarine
TNW	Tactical Nuclear Weapons
UDF	Union pour la Démocratie Française (Union for French Democracy, center-Right French political coalition)
WEU	Western European Union

Something will be left of Gaullism even after de Gaulle, but what?
and how much?
—Alexander Werth, *De Gaulle* (1965), p. 9

Is Gaullism the work of one man . . . or does de Gaulle express a coherent
doctrine adapted to the needs of our time? If the latter is true,
Gaullism has every chance of surviving to influence the future.
—Robert Aron, *An Explanation of de Gaulle* (1966), p. 175

In foreign policy, France without de Gaulle would probably
still be Gaullist.
—David P. Calleo, *Europe's Future* (1965), p. 160

No study of France in the Gaullist era can avoid. . .asking if his place
in the history books of tomorrow will be that of a man who changed the
course of history, or merely that of a brilliant parenthesis.
—Stanley Hoffmann, *Decline or Renewal?* (1974), p. ix

France, the only West European nuclear power along with
Great Britain, present on five oceans and four continents, has chosen
to ensure her security by herself to guarantee her independence and
maintain her identity. . . . The choice of an independent defense,
based on a strategy of autonomous deterrence and accepted by a large
majority of our compatriots, permits her to affirm a will
to defense that is, moreover, uncontested.
—*Loi de programmation militaire pour les années 1990–1993*, preface

Part One

THE GAULLIST YEARS

CHAPTER ONE

Perspectives on de Gaulle

THE VERY distinctive elements of the Gaullist model for French national security—the absolute need for independence in decision making, a refusal to accept subordination to the United States, the search for grandeur and *rang*, the primacy of the nation-state, and the importance of national defense—can be explained in a number of different ways. Some authors have seen Gaullist principles as primarily pedagogical tools, meant to reinstill spirit in a tired old country and to inspire the French.[1] Others believe that Gaullist goals such as French independence and prestige were not necessarily means toward such an end but were for de Gaulle ends themselves, values that needed no other justification.[2] Still others have tended to attribute Gaullist principles and policies to the personal objectives of the ambitious General himself.[3]

Debates about these various explanations have gone on for years and, happily, need not be resolved here; this study is more concerned with the consequences of Gaullist policies than with their origins. Nonetheless, it would be impossible to discuss the legacy and merits of Gaullist security policies without some sense of the ideas that were behind them. Particularly in the United States, where Gaullist thinking has generally been a subject of great incomprehension, it seems useful to ask some basic questions about why Gaullist policies were what they were. How did General de Gaulle see the world? and Why did that lead him to act as he did? What were the intellectual and emotional roots behind Gaullist ideas about France and national security? Why was de Gaulle so obsessed with France's status? and Why did he insist French defense be "independent"? It is not necessary here to attempt a conclusive interpretation of this rather colossal figure (a task Jean Lacouture has rightly likened to climbing a mountain),[4] but it does seem useful to reconsider de Gaulle's views on some topics (such as the nature of change, the nation-state, French exceptionalism, and national independence) that are fundamental to understanding his worldview and its influence upon the French.

WHY START WITH DE GAULLE?

One of the central questions posed in this study is whether the Gaullist objectives of French national independence and grandeur have been compatible with that of European security. It asks whether de Gaulle's national security legacy has been in the French and European interest and how de Gaulle's ideas and policies influenced the ideas and policies of his successors. To frame the French security dilemma in this manner, however, presupposes the Gaullist era to be a logical starting point, a model with which to compare later French policies. It implies, possibly perpetuating the Gaullist myth of a Fourth Republic indentured to the West and voluntarily dissolving itself into a hybrid "Europe," that de Gaulle's resistance to superpower hegemony and assertion of French independence was a wholesale break with the past, a sort of founding act (or to critics, an original sin). It begs a number of questions about continuity and change: How much continuity can be identified between the policies of de Gaulle's predecessors—the leaders of the vilified Fourth Republic—and those of the General himself after 1959? Was present policy not simply "French" before it was "Gaullist"? Can we not trace "Gaullist" policies and aspirations back at least as far as the Treaty of Versailles—if not back to Napoleon or Louis XIV? Why begin this study with de Gaulle?

To be sure, the particular security policies of French governments after 1958 did not emerge from nowhere. Numerous analysts have shown the considerable similarities between the expressed security interests and policies of de Gaulle's Fifth Republic and those of the preceding period.[5] The Fourth Republic was not the incompetent, lackey regime depicted by de Gaulle but was similarly resentful of the policies of the Atlantic Alliance and, like de Gaulle, sought to use what leverage it could to assert France's role in the world. The policies developed and pursued in France in the 1960s, now so readily identified as "Gaullist," in fact have roots that were clearly planted in the years that preceded the General's return to power. Fourth Republic leaders had to make national security policy in the same bipolar world and divided Europe as de Gaulle would, a world in which French prominence, like that of other European states, was drastically reduced. Their strategic choices in this environment—an anchor in the NATO Alliance, solidifying Western Europe to resist the Communist East—were inevitably dictated by the compelling circumstances of the period but were no less influenced by the particular French desires of national revival, the maintenance of a global role, and influence on, if not freedom from, the dominant United States. Attempts to assert these traditional and particular French aspirations were manifest from the early days of the Western Alliance: the insistence on including "Algerian departments" in the protected zone of the 1949 NATO treaty; the proposals and demands of various French governments for tripartite (with Britain and the United States) direction of the alliance; the constant insistence on military superiority in continental Europe, especially over a reconstructing Germany; the efforts, regardless of cost, to maintain overseas colonies and influence abroad; and, finally, the decisions taken toward the creation of a national nuclear program and strategic nuclear force were all areas in which France refused to accept lightly the developing status quo as directed by Washington. Admittedly, the French Fourth Republic was far from able to execute the stubbornly independent policy propagated by de Gaulle, and its tolerance for subordination was certainly much greater than the General's. But the impression that French leaders during these years had forgotten France's grand past and former world role and were now happily indentured to the United States and NATO is no more than a rather superficial, and sometimes convenient, myth. Just as post-Gaullist leaders have not called into question the fundamental decisions of the Gaullist years, the Fifth Republic did not raze the foundation left to it by the Fourth but built on it.

But if all this is true, Why start with de Gaulle? Why assess present French policies in the light of Gaullist ideas and doctrines if these represent nothing more than continuity themselves? The answer should become clear in the analysis of the security policies of the Gaullist period that forms part 1 in this book. The Gaullist years may not represent an entirely new era in the history of France, but in a number of ways, they set a standard for continuity and change.

De Gaulle's worldview and political priorities implied a very specific set of rules for national policy, and his conviction was instrumental in the realization of some of the very same goals that had escaped previous French governments. True, the leaders of the Fourth Republic prefigured de Gaulle in their resistance to American hegemony, in their broad conception of France's international interests, and in their claims to a share of the leadership of the Atlantic Alliance. But it was not until the Gaullist era that these diverse aspirations were translated into a coherent overall policy and were backed by sufficient political means and will. The security policy of the Fourth Republic was marked by vacillation, indecision, and an unwillingness or inability to take risks. The governing parties of the regime's weak coalitions were slaves to those coalitions and could never put together the political combinations necessary to assert their aims and to challenge the international status quo, even when they felt it was in their interests to do so. It was only with the advent of the Fifth Republic—with its strong executive, new constitution, and charismatic leader—that these loosely scattered goals were formulated and could be executed. De Gaulle did somewhat more than "symbolize and accelerate trends that could not be stopped," as historian Paul Kennedy has justly written.[6] He also gave those trends a rather significant boost, endowed France with the means to see that they were fulfilled, and convinced his successors that his own goals were the proper ones for France to pursue.

No one can easily deny the continued influence of Gaullist ideas, policies, and practices over French security policy from 1969 to 1989. Whatever one thinks of the particular road France has taken in its European and alliance policies since the 1960s, it is clear that those policies have been determined to a great extent by the Gaullist worldview and that they would have been very different had de Gaulle not come to power in 1958. If Charles de Gaulle's vision of France's defense was in many ways a continuation of the vision of the Fourth Republic, and if some Gaullist aspirations were echoes of French goals from before that, the Gaullist years are still fundamentally unique, and their legacy has been lasting, clearly definable, and highly consequential. The Gaullist years represent a crystallization of traditional French attitudes toward national security into a coherent, well-articulated and largely implemented doctrine. To study the ideas of Charles de Gaulle in the context of this book, then, is not to "personalize" the policies of an entire nation but simply to recognize the inordinate role of a single individual on those policies. De Gaulle shaped French policy in ways that probably cannot be reversed, and it would be wrong to see his tenure as merely one more episode, albeit a remarkable one, in the recent history of France.

DE GAULLE AND CHANGE: THE PROVISORY AND THE PERMANENT

One of the most important lessons from a close reading of de Gaulle is the emphasis that he placed upon the importance of particular circumstances and the need to understand the nature of change. Despite his historical reputation for intransigence and stubbornness, de Gaulle the statesman had a remarkable capacity to adapt to an evolving environment. It is often said that de Gaulle was pragmatic, that he held to certain broad principles but was flexible in their application. What seems more accurate, and indeed more important, is that de Gaulle was able to evolve in his ideas as well as in his tactics. To be sure, the "man of June 18," isolated in his refusal to accept the "inevitable" in 1940, was scarcely one to let the course of events inflect his views or his comportment where France was concerned. But he was also too aware of the force and limits of circumstances, and too intelligent, to resist the "winds of change" when their course was obvious and when the stake was something less than the survival of France. De Gaulle was not always the Don Quixote figure he sometimes seemed, all too ready to throw reality to the wind and challenge the inevitable. He knew what he ultimately would have to accept and when he had to accept it. This capacity, moreover, was an important element in de Gaulle's own philosophical worldview, for that view presupposed a highly dynamic world where success required perpetual adaptation to changing circumstances.

Some things on the international stage, like nations and peoples, were close to eternal for de Gaulle. "France," he wrote in his *Mémoires d'espoir* (Memoirs of hope), "comes from the depths of time."[7] But most things, like governments, individual leaders, or political ideas, continually come and go over the years. De Gaulle's use of language itself indicated this belief: he consistently spoke of *"les Gaulois," "les Germains,"* and *"les Russes"* rather than their most recent manifestations and seemed to dismiss the ultimate importance of the regimes that for him were "presently in power." The Soviet Union, the German Democratic Republic (GDR), and even the Federal Republic of Germany were only temporary representations of the eternal peoples of Europe.[8] One of the General's favorite ways of prefacing his remarks, "Things being as they are in the world as it is" is the classic expression of this attention to context and emphasis on circumstances. He said it most clearly in his *Mémoires de guerre* (War memoirs): "In the incessant movement of the world, all doctrines, all schools, all rebellions have only one time."[9] Like his father, the history teacher, Charles de Gaulle was well aware of the constant evolution of events that perpetually changed the world.

Such respect for change and adaptability is evident from early in de Gaulle's career and is clearly foreshadowed in his early writings. One of the principal arguments in his first book, *La discorde chez l'ennemi* (Discord among the enemy, 1924), for example, was that the German military in World War I, by holding on too tightly to its winning doctrines of 1866 and 1870, had lost its chance to win the Great War. The French, too, had almost lost by trying to revive the *offensive à outrance* that had prevailed among the breech-loading rifles and cavalries of 1870 but was fantastically inappropriate in a war of trenches and heavy artillery. This, of course, was fundamentally the same critique—reversed this time—that de Gaulle would later make against the French military in *Vers l'armée de métier* (Toward the professional army, 1934): by failing to assess the present circumstances, which called for armored mechanized divisions capable of taking the offensive, French military commanders held on to a doctrine that was no longer germane to events. And as de Gaulle argued in *Le fil de l'épée* (The edge of the sword, 1932), both warfare and diplomacy were constantly changing. The Cartesian French mind sought clarity and order, and ceaselessly tried to construct a priori doctrines. But invariably, those doctrines failed to take account of the changing circumstances that were supposed to have guided them in the first place.[10]

As a national leader, de Gaulle was mindful of his own principles, and his foreign policies showed great sensitivity to changing global conditions over the decades. Take, for example, de Gaulle's position on French overseas colonies—"the Empire." Never in the General's long life did he change his view on the importance of French grandeur and the destiny of

France's global role. But he was not blind to the fact that World War II released forces in the colonies that could not be contained, even with all the political will he might muster among his compatriots. For this nationalist soldier to preside over the transformation of the empire and become the sponsor of Algerian independence was an extraordinary homage to his willingness to adapt.[11]

Another striking example of de Gaulle's sensitivity to circumstances was the evolution of his thinking about Germany. After World War II, of course, de Gaulle was vehemently opposed to the recreation of a centralized German state, and he sought strong guarantees and heavy reparations for France. Three times during the past seventy years, after all, France had been invaded from the east, and de Gaulle himself had fought in two Franco-German wars. In the first, he was wounded twice and taken prisoner, and in the second, he saw his homeland defeated, occupied, and embarrassed by Germans. As the leader of the Rassemblement pour la France (RPF) in the late 1940s, de Gaulle thus demanded (with the support of most of his fellow citizens) that the old German Reich be "dismembered," that the Rhineland be demilitarized or detached from the rest of Germany, and that the Ruhr be given an international status, with France to receive some of its coal.[12]

By 1958, however—after nearly one decade of successful democracy, the honorable leadership of Chancellor Adenauer, the creation of a West German army, and the Federal Republic's membership in NATO and the European Economic Community (EEC)—de Gaulle knew the Federal Republic could not be broken up or demilitarized. He recognized that geographic truncation, military guarantees, and Germany's outright subordination were just not going to happen, and rather than continue to seek assurances against France's *"ennemi héréditaire,"* de Gaulle chose instead to embrace it. By 1959 he had made Franco-German reconciliation the cornerstone of his European policy and was calling reunification "the normal destiny of the German people."[13] Given de Gaulle's own personal experiences and past perspectives, the importance of this particular adaptation cannot be overstated.

De Gaulle also evolved where conditions dictated change by recognizing the "great civilization" of China (whereas he had previously denounced the "yellow hordes"), by understanding the revolutionary nature of nuclear weapons earlier than most, and by accepting and taking advantage of the Common Market he had once rejected. No one has put it better or more concisely than Raymond Aron, "[De Gaulle] had the intelligence to renounce his conceptions when they were overcome by events."[14]

To impute to de Gaulle a rigid and unchanging view of the world is, thus, to overlook a key element of French policy during the first decade of

the Fifth Republic. Gaullist policies, no matter how stubbornly implemented, no matter how forcefully defended, were based on a careful and,
it must be admitted, often very perspicacious assessment of the global
context and how it had developed. From the perspective of the 1990s, the
value of such a dynamic view of history has only been reconfirmed. The
point has obvious implications for France today.

DE GAULLE AND THE NATION-STATE IN EUROPE

It is not very original—but it is surely accurate—to say that at the heart
of de Gaulle's worldview was his concept of the nation-state. As de Gaulle
himself put it, "Nothing is more important than the legitimacy, the institutions and the functioning of the State."[15] Where European security and
defense are concerned, the most important observation that emerges from
this view has been a potential incompatibility between the requirements
of a great and independent state and those of a cooperative, interdependent one. Especially in postwar Europe, where formerly great nation-states
no longer seemed viable in a bipolar world and where security was no
longer a question of uniquely national military capabilities, the Gaullist
concept of the nation-state came under strain. Truly independent national
policies, and particularly the special role and interests for France claimed
by de Gaulle, did not seem to fit with the integration and military cooperation viewed as necessary by France's neighbors or by the governments of
the Fourth Republic.

De Gaulle's emphasis on independence and jealous guarding of French
sovereignty were, in fact, the most fundamental source of conflict within
Western Europe and with the United States during the Gaullist years. The
legacy of these quarrels has not lost its force. If a state claimed the unin-
hibited right to decide for itself, how could the European Community—
based on compromise and consensus—function? How could the Atlantic
Alliance, the hierarchical organization of military resources, be effective?
If a state had to have rights equal to all others, such as the right to nuclear
weapons or to be free from foreign troops, what did that imply for the
Federal Republic of Germany? Finally, how could Europe, made up of
separate nation-states, ever pool its resources to assume responsibility for
its own defense, a goal de Gaulle always claimed as his own?

The national independence that might have seemed unexceptional for
one state in isolation thus caused thorny problems in a system of closely
interdependent states. France's independence under de Gaulle was being
achieved at the expense of its allies. What was in the interest of one actor
(in this case France) was not necessarily good for the whole (Europe or
the West). De Gaulle's France, it seemed, was like the delinquent hunter

in Rousseau's metaphorical stag hunt. France was choosing to kill a rabbit for its own dinner while the stag that might have fed everybody got away. There seemed to be a contradiction between Gaullist nationalism and the practical requirements of the Europe de Gaulle claimed to support. Why, despite all this, did de Gaulle believe the nation-state still to be so important and so difficult (indeed, impossible) to replace?

De Gaulle justified his concept of the nation-state in terms of legitimacy and efficacy. The nation-state was morally fundamental because it was the only entity that legitimately represented the people who felt attached to it, and it was practically fundamental because it was the only political community that could effectively serve a society's interest. Any other political organization, de Gaulle believed, would leave that society vulnerable to the domination of an outside power (a Piedmont, a Prussia, or, now, the United States) or to the will of foreign technocrats (such as those in Brussels) who had no legitimate base of support. De Gaulle's view was that only the nation-state had both the legitimacy necessary to govern and the practical ability to do so.

Legitimacy, for de Gaulle, was born in history. Nations, especially in long-civilized Europe, were "very different from one another, [each one with] its own soul, its own history, its own language, its own misfortunes, glories and ambitions."[16] Their individual qualities, defects, and habits were clearly delineated and could not be made over or quickly changed. The structures created by those nations—nation-states—were, therefore, the recipients of historical legitimacy. As the state, moreover, had throughout history been the entity responsible for national defense, itself the state's raison d'être, only it could claim the ultimate right to take the vital decisions of government. "If a government were thus to lose its essential responsibility [national defense], it would lose, at the same time, its justification."[17]

Thus, states were "the only entities that have the right to order and the authority to act."[18] They were legitimate because they, more than any other entity, "were based on the interest and the feeling of the nation."[19] For centuries, people had felt bonded to their particular nations, and the nation-state was the apparatus to which they looked for leadership, order, and security. Artificially created communities (such as the Soviet Union), without historical legitimacy, would never have internal support.

National legitimacy thus came primarily from the respect and support of citizens for their *patrie* and the affinity they felt for their compatriots. This was an argument similar to the nationalist theories of nineteenth-century French thinkers like Hippolyte Taine, Numas Denis Fustel de Coulanges, and Ernest Renan, as well as of nationalist republicans like Giuseppe Mazzini. People naturally seek a community in which they feel comfortable and to which they will be loyal in exchange for this comfort. They have a common sense of belonging and share history, religion, language, and tradition. They have made similar sacrifices for this community and are prepared to make others. This, in fact, was the very definition of a nation as such thinkers understood it.[20]

Such loyalty, or civic duty, is impossible where the community is vague, heterogeneous, or lacking the unity that a nation-state can provide. It would be impossible to build a lasting political community on a multinational entity and expect it to function or survive. Thus, only a state—and only a democratic one because it provides for the expression of a people's "general will"—legitimately represents the people whose support it requires.

Nation-states had this primary role to de Gaulle, though, not only because they were legitimate representatives and valid actors but also because they were the only actors capable of real achievement. It was a simple matter of organization and authority: the state was the only unit that could act with sufficient power, authority, and skill. Other organizations could certainly produce similar bureaucracies, but none, without the cohesion that history had delegated to the nation-state and the popular loyalty that was necessary to support it, could ever effectively act in those great matters on which government must decide. Governments sometimes had to make very difficult, unpopular decisions, and they could only do so if they were founded upon popular legitimacy and consent. In de Gaulle's own words, supranational organizations "have their technical value, but they do not have, they cannot have, political authority, and consequently, political efficacy."[21] For Charles de Gaulle, not only was the nation-state the only legitimate representative of individuals and social groups but only the nation-state could effectively act in their interests.

These general points about the nation-state had a particular implication for the French case because of France's weak position, and weak state, after World War II. The French had lived through a period of enormous difficulty and even embarrassment and needed more than the bland, divided leadership of the political parties. The Third Republic had fallen in defeat and disgrace, and now the Fourth was built on a weak constitution whose ratification had only been supported by a minority of the French. Could such a France ever expect to climb back into the first echelon on nations—let alone provide for its most basic national interests like security—with "integration" as its highest motivating goal?

For de Gaulle, supranational integration was a process, not an end in itself, and it was used by its advocates as a smokescreen for inaction. It would not amount to a regeneration of Western European states but, rather, lead to relinquishing the ability to defend their interests. Not only would France lose its ability to act if it were integrated into a European federation but so would the other European states as well. An inevitably artificial federation in Europe, de Gaulle believed, would lead either to an entity in which nothing would get done, or worse, one that would be dominated from the outside, that is, by the United States. De Gaulle preferred a France capable, if necessary, of acting alone to a federal Europe whose lack of consensus or authority would risk leading, he believed, to the absence of any policy at all.

The "Europeans" in France, committed to the supranational community opposed by de Gaulle, of course disagreed, and their response to de Gaulle is worth considering. To them, the French could better preserve themselves and their state by combining their resources with those of others. Using logic opposite to that of de Gaulle, it was by *failing* to do so that they risked disappearing as major actors in the world. As Alfred Grosser asked in 1961, "Why not add [France's] weakness to that of others to create a common strength, capable of thwarting one superpower's threat and inspiring the other's respect?"[22] The "Europeans" denied the Gaullist charge that they wanted to give up the dream of a restored and more powerful Europe and argued instead that they were merely at odds over how to get there. For them, if Europeans wanted to demonstrate their independence vis-à-vis the superpowers (de Gaulle's own objectives), it was only by joining their nation-states that they could do so, not by reinforcing them.

De Gaulle's conviction that the nation-state remained the primary and most legitimate actor in world affairs put him squarely in conflict not only with his political opponents but also with some of the ideas developing in the emerging field of international relations theory. Many theorists were beginning to argue that the world system based on nation-states since the Treaty of Westphalia in 1648 was coming to an end. The post–World War II era would be increasingly influenced by transnational, or even "supranational," organizations. Already, before World War II, a number of writers were postulating the demise of the nation-state, arguing along with Pierre Drieu La Rochelle that "the era of nations was ending, giving way to the era of continents." Arnold Toynbee, the historian, implied in his work that the nation-state was an improper unit for political analysis. E. H. Carr, writing of "nationalism and after" in 1945, asserted that "we shall not see again a Europe of twenty, and a world of more than sixty independent states." And later, in an influential article from 1957, John H. Herz argued that nuclear weapons, by rendering the borders of territorial states "permeable," had tended to "obliterate" the meaning of the unit. These thinkers had begun to consider the influence of nonstate actors in world affairs and many began to reach the conclusion that national distinctions were blurring.[23]

De Gaulle's opponents had other, less theoretical reasons for calling for the end of the state-based system, particularly in Europe. Although Americans and Europeans had some important differences in perspectives and interests, some of these arguments were put forward on both sides of the Atlantic. Of these, the most widely shared and most valid were the following: a federal Europe would (1) prevent European nations from resuming the internecine warfare that had destroyed them twice in three decades; (2) provide a means for controlling Germany, the country seen as most responsible for this bloodshed; and (3) help create a counterweight on the Eurasian continent to the newly threatening Soviet Union. To those of this mind-set, the stubborn persistence of a European "nationalism," like that of the pretentious de Gaulle in France, could only frustrate the achievement of these worthy goals. To federalists like Jean Monnet and EEC Commissioner Walter Hallstein, de Gaulle's fetish for the state was anachronistic and would be an obstacle to objectives as grand as the end of war in Europe and continental free trade as long as it remained. Of course, argued the "Europeans," nation-states in Europe had their different languages, religions, cultures, and cuisines but so did regions, and within them counties, and within them cities and towns. In fact, so did territorial groupings larger than the state. Did not the Atlantic Community share many values and customs? The unit around which "societies" were formed had begun with the family and moved to the tribe to the city-state to the nation. Why could this natural progression not extend to the continental level where values and interests were shared?[24]

In this sense, "national" borders were artificial. What was worse, they provided the pretext for emotional nationalism, whose vulgarization had in the past caused not only trade wars but real wars, most recently in the disaster of 1939–1945. Thus, arguments like de Gaulle's that nation-states were the only "legitimate" units of action were not only unsubstantiated but ultimately very dangerous. Moreover, the federalists did not believe (in direct opposition to de Gaulle) that a state-based organization was necessary to the effective functioning of government. What it took to run an economy, and even to make foreign policy, was competence, not the "loyalty" of the masses to one flag or another. In a European version of the American "best and brightest," the technocrats of the Communities believed that they could manage the Continent's affairs more effectively than the numerous minibureaucracies and governments of the individual states.

This debate of historic proportions, thirty years later, has largely died down and has been tempered by pragmatism on both sides. In France, few "Gaullists" remain who feel the need to assert the centrality of the nation-state as strongly as the General did, and just as few "Europeans" still believe in the inevitable disappearance of the state. Whereas on one hand the great successes of the European Community have demonstrated the need for cooperation and the pooling of national sovereignty, the breakup of artificial federations in Eastern Europe and the USSR, as well as the disturbing growth in the xenophobic extreme Right in Western Europe, are reminders of the importance of the legitimate national community. If the early European federalists were thus right to stress the need for European integration in an interdependent world, de Gaulle was also right to underline the importance of the true pillars of Europe, the states. What is important here, in any event, is not to identify the "winner" in this great debate but simply to understand Gaullist arguments and to put them in context. De Gaulle's concept of the nation-state was not an eloquent excuse for xenophobia, as some critics would have it, but a coherent vision of political organization that still influences France today.

DE GAULLE'S "IDEA OF FRANCE"

Was it de Gaulle's concept of the nation-state that caused problems in Europe or was it, rather, his concept of *France*? Was the General saying that nation-states as such had a special right to autonomy or that these rights were reserved for France, that France alone was "dedicated to an exalted and exceptional destiny?"[25] In other words, to what extent were de Gaulle's arguments for the primacy of the nation-state based more on the pursuit of uniquely French goals than on the social and political logic just discussed?

The particular French desire to play a special role in the postwar world can be rationalized in several ways. Some of General de Gaulle's more brilliant defenders have eloquently made the case that his pursuit of grandeur was a reasonable and practical strategy for reaching certain legitimate ends.[26] One of the primary justifications for Gaullist policy and style was that postwar France was demoralized and could only be redressed by recovering a certain amount of respect in the world. The feeling of national sovereignty was necessary for national achievement. Moreover, the argument runs, in a global system paralyzed by the superpower blocs, an internationally powerful and assertive France was essential to the creation of the strong West European force that could alone break apart this pernicious bipolar structure. A prominent world role for France was, thus, in the interests of both the country and the international system.

To attribute to Charles de Gaulle a strategy of cold rationality where France was concerned, however, would be to misread a fundamental element in his view of the world. His political arguments for the necessity of

French grandeur were usually coherent and often persuasive. They have given subsequent French leaders—men who did not share de Gaulle's view of society and of the world—ample reasons to accept the policies Gaullist ideas implied. And they have, arguably, helped unite the independent-minded and usually contentious French around a set of national goals to which the majority of them still aspire. But to this intellectual who admired the emotive, mystical works of Charles Péguy and René Chateaubriand, the importance of France's international stature was something more than a simple calculation of national interest. De Gaulle's vision of France was also based in part on an a priori concept that he felt no need to justify in any other way: France had a special right and duty to play the role of a world power simply because it was France.

To de Gaulle, more than numbers and material factors were involved in the determination of human and national enterprises. Like the philosopher Henri Bergson, whose works he read as a youth, de Gaulle believed there was more to life than simple scientific calculations that ignored intuition and élan. Marshal Pétain's armistice with the Germans in 1940, for example, was just the sort of supposed realism that overlooked intangible factors like human and political will. The same was true for the Fourth Republic's resignation to Atlanticism or its grudging acceptance of France's decline as a world power. In this sense, it is not difficult to read in de Gaulle an element of what might be called irrationality; he would never have denied that his view of France stemmed from something more than an impassive analysis of the political utility of the state. De Gaulle's *"certaine idée de la France,"* he admits in his *Mémoires de guerre*, was inspired "by sentiment as much as by reason."[27]

Returning to power in 1958, de Gaulle reasoned that "France must fulfill her mission as a world power. We are everywhere in the world. There is no corner of the earth, where, at any given time, men do not look to us and ask what France has to say. It is a great responsibility to be France, the humanizing power par excellence."[28] In other words, "France, because she can, because everything summons her to do so, *because she is France*, must lead a global policy in the center of the world."[29]

Not only was France destined for a great role on the international stage, but that role was in the interests of all humanity. At the end of 1967 de Gaulle explained that "Our action is aimed at reaching goals . . . that, because they are French, are in the interest of mankind."[30] It was because of the "genius of France," that French "power and grandeur . . . [were] directed toward the well-being and fraternity of mankind" and not exclusively toward the French people.[31] And by adopting France's "great and generous" plan for Algerian independence, "the French people [would] contribute, once again in its history, to the enlightenment of the universe."[32]

This vision of a "special" France, similar in some ways to America's "Shining City on the Hill," was of course not an innovation of Charles de Gaulle. For more than two hundred years, (since the French Revolution, if not since the time of Louis XIV) the idea of playing the role of *nation phare* had tempted the French, and history had given them a sense of national importance in international affairs. Expressed in the famous *mission civilizatrice* of colonialism, this particular French feeling of national eminence, if not superiority, was carried through into the Fourth Republic and remained imbedded in the country's consciousness notwithstanding the experience of World War II.

Because they have believed that past French greatness had conditioned the world to look to France for inspiration, the French have had a strong tendency to view their national interests in general or systemic terms. French rights are thus "human rights" (as the revolutionaries put it), and France's rebirth as a great power is to take the form of a "Europe from the Atlantic to the Urals" (as de Gaulle used to say). France's greatness was to be universal. De Gaulle's Europe, as Jean Lacouture described it, was to be a *"Europe tricolore."*[33]

Was this part of the grand design meant to inspire the French, to give them something in which to believe, or was it simply deeply and sincerely felt? The correct answer is certainly both, but the latter explanation should not be neglected. Stanley Hoffmann was undoubtedly correct when he wrote that when de Gaulle "talks to the French about their greatness . . . it is in order to get them to adapt to, and to act in, the world as it is."[34] De Gaulle was only too well aware of the need to motivate his compatriots, he had denounced the failure of his predecessors to do so, and he very skillfully managed to stimulate, inspire, and unite a wide range of French people, not an insignificant or easy task. But whereas some of de Gaulle's rhetoric—the "flattery for reform" to Hoffmann—was doubtless employed toward the end of lifting France's spirit, it is probably also true that Charles de Gaulle really believed that his country was "exceptional" and that it had universal qualities. There is no doubt that the strategist in de Gaulle used what French historian Odile Rudelle has called "operational language," designed to rally his compatriots.[35] France in the late 1950s was indeed demoralized, having gone through perhaps the most trying two decades in the country's long history, and badly needed a clear mission. But the patriotic passion and national sentiment of Charles de Gaulle cannot be reduced to tactics alone.

De Gaulle, it should not be forgotten, had been influenced as a young man by the nationalist tradition that played a prominent role in the intellectual life of France in the early twentieth century not only by the mystical nationalism in the Catholic tradition like that of Péguy but also by some of the more fervently nationalistic ideas of Maurice Barrès and

Jacques Bainville. He may have avoided the excesses of some of these champions of French virtues, but he shared their ambitions for France. The young de Gaulle was a member of a generation of nationalist, traditionalist young intellectuals marked by the country's unfortunate experiences of the recent past, such as Sedan, the Paris Commune, Fashoda, and the Dreyfus affair.[36] Nothing had moved de Gaulle more, he later wrote, than memories and symbols of past French failure and past French success.[37]

De Gaulle's nationalism, moreover, preceded the Fourth Republic and was not a result of it. He had seen the extent to which dependence on Great Britain had cost France between the two world wars when a lack of British support and diverging British and French interests had constrained France and led to her demise. It was thus not surprising that the post–World War II dependence on the United States evoked bitter memories and not surprising that de Gaulle, the statesman, pursued uniquely national goals first.

Even when used at the same time toward obviously calculated ends, de Gaulle's profession of faith in the universal values and special role of eternal France seems to have been a genuinely felt conviction. No one can deny that Gaullist language gave the French something to believe in, a reason to forget the crisis of confidence that had plagued the country from June 1940 to May 1958. But it is also probably too apologetic to suggest that Gaullist rhetoric had exclusively calculated and purely pedagogical roots. De Gaulle was certainly sincere in the almost religious faith he expressed in France. Even if one accepts that French exceptionalism was used by de Gaulle for psychological purposes, it is important not to overlook the genuine sense of France's "manifest destiny" that he felt.

INDEPENDENCE AND GRANDEUR AS GOALS AND MEANS

Not even a brief discussion of Gaullist perspectives would be complete without considering the twin concepts of independence and grandeur, for these two notions were at the heart of Charles de Gaulle's international policies and have left a highly influential legacy in France. Especially in the area of national security, no politician in France has been able to neglect the theme of French independence, and attempts even to put the notion into perspective have brought immediate and consequential public and political reaction. French grandeur, too, is still important; the French feel they are destined to play leading global and European roles and are loath to renounce them.

As already pointed out, neither of these notions was invented by de Gaulle, and both have been salient elements in French history. In this sense, de Gaulle played on rather than created French political culture and myth. But de Gaulle's construction of a foreign policy inspired in rhetoric and fact by grandeur and national independence—and especially the arguments about French national security born from it—make an exploration of the meaning of these concepts indispensable to an understanding of the Gaullist security legacy. The two notions can be analyzed together not because they are interchangeable but because they were so integrally related to one another. Indeed, it can be argued that independence was more than anything else the means de Gaulle believed necessary to achieve grandeur: France had to be free enough "to seek her rightful place in the world."[38] Sifting through the various arguments in the literature about de Gaulle, two very broad, and very different, interpretations emerge.

The first interpretation, most commonly found among de Gaulle's domestic political rivals and academic critics, among "Anglo-Saxon" opponents (like those in the U.S. State Department), and in neighboring countries in Europe, is the more critical of the two.[39] It tends to take the two terms literally and professes to see international stature and total freedom of action as the goals of France in and of themselves. It questions the inherent value of grandeur as a goal and argues that de Gaulle's pursuit of national sovereignty was both harmful and unrealistic. It also raises questions about Gaullist style and tactics, no matter what goals were involved.

"Independence," in the more extreme version of this analysis, meant largely denying the reciprocity of external relations and pretending that France could exercise complete autonomy in dealing with the world. Resentful that the Allies had thwarted French ambitions after the first world war and ignored him personally during the second, this argument runs, de Gaulle stubbornly pursued the illusion that he could avoid such dependence in the future. Regretting France's loss of power and influence in the world, the General, who saw himself as Joan of Arc, tried to restore France's old role but failed to admit he had too few resources to do so. Independence meant trying to seal France's fate from that of others, a strategy that seemed especially absurd when it meant a national defense that refused to admit its geopolitical limitations.

"Grandeur," this argument continues, was in part a product of personal ambition and in part an anachronistic vision of France that had implanted itself in the head of this one-time historian of *La France et son armée* (France and her army). De Gaulle here is seen obsessed with his own country (if not with himself, if he distinguished between the two at all), a preoccupation that produced an often bothersome insistence on national achievement. Grandeur meant great projects, *"vastes entreprises"* often disproportionate to the means at hand. In the words of John

Newhouse, de Gaulle was a "quixotic European separatist" who had "no tolerance for the limits of power." It was his nationalistic "grandeur" that stood in the way of great achievement for Europe: "He, and possibly only he, could have mobilized the countries of Western Europe into a community that could play something approaching the role he insisted belonged to France alone."[40] Many have seen in de Gaulle a "Louis xiv complex," a thirst for glory and power and the conviction that one had a divine right to both.

Some of de Gaulle's more vehement critics had ulterior motives, and their arguments were often exaggerated. But a more subtle critique makes some valuable points. De Gaulle's personal pride and relentlessly national perspective did, it must be said, often get in the way of generally beneficial international cooperation, and his insistence on keeping his own hands free was not appreciated by France's European and Atlantic allies. Surely de Gaulle did not, as Robert Aron wrote in 1966, "[oppose] every major effort . . . to establish European co-operation," nor did he "[do] all he could to prevent it" as Jean-François Révél concluded over two decades later.[41] But his emphasis on France's independence and grandeur did slow progress toward European unity in important ways.

It was also true, as these critics argue, that de Gaulle's wartime experience left him with an intense aversion to having to act as *demandeur*; de Gaulle did not like being a subordinate partner (although his Fourth Republic predecessors, after all, were not immune to this aversion either). De Gaulle's rhetoric, moreover, often seemed to suggest that he viewed independence as a value in and of itself. To assert that "independence means that we decide ourselves what we must do and with whom, without it being imposed upon us by any other state [or] collectivity," as de Gaulle did in 1966 (after repudiating the NATO military command), seemed to reflect a belief in unmitigated autonomy.[42] And the "rule" de Gaulle defined for France as described in his *Mémoires d'espoir*, "that what we say and do be done independently of others," can be seen as independence for its own sake.[43] Should not an aim in international affairs be to do things *with* others where possible? In the critical area of national security, the continual refusal of integrated defense (which seemed vital) and the equally persistent insistence on an independent nuclear deterrent (which seemed useless and dangerous) seemed to flaunt the country's willingness to go it alone and to presume its ability to do so.

Finally, as with the notion of independence, this interpretation of Gaullist grandeur also provides some useful insights. The belief in France's universal mission often appeared to others as just the sort of hegemonic pretention of which the "superpowers" were accused by de Gaulle himself—de Gaulle's Europe of states would fall under French hegemony in the same way an Atlantic Europe fell under American. (France's neighbors never forgot de Gaulle's 1958 proposal for a tripartite leadership of NATO that would exclude them.) It also implied a hierarchization of nation-states, with France, naturally, at or near the top. De Gaulle's preoccupation with his own and his country's stature gave the impression that he shirked international responsibilities and failed to see success in anything broader than a national perspective.

Thus, there was ample reason to suspect the motives behind the twin themes of independence and grandeur, and the roots of the great exasperation and diplomatic damage caused by this Gaullist creed are easy to trace. But despite the evidence for this reading of de Gaulle, can the General's conception of independence and grandeur be explained in any other way? What was de Gaulle's own explanation of it? Was it the counterproductive and irrational pursuit of exclusively national interests for the sake of it, or was it part of a more coherent, and more rational, overall strategy? For all the good questions it raises, the above analysis is incomplete; it fails both to give enough weight to the circumstances so critical to de Gaulle and to consider the more subtle intentions behind the often brutally straightforward Gaullist style. It fails to take into account the intended gap between rhetoric and reality. A second interpretation of the two concepts, more sympathetic but not uncritical, puts Gaullist intransigence in a different light.

First, when studying Gaullist policy, the tactics and rhetoric made necessary by weakness must be taken into account. De Gaulle, in fact, knew how feeble a position he was in and only increased his obstinacy and will to compensate. He was carrying through with the *du faible au fort* tactics toward his great Allies in World War II: "Limited and alone as I was, and precisely because I was so, I had to climb to the heights and never then to come down," explained de Gaulle in his war memoirs.[44] And as he said to Winston Churchill, "Where are my means? . . . I am too poor to bend."[45] Far from having the exaggerated sense of power for which he is often blamed, de Gaulle was all too aware of his weakness. Indeed, it is this very weakness that explains in part his desire to have his hands so free.

Independence to de Gaulle was more than an end in itself. It was a way to make sure French interests would not be overlooked by bigger, stronger powers or even smaller ones that did not share France's goals. Because states had different interests, it could not be in the interest of France to sacrifice its ultimate freedom of decision to anyone. Alliances, such as NATO and the European Economic Community, were fine and even necessary, and de Gaulle certainly took advantage of both. But their purpose was to facilitate cooperation, not to replace it with hierarchy, hegemony, or subservience. Little could be gained, de Gaulle believed— but much could be lost—by letting others make one's decisions.

Independence, moreover, was in de Gaulle's concept a catalyst for self-confidence, pride, and subsequent achievement. It was the sense of responsibility that was indispensable to the realization of one's goals. Even more important, pursuing a rhetorical goal of independence was the best way to avoid the *feeling* of dependence, a condition with degenerating effects. If a state began to think of itself as a dependent, as nothing more than a passive follower, it was just one step away from giving up its interests all together. Dependence only bred resentment, which was healthy for neither partner in a relationship. This conviction was doubtless one of the driving forces behind the General's hostility toward the Fourth Republic, a regime that he believed was committing suicide, voluntarily giving up.

Given these perspectives, it is not difficult to see why de Gaulle insisted so strongly that France's defense should be independent. To the author of *La France et son armée*, there was a historic link between a country's military history and its very existence as a nation. And because defense was "the first duty of a state," no state could maintain authority in the eyes of its citizens if it was seen to rely on a foreign power for its very existence.[46] Thus, even if it "went without saying" that French strategy would be coordinated with that of France's allies, and if it was "infinitely likely" that French troops would fight alongside their allies in case of war, it was indispensable that France have its own say.[47] General de Gaulle, after all, had had ample experience trying to ensure French interests during a war conducted under a foreign integrated command, and that experience had not been altogether auspicious.[48] How could the particular interests of France be protected if the means to protect them were not under France's own control?

In conclusion, independence for de Gaulle was part of an overall strategy for ensuring French interests in what de Gaulle believed to be an environment hostile to, or at least indifferent to, those interests. But it was not the belief that national isolation was possible in the modern world. Just as Gaullists caricatured the dependence and subordination of the leaders of the Fourth Republic, the General's own views have often been exaggerated or misread.

GAULLIST IDEAS AND GAULLIST POLICIES

De Gaulle's worldview was a rich and complicated one about which much more could be said. The point here, however, has simply been to provide some insights into the key ideas behind the policies that emerged from that worldview. As will become quite clear in subsequent chapters, the consistency between Gaullist ideas and Gaullist policies was remarkable, as was the consistency between Gaullist policies and the ones pursued by de Gaulle's successors. For better or for worse, Gaullist ideas have left a legacy that has heavily influenced—and at the same time closely reflected—the perspectives and preoccupations of the French. As one turns to the security policies that emerged during the Gaullist years, the fundamental principles behind those policies will be worth keeping in mind.

CHAPTER TWO

The Missing Pillar

FRANCE'S ROLE IN THE DEFENSE OF EUROPE

IN THE 1950s AND 1960s

LARGELY THROUGH de Gaulle's intransigence during and after World War II, France had ensured itself at least a nominal place among the world's powers—as an occupying power in Germany, on the exclusive United Nations Security Council, and in Berlin—and repeatedly claimed to merit a leading role in NATO. France was easily Western Europe's largest national territory, had one of its largest populations, and was strategically located and endowed with significant natural, economic, and industrial resources. Yet, France played a remarkably small part in the common defense.

To be sure, as a founding member of the Atlantic Alliance that defended Europe, France was the home of NATO's Supreme Headquarters (SHAPE), the Central Force command center (AFCENT), the NATO Defense College, thirty U.S. military facilities, and thousands of NATO soldiers. But although these support and logistical assets were integral parts of the alliance's defense structure, they were not sustained in any large part by France. At the time of the withdrawal from NATO commands, only two French army divisions and a total of seven tactical air wings were assigned to NATO.[1] Of the thirteen major commands divided among alliance members, France only ran one of them, and it was a subordinate one.[2] The country that only one decade previously boasted—not without some justification—of having "the greatest army in the world," was conspicuously absent from the structure in place to defend Europe. Although there was never any question that France would be implicated in any conflict on the continent—by the extensive NATO military and logistical presence in France, by the requirements of the Western European Union (WEU), and especially by the natural logic of geography—the French army was simply not significantly involved there.

By all historical measures, this situation was an aberration. A leading European and world power since the sixteenth century, having the largest army in Europe since World War I (when it mobilized no less than four million men), and traditionally insistent on maintaining forces at least equivalent to those of other European powers, France suddenly found itself lagging behind. Not only was military power in Western Europe for the first time primarily American but even among the Europeans themselves it was not long before the French found their contribution dwarfed by Germany's, despite the fact that the Federal Republic did not even have an army until 1955. Even Great Britain, against all historical precedent, maintained a larger contingent on the European central front than did France.

It is also worth noting that this situation was well in place long before the much-blamed deviation of funds toward the strategic nuclear force or the 1966 decision to withdraw from NATO's integrated military command. Nuclear spending did, as will be seen, rob French conventional forces of sorely needed funding, but it never played the role often assigned to it as the exclusive or even dominant reason for France's limited role on the central front. France did not want that role and, indeed, had never played it. It was neither the force de frappe nor Gaullist hostility toward NATO that prevented a leading French role in European security; both followed rather than caused what must be considered a lasting reality of the postwar period—the absence of a French military "pillar" in Europe.

The origins of this missing pillar are worth exploring. I argue in this book that the gap between France's nationally oriented policies and the requirements of European defense narrowed significantly over the 1970s and 1980s. But how did this gap appear in the first place? Why were the French so dispensable on Europe's central front before and during the Gaullist era? And why did the French contribution to European defense become more important over time?

To answer any of these questions, it is necessary to look back at France's military role in Europe during that earlier period. If, during the 1970s and 1980s, the French role in Europe's conventional and nuclear defense was widely recognized as important, such an observation was not as "obvious" during de Gaulle's time. Indeed, with more than twenty years of hindsight, the military situation in Europe in the 1950s and 1960s might seem rather curious. Why were the French so absent from the military picture in Europe during the 1950s and 1960s?

THE MISSING PILLAR DURING THE FOURTH REPUBLIC

A minimal French involvement in West European defense was not a situation de Gaulle created but one he inherited. The policies and practices of the Fourth Republic presaged Gaullist policies in a number of ways, and what appeared to be a great break with the past—de Gaulle's pursuit of grandeur and disagreements with NATO—was, in fact, not so great a change. At no time since the collapse of the Maginot line in June 1940 was Western Europe the French army's primary concern, and at no time after 1950 did French troops play a leading role there.

From the very start of the postwar era, France was more preoccupied with its global than with its European role. It was not long after V-E Day that the French army, already largely decimated by the events of June 1940 and still stunned by the experience, had to take up arms abroad. Four years of war had unleashed feelings of nationalism and desires for independence in the French empire and trying to thwart these desires became the overwhelming focus of the French army for more than a decade after World War II. Desperately in search of a role—and of an opportunity to save face—after the 1940 debacle, preserving the empire and stopping Communist-supported *guerres révolutionnaires* became the primary preoccupation of army leaders. Embarrassingly unprepared to meet the last enemy, the military vowed that this one would be contained. Similar feelings drove politicians in Paris, who felt that lost prestige could only be regained quickly by reestablishing the manifestations of world responsibilities.[3]

The most consequential quagmires of the empire were, of course, the debilitating Indochina war, which began just as World War II ended, and the disaster in Algeria, which eventually brought down the regime. The rebellion in Indochina broke out just months after the armistice with the Germans, and the revolts in Algeria began just a few weeks after nine years of Southeast Asian war. It was as if the French were destined to be continually at war for a generation. This colonial priority also had implications for Europe, fast becoming host to the highest concentration of military power the world had ever known. A country pouring its money and its soul into Asian and African wars and preoccupied with reasserting a world role was neither well placed nor well disposed to provide a large quota of foot soldiers along the central plains of Europe, particularly in an alliance dominated inevitably by the Americans.

These colonial conflicts and efforts to maintain France's global role affected France's capacities in Europe in a number of ways. The first was a flagrant financial problem, which was particularly critical in Vietnam. Maintaining troops and sending heavy material halfway around the globe while trying to reconstruct a war-ravaged domestic economy in France was not an easy or inexpensive task. Despite increasing American financial and armament support after 1950 (spurred by the shock of the Korean War), the Indochina conflict began to strain French budgets at the expense of domestic reconstruction and contributed to an inflation that was rapidly getting out of hand. Notwithstanding American military aid, which by 1954 was providing for no less than two-thirds of the French war effort, the Indochina conflict cost France nearly eight billion dollars.[4] To put this cost in perspective, this was nearly twice as much money as France had received from the entire Marshall Plan.[5]

The Algerian War, if closer, was not cheap either. For nine years, France trained, fed, and equipped up to six hundred thousand soldiers for service in this North African "department." Although it is probably impossible to establish precisely what all this cost in the aggregate, it is indicative that by 1962 an exceptional 68 percent of the French military budget—itself nearly 5 percent of GNP—was going to "operations," a direct result of the overseas war. Moreover, added to the conflict's official costs must be the huge economic opportunity cost of sending such a large proportion of the country's young labor force abroad as conscripted soldiers. During a period of tight labor supply, worsened by negative demographic trends and a slowing of the postwar migration from agriculture to industry, the war had economic consequences well beyond the numbers found in the military budget. In short, fighting two colonial wars back to back was not only a human tragedy for France but an economic disaster that had implications for France's military role in Europe.

The second major consequence of France's two colonial conflicts (more important where European defense was concerned) was their decimation of French fighting forces. Although the recruitment of foreign troops and the ban on sending conscripts to Indochina kept the numbers of French soldiers there relatively low (never more than seventy thousand), the drain on the officer corps was much more serious. From 1945 to 1954, nearly twenty thousand French officers lost their lives in Indochina; each year of the war saw the disappearance of the equivalent of an entire Saint-Cyr graduating class.[6] While Fourth Republic leaders in Paris were haggling over the sort of role French troops theoretically might play in Europe, the ostensible leaders of those troops were for the most part bogged down in ricefields 12,000 kilometers away.

In Algeria, of course, ordinary soldiers from the Metropole were not spared as in the Far East. A 1954 North Atlantic Council decision had given France the right to exclude from NATO "forces intended for the defense of overseas territories" and even to separate those "designated" for overseas duty that were stationed in France, leaving the door open for the diversion of French troops.[7] As the war grew, calling for ever-increasing numbers of French soldiers in the "pacification" campaigns, this clause essentially deprived NATO of anything like a full contingent of French forces. Although France had promised twenty divisions for European defense at NATO's Lisbon conference in 1952, by the time de Gaulle was called to power, NATO had never received even half that total. Three of the most modern mechanized divisions, already in great demand in Europe, were sent (with NATO's reluctant approval) to Algeria between

1956 and 1958, where they joined what was already more than one-half of the *armée de terre*. As put succinctly by the historian of the French army, Jean Planchais, "Algeria [was] devour[ing] continental defense."[8]

Planchais did not overstate the case. At the high point of the fighting, nearly one-half million French troops were in Algeria, including most of the experienced and combat-tested professionals who had fought in the Far East. That year, 1959, was also when de Gaulle became the first president of the Fifth Republic. France was contributing only 2 of NATO's more than 21 divisions on the central front—the same number as Belgium and the Netherlands, and notably fewer than the Federal Republic's 7, the United States' 5, and Britain's 3 divisions.[9] The following year, while the French army had just 253,000 troops stationed in France and in West Germany combined, it maintained 418,000 soldiers in North Africa.[10] From 1958 to 1961, there were times when more than 500,000 French troops were stationed in Algeria, a contingent much larger than any postwar French standing forces made available for European defense (table 2.1).

Finally, the colonial wars not only drained French men and money from Europe but also led to force structures largely incompatible with those of France's allies in the European theater. While France was training its soldiers to hunt out rebels in the countryside or in the mountains, to resist the tactics of small clusters of relatively untrained guerrillas, or to conduct psychological warfare, NATO Europe was relying on the heavy arms—tanks and artillery—needed to stop the supposed one hundred plus Warsaw Pact divisions. Even if French troops from Algeria could have been quickly flown back to the continent if hostilities developed, it is doubtful that they would have been of much use. For a "European defense" that meant halting a Soviet invasion, French forces were not only absent but entirely unprepared.

None of this is to suggest, of course, that the French of the Fourth Republic were not committed to the Western cause or that they were somehow indifferent to the fate of their allies in Europe. On the contrary, many French leaders of the time were among the most fervent supporters

TABLE 2.1
French Military Manpower and Its Location in 1960

	Army	Air Force	Navy	Totals
In France	203,000	82,000	48,000	333,000
In Germany	50,000	8,000	0	58,000
In North Africa	418,000	43,000	14,000	475,000
Other overseas	65,000	0	0	65,000

Source: Lothar Ruehl, *La politique militaire de la Ve République* (Paris: Presses de la Fondation Nationale des Sciences Politiques, 1976), p. 328.

of the Atlantic and European military alliances—both largely French in-spired—and they rarely hesitated to trumpet their common values and shared civilization with Europe and with the United States. They wanted to maintain, as former Prime Minister Edouard Herriot put it, "this fra-ternity that is based on our common political origins [and] on the identity of principles on which our two democracies are founded."[11] Since the momentous "double fracture" of 1947, when France split both internally and externally, and when realistic hopes for a French mediating role faded, most of the French saw their choice as all too clear: to accept an Atlantic-oriented Western Europe or to bear a Soviet-dominated one. Aside from the Stalinist Parti Communiste Français (PCF) and a small group of intellectual "neutralists," all French political movements, on the Left and on the Right, were convinced of the seriousness of the Soviet threat and the need for the United States to counterbalance it.[12]

At the same time, however, these same French leaders maintained their conviction that France had its own special responsibilities and never gave up their fight to reestablish French independence and stature in the world. For many in Paris, France's "position as a great power [was] definitely at stake [in Asia]," and "[French] soldiers fighting over there [had] the inten-tion and impression of also defending civilization, cultural interest, and the glory of France."[13] Grandeur and rang were not Gaullist inventions. To the leaders of the Fourth Republic, sharing democratic values with the United States and admitting the need for American military power in Eu-rope was not the same as resigning themselves to a subordinate role. The Americans were constantly reminded of French interests and incessantly, if often fruitlessly, urged to take them into account. However committed to the common cause and however soberly convinced of France's need for the United States, only the most "realist" of the French had given up aspirations of recovering a leading global role.

Many of the leaders seeking to reestablish French influence, particu-larly those in the army, firmly believed that a closely knit Atlantic rela-tionship was France's best hope for restoring lost prestige. De Gaulle, of course, believed this to be folly: the United States, like any great power, would seek to promote American interests, not French ones. But most of the Fourth Republic's political and military elite was convinced, or at least hoped, that the Americans would recognize Paris's role in the global fight for Western values and that Washington would supply France with modern arms, money, and political support. The battles France was wag-ing to hold Indochina and Algeria, as well as the expedition into Suez, were all efforts toward the common goal of defending the West from communism and the radicals of the Third World. "We are the supporting pillar of the defense of the West in Southeast Asia," French President of the Council Vincent Auriol argued to John Foster Dulles in May 1952, "If this pillar crumbles, Singapore, Malaysia and India will soon fall prey to Mao Tse-tung." The French fight to maintain the empire was, thus, a more appropriate French contribution to Western defense than a major presence in Europe would have been. What was the difference, the Fourth Republic's leaders argued, between containing communism on the Elbe and containing it abroad?[14]

However sincerely the French may have believed this logic—and they were not, in fact, always sincere—it was clearly unconvincing to the Americans, who believed that the global aspects of the fight against communism were best left to them and in places of their own choosing. Though the United States backed heavily (and apparently wholeheartedly) the early French effort in Indochina, by the 1950s they believed that the French were essentially interested in perpetuating European colonialism rather than containing the Soviets abroad. The Pax Americana aimed at a Third World of independent, Western-oriented, liberal nation-states under American patronage, and the United States had little interest in harnessing its own prestige to a dying European imperialism.

Given the seemingly endless colonial conflicts that drained French military power, money, and attention from Europe, French forces and military leadership were, frankly, rather marginal to the alliance's strategy for continental defense in Europe throughout the 1950s. The France of 1958 still had a wealth of resources, a large military, a nascent nuclear force, and a certain amount of worldwide diplomatic influence, but it was not a major contributor to its own direct security.

THE MISSING PILLAR DURING THE GAULLIST YEARS

Noting France's traditionally small role in postwar European defense puts Gaullist strategy in a different perspective. The gradual "withdrawal" of France from NATO, which began with the removal of French naval forces from the Mediterranean command in 1959 and reached a peak with the French departure from the alliance's military integration in 1966, was not the sudden crisis it might superficially appear to have been. Because the French contribution to NATO forces was not very critical to begin with, the military implications were not overwhelming when French troops were formally withdrawn. Rather than saying de Gaulle tore down the French pillar from the NATO temple, it might be more accurate to say he refused to erect one that had never been there in the first place. The contrast between Gaullist "neutralism" and Fourth Republic "subservience" is thus a double caricature, and if de Gaulle stretched and flaunted France's distant military role in European defense, he did not originate it.

If de Gaulle did not bring about this peculiar situation, in which a leading European power was not very involved in European defense, why did Gaullist policies bring about such controversy and conflict? If the French military contribution to NATO at the time of de Gaulle's 1966 withdrawal was, as one military analyst wrote at the time, "not really vital,"[15] why did de Gaulle's NATO policies raise so much more ire than those of his predecessors? Why was the Fifth Republic seen as so sharply different from the Fourth?

The answer is twofold, with both an internal and external component. It has to do not only with the changes taking place within France as de Gaulle reoriented French policy around the principle of national autonomy and a strategic nuclear force but with the international trends affecting military strategy in Europe. The changing internal priorities of de Gaulle's Fifth Republic meant that France would not increase its commitment to Europe even if it now could. The changes in the international strategic balance, however, suggested that some day France would have a much more vital role to play than formerly. The differences in security policy between the Fourth Republic and the Fifth were more than a question of style.[16]

When internal factors are considered, several differences between de Gaulle and his predecessors spring easily to mind. First, de Gaulle's aloofness from the alliance, in contrast to that of the Fourth Republic, was deliberate, put forth with conviction as a specific means toward a lasting end—the achievement of French military autonomy. Whereas French leaders before 1958 argued that France's military shortcomings in Europe were a temporary result of action they were taking abroad in the name of the common cause—the security of the West—de Gaulle seemed to be making a permanent and voluntary policy out of truancy in Europe. Whereas the Fourth Republic pushed for more influence within the integrated alliance, even while putting few of its own forces within it, de Gaulle denounced the very concept of integration. Whereas the Fourth Republic was grudgingly prepared to accept the principle of American direction in exchange for actual American protection, de Gaulle refused the former on the grounds that the latter could not endure. Thus, even as past impediments to the European role disappeared—the colonial wars ended and the French economy boomed—the long-awaited French contribution to the standing forces of Western Europe never came. Not surprisingly, de Gaulle was seen as a much more serious and potentially destabilizing challenge to the alliance than his equally delinquent but rather more pliant predecessors.

The second set of reasons a missing French pillar had greater impact under de Gaulle than it had under previous governments had less to do with France itself than with the situation developing around it: France's role in Europe was beginning to matter. Put another way, it was not only de Gaulle's stepped-up intransigence and louder voice that made his quest for independence stand out but the effect that such a quest had in a changing situation. France was no longer the ravaged country that had almost disappeared in the war but was now one of a number of increasingly prosperous European states whose contribution was becoming necessary to a security alliance that the United States could no longer afford to run alone. As the United States lost its exceptional nuclear superiority and became vulnerable itself, the changing balance of global power began to suggest that the Americans would need a greater defense contribution from these European states, making the continued French refusal to commit itself all the more disturbing to allied relations. It was not that France's security was no longer secure behind the American strategic shield—in fact that shield was still strong enough to free France from choices and obligations with which it would otherwise have been faced. But as America began to decline from omnipotence, France's absence from Europe was more portentous than before.

It is unnecessary here to present a detailed narrative of what de Gaulle did in the security policy field. It is well known that France did not become an integral part of NATO or of any other European defense, and a number of excellent studies exist already that detail the events and choices of these years.[17] Instead, in the rest of this chapter I focus on three questions about France's role in Europe during the 1960s that emerge from the considerations just discussed: (1) Why did French forces remain so marginal to European defense even as de Gaulle liquidated the apparent sources of their weakness? (2) What, if anything, were the contemporary and potential roles of the emerging French nuclear force? and (3) Given the context alluded to above, in which French security was apparently ensured by other means—NATO and the American nuclear protectorate—to what extent did France's continued absence from European defense make any difference at all? These issues are taken up in turn.

EXPLAINING THE "MISSING PILLAR" UNDER DE GAULLE

Why did Gaullist France not play a leading role in Europe's defense? De Gaulle, it is said, replacing the weak and unstable governments of the Fourth Republic, restored the morale of the French and renewed their *esprit de défense*, got safely out of the empire while preserving an inspiring world role, rebuilt a strong French defense around solid principles, recaptured the loyalty of the army, and provided the money to pay for military force. Such a successful national revival obviously suggested a greater capacity to play the sort of leading military role that some Gaullist ideas—like the indissoluble link between the army and the nation, the primacy of national defense for government, and the grandeur of France—seemed to imply. Moreover, as will be seen, as the nuclear protection and military leadership of the United States became more suspect, a major French contribution to European defense began to appear more imperative than ever. Why, though, did the French military role in Europe remain limited just when both its potential and the need for it seemed to grow?

Some of the reasons for France's failure to play a greater role remained the same as they had been in the 1950s: an interest in reestablishing a French presence overseas, a traditional resistance to American hegemony, budgetary constraints, and until 1962, colonial conflicts, all played their part. But with the 1960s and Gaullist leadership also came new goals, rules, and justifications for French forces and their planned employment in Europe. The tenacity with which these new objectives were pursued made for a striking contrast with the results of previous policy, and if the Fourth Republic was no more involved in European defense than the Fifth, neither the reasons for this uninvolvement nor its extent were quite the same. Just as certain "Gaullist principles" made a leading French military role in Europe seem natural, they also explain why in the circumstances of the time that role would not be forthcoming.

The first Gaullist explanation for the absence of French force in Europe was the General's absolute refusal of military integration, particularly in coalition with the imperious Americans. The leaders of the Fourth Republic, of course, were not enamored of the idea that their American colleagues made all the major decisions about Europe and were able to dictate the direction of the Atlantic Alliance. But if these French leaders often protested stubbornly and at times exasperated their transatlantic partners, they never threatened the concept of alliance integration itself. De Gaulle's opposition, on the other hand, would prove to be much more fundamental.

Many in Europe and the United States, of course, had long assumed that once France finally extracted its army from North Africa, a greater contribution in Europe would be forthcoming. If the argument in Paris throughout the 1950s had been that French forces were only absent from Europe because they were fighting freedom's battles on other fronts, the elimination of those fronts should have brought the troops home; French military resources could finally be put toward European defense. Yet, despite the urging of people like U.S. President John F. Kennedy and Secretary of Defense Robert McNamara, anxious to see combat-tested French forces replace the "temporary" American troops in Europe so that they could be used elsewhere, de Gaulle resisted. For Kennedy and the Americans, whose own forces were being built up to fight "two and a half wars" around the globe, and whose new strategy of flexible response required much higher force levels in Europe, a greater contribution from the Allies—including and, perhaps, especially France—was imperative. But although de Gaulle had just freed a potential half-million troops for other duty by bringing the war in Algeria to an end, he had no intention of placing them at the disposal of the American leaders. To do so would not only lead to the abdication of responsibility implied in the serving of someone else's grand design but would put France's own destiny in the hands of others. Jean Lacouture captures best the General's thinking: "He had not pulled his army out of the Algerian djebels in order to turn them into sacrificial pawns in a coalition directed at Washington's discretion."[18]

The importance that de Gaulle placed on a *national* command for a *national* army is well known. "The principle that dominates everything," he argued while combating the plan for a European Defense Community in 1951, "is that an army fights for its country, under the authority of its government, and under the orders of its leaders."[19] Doubtless influenced by his formative period as a captain in World War I, when patriotism was the motivating source of soldiers on both sides, de Gaulle was convinced that only when a man fights for his flag can he make the sort of contribution required in war. "Ardor, confidence, and obedience" could only be mustered by serving in a national command.[20] But this was not the only prerequisite for a national defense. Not only did French forces have to be commanded by French leaders, but for France to play the role it was due the country as a whole had to be made to feel important. If French soldiers were no more than pieces on America's European chessboard, how could they ever contribute to winning the game of chess? How could they ever influence how the game was played? Sacrificing pawns was sometimes in the interest of protecting the queen, but it did not do much for the pawns themselves.

Consistent with this logic was another reason not to integrate with NATO after Algeria—the psychological needs of the French army. For de Gaulle, as noted in chapter 1, nothing was more fundamental than the relationship between an army and the nation it was to serve. The two were linked organically and separation was fatal; this France had just learned. As the Algerian War was being brought to an end, the deep wounds of the army's loss came forth: an officer corps that had vowed after leaving Indochina "never again to die for nothing" had obvious difficulties in swallowing another defeat because of the politicians back in Paris.[21] Thus, it was critical that the French army, after feeling betrayed in both Indochina and Algeria, be reintegrated into the nation, which meant that it would now serve primarily in France. For de Gaulle, it was "absolutely necessary, morally and politically, for us to make our army a

more integral part of the nation. Therefore, it is necessary for us to resta-
tion it, for the most part, on our soil; for us to give it once again a direct
responsibility in the external security of the country; in short, for our
defense to become once again a national defense."[22] French soldiers could
not be asked once again, by being assigned to an American-run alliance,
to meet goals that were not their goals, to risk wars that were not their
wars; they had to be brought back home and be given a truly national
mission.

De Gaulle, then, in a fundamentally different manner from his predecessors, opposed not only military integration (which his predecessors
had favored) but, more specifically, national subordination (which they
could not prevent). If France could somehow have been the cog of a truly
European defense, perhaps de Gaulle would have found a way to join it.
But as long as Europe had to depend so heavily on Washington for protection, de Gaulle preferred a different role. The real obstacle to a greater
French role in European defense in the 1960s was not that France did not
want to cooperate with the Europeans but that France did not want to be
directed by the United States.

It would be difficult to argue, however, that the aversion to integration
and abstract desire for independence alone kept France from playing a
leading role in its own defense. A country that wanted to avoid a subordinate role in conventional defense would probably build up its forces
rather than cut them back. A country that saw itself as a natural leader of
an alliance would probably look for prominence and leverage within that
alliance rather than place limits on its contribution to it. Yet France,
throughout the 1960s, saw the size, strength, and equipment of its conventional forces decline relative to those of its neighbors. Why did France,
even while avoiding integration and the alliance, not build up its forces in
France? Why did French military budgets overall, but especially conven
tional military budgets, decline? And why was French military investment
not concentrated in the areas—such as tanks, armored vehicles, and logistical means—which a stronger fighting force seemed to require?

The answer most often given, of course, was that these were all consequences of the unyielding French commitment to build a national nuclear
force. Given the priority of such a costly new program, it is said, conventional forces inevitably bore the brunt of the financial limitations. As an
all-encompassing explanation for French conventional military weakness, however, the costs of the atomic force can easily be exaggerated.
The French conventional role in NATO defense, as previously suggested,
would doubtless have remained circumscribed whether the nuclear experiment existed or not, and as French officials often pointed out, major
conventional programs would have cost as much as or more than the
nuclear force anyway. Still, there is no question that France's nuclear programs competed for resources with its conventional ones and that the

former often won the competition. Although assessing the relative importance of French nuclear spending is a complicated and often controversial task, even a brief analysis can be instructive.[23]

The military program law of 1960–1964 set for itself the goal of realizing the bases for a French national deterrent force. The funding it allocated to the new nuclear force—FFr6.3 billion out of a total allocation for military procurement of FFr11.7 billion—included primarily the production of the first fifty Mirage ivs and a stock of atomic bombs, the Pierrelatte isotope separation plant, and the research and development of ballistic missiles. In contrast to later program laws, this multiyear effort only covered a small portion (less than 40 percent) of spending on military equipment and no operating expenses at all.[24]

The second program law (1965–1970), which covered 69 percent of military equipment programs, was also focused on the nuclear force, specifically on the development of new nuclear materials (including thermonuclear bombs), new launching vehicles (submarine launched ballistic missiles, land-based IRBMs, tactical nuclear missiles) and twelve additional Mirages. In this program law—which covered six years instead of four, and which was written in 1964 francs—projected nuclear spending rose to FFr27.3 billion out of a total of FFr54.9 billion.[25]

Looking only at the program laws can be misleading, however, because they represent only government projections of what would be necessary for certain programs, not what would in fact be spent. The two laws took no account of an inflation rate of nearly 4 percent; underestimated the costs of certain programs; allowed the government to reallocate programmed funds from conventional programs to nuclear ones; and largely overlooked certain operational and maintenance costs associated with the nuclear force.[26] If one looks instead at what was actually disbursed, one gets a slightly different and much more accurate picture of the relative financial drain of the force de frappe. The actual nuclear share of the defense equipment budget, according to figures based on parliamentary reports compiled by Jacques Percebois, is indicated in table 2.2. As can be seen, especially toward the late 1960s, spending on the force de frappe compared to other military programs was thus clearly substantial.

Even these figures, however, must be put into perspective. It is important to remember that they refer not to the defense budget as a whole but only to the portion of it devoted to military equipment. French military budgets are divided into two parts, Title iii (operations) and Title v (equipment), and throughout the 1960s Title iii (because of the delays in disbanding the huge conventional contingents from Algeria) was usually much greater than Title v (see table 2.3). In other words, noting (in table 2.2) that the nuclear force consumed close to half of Title v spending, and (in table 2.3) that Title v spending was on average just under one-half of the overall defense budget, one can conclude that the French nuclear force

TABLE 2.2
Cost of Nuclear Forces as Share of
Military Equipment Spending under de Gaulle

Year	Percentage
1960	9.30
1961	15.84
1962	22.23
1963	31.06
1964	40.67
1965	48.56
1966	49.48
1967	51.42
1968	48.27
1969	41.07

Source: Jacques Percebois, "Economie de l'effort d'armement," in Université de Franche-Comté and Institut Charles de Gaulle, *L'aventure de la bombe: De Gaulle et la dissuasion nucléaire, 1958–1969* (Paris: Plon, 1985), p. 118.

as a share of overall military spending throughout the 1960s was approximately 25 percent.[27]

To what extent did the allocation of one-fourth of the French defense budget to nuclear forces contribute to the starving of conventional forces, those more necessary for a European role? Had the French military budget been rising or even stable, the impact of nuclear spending might not have been very significant. France at this time was drawing down forces from a costly foreign war, and the resources previously devoted to Algeria could have then been applied to the nuclear force. As it turned out, however, not only did French defense budgets not rise or remain stable but they declined continuously and sometimes sharply throughout the period (see tables 2.4 and 2.5).

General de Gaulle, of course, was scarcely one to overlook the value of a strong and well-funded military force, but he was also highly attuned to

TABLE 2.3
Budgetary Credits by Title, 1960–1969 (percentage)

Year	Title III	Title V	Year	Title III	Title V
1960	64.3	35.7	1965	50.1	49.9
1961	65.8	34.2	1966	48.8	61.2
1962	67.6	32.4	1967	48.2	51.8
1963	57.8	42.2	1968	48.0	52.0
1964	54.1	45.9	1969	50.7	49.3

Source: Livre blanc sur la défense nationale (Paris: Ministère de la Défense Nationale, 1972), 1:60.

TABLE 2.4
Defense Budget as Share of GNP, 1960–1969 (percentage)

1960	5.5	1965	4.3
1961	5.1	1966	4.1
1962	4.7	1967	4.1
1963	4.5	1968	4.0
1964	4.3	1969	3.6

Source: Ministère de la Défense Nationale, *Livre blanc sur la défense nationale* (Paris: Ministère de la Défense Nationale, 1972), 1:60.

the need for French economic revival and convinced that the state would have to use its resources to promote economic growth, technological prowess, and industrial success. Feeding and housing hundreds of thousands of conscripts, even based in France, was not the formula for such success. Like his counterpart, Eisenhower, in the United States, de Gaulle was sensitive to the concept of sufficiency in defense spending and fundamentally conservative about balancing his national accounts. Rather than devote his Algerian "peace dividend" to his nuclear force, then, de Gaulle paid for that force with what he already had, and it was inevitable that French conventional forces would feel the strain. Nuclear programs were taking up an increasing portion of the budgetary pie, and the pie was getting smaller.

As one might expect in this context, the delivery of conventional equipment to French troops fell far behind schedule. Even where attempts were made to furnish the now smaller French army with adequate conventional forces, procurement goals were never met. The 1960–1964 program law, for example, foresaw five (1959-type) divisions of approximately twenty thousand men, each of which was to include two infantry brigades, one armored brigade, heavy artillery, reconnaissance aircraft, and helicopters. In 1962, Armed Forces Minister Pierre Messmer repeated this goal, calling for the deployment by 1970 of "five or six mechanized divisions and one or two aeroportable divisions," which would be

TABLE 2.5
Defense Budget as Share of National Budget, 1960–1969 (percentage)

1960	28.5	1965	22.5
1961	26.7	1966	21.8
1962	24.7	1967	20.7
1963	23.9	1968	20.0
1964	23.0	1969	17.9

Source: Ministère de la Défense Nationale, *Livre blanc sur la défense nationale* (Paris, 1972), 1:58.

equipped with 1,500 tanks (new AMX-30s), 3,500 armored personnel transport vehicles, 400 self-propelled cannons, and 900 helicopters.[28]

By the following year, however, it was already apparent that these hopes would not be realized. Messmer began to revise his projections, now calling for a total of only six divisions, smaller than those originally foreseen.[29] In 1963, France still had only two partially modernized divisions in West Germany (a total of six fully manned brigades), and three light, and poorly equipped, divisions in France. As the nuclear force took an increasingly greater share of a shrinking military budget, production of AMX-30 tanks and other equipment was delayed, and several major projects—including multiple independently targetable reentry vehicles (MIRVs), nuclear-powered hunter submarines, heavy lift helicopters, and a vertical takeoff airplane to be built with Great Britain—would be canceled altogether.[30] Primarily because of the lack of equipment, as late as 1966 still only four of the new divisions existed. In 1967, the decision was taken to form the planned fifth mechanized division out of units taken from the existing divisions whose troops were thus reduced by 20 percent. Now France had its planned five new divisions, but they were lighter than foreseen, less flexible, and only at 80 percent strength. By the end of 1967, Messmer had to admit that the modernization of the land army was three years behind the schedule established in 1964.[31]

In the end, then, although a large French contribution to conventional defense in Europe was never in the cards, one can conclude that if the nuclear force was not the only or even principal factor limiting France's conventional military contribution, it was at least responsible for maintaining a certain limit on the capacity for it. The fact that greater conventional force levels and better equipment were programmed in the first place but not met, the traditional desire in Paris to maintain land forces at least equal to Germany's (for political if not other reasons), and de Gaulle's need to satisfy the army suggest that not all the conventional force cutbacks were intended elements of an overall strategy. The cost of the force de frappe was far from *the* cause of weak French conventional forces in Europe in the 1960s, but it did help contribute to a difficult situation that would not soon disappear.

Blaming the resistance to American hegemony and the material inadequacies of French conventional forces for France's aloofness from NATO, although perfectly factual, overlooks an even simpler explanation that must also be mentioned. France failed to assume a large military role in Europe not only because of the constraints discussed above but because French military strategy did not require such a capacity; in fact, it specifically opposed one. No matter what they might have been able to contribute to conventional defense had they wanted to, the French refused to provide the military means that would suggest a willingness to fight an inevitably catastrophic conventional war in Europe.

French doctrines of "pure" or "absolute" deterrence will be discussed in detail in chapter 3. Here it is necessary only to note that as these doctrines developed, emphasizing the threat of nuclear retaliation to a classic ground attack from the East if that attack threatened French survival, the argument *against* maintaining a credible conventional defense took on greater logic. Nonnuclear defense had only to be strong enough to require that any Soviet attack be large enough to make plausible the threat of nuclear retaliation; any more than that only made a nuclear response less likely and conventional war more so. In this way, the French military leadership could justify some of the conventional force reductions and failure to fill a NATO role. These reductions were more compatible with the army's desire for the lighter and more mobile units adequate for their preferred strategy of proportional "massive retaliation." Because conventional forces were meant only to buy time enough to threaten a French nuclear response, a viable conventional defense was undesirable. In short, if Western Europe were "too prepared" conventionally, it risked making Europe "safe for the next war" something that the French, naturally, wanted to avoid. America's doctrine of flexible response was an unacceptable battle plan for those who lived on the potential battlefield, and if de Gaulle's European neighbors would acquiesce and reluctantly supply the forces it called for, de Gaulle himself would not.

FRANCE'S NUCLEAR FORCE AND EUROPE

The second main question to answer about France's role in European defense under de Gaulle concerns not the opportunity cost of the nuclear force but the potential utility of that force. If France sacrificed some of its capacity for a strong European army to build a national nuclear force and to help make its deterrent effect credible, what sort of role was this nuclear force meant to play? To what extent, if any, was French conventional power in Europe traded off for a French contribution to nuclear deterrence? Was the force de frappe meant to be a "European deterrent" in the future?

The developments leading to NATO's recognition of the contribution to deterrence of "small nuclear forces" at Ottawa in 1974 and the subsequent modernization of the French strategic force can easily lead one to forget just how marginally useful those forces were such a short time before. Throughout de Gaulle's tenure, the force de frappe was far more a symbol of independence than a serious enhancement of deterrence in

Europe. Wolf Mendl has accurately described it as more a *"force de persuasion"* than a *"force de dissuasion"*; in the 1960s, the French deterrent was not very credible militarily.[32]

Although France had surprised almost everybody by managing a nuclear explosion in a test at Reggane in the Sahara as early as February 1960, it did not have the means to deliver any nuclear device at all until 1964, when the first Mirage IVs became operational and received atomic bombs. The other, and more important, elements of what is today France's nuclear triad, the 18 intermediate-range ballistic missiles (IRBMs) deployed in hardened silos at the Plateau d'Albion in Provence and the nuclear submarine force of strategic missiles, were not to be operational until the 1970s.

Given this relative weakness—the superpowers were amassing megatons and ballistic missiles—it is not surprising that at first, the Gaullist force de frappe was more an object of derision than a serious element in the defense planning of the West. The so-called bombinette was not only attacked by de Gaulle's political opponents like François Mitterrand (who called it "ineffectual, costly, and dangerous") but by those more sympathetic to both a strong defense and to de Gaulle himself.[33] Raymond Aron, for example, once a follower of de Gaulle's RPF and always a realistic defender of the need for nuclear deterrence, believed the French nuclear force to be a "wholly insignificant, not to say non-existent, contribution to deterrence."[34] In his 1963 book *Le grand débat* (published in English as *The Great Debate*, 1965), Aron argued that the force de frappe was (1) too expensive (it drained limited funds not only from the necessary minimum of conventional forces but from nonmilitary scientific research); (2) not a credible replacement for the American deterrent (even when France would have built its three nuclear-armed submarines, the Americans would have forty-one); and (3) beyond French means (France's defense budget was only one-fifteenth the size of the Americans', and France not only would have to build from scratch the submarines and missiles to go with them but secure command posts and means of communications). In other words, the French contribution to American deterrence was based on "nothing more substantial than a sinister comedy of irrationality."[35]

Similarly, *Le Monde*'s military correspondent Jacques Isnard wrote sarcastically in 1968 that "If we accept the most optimistic hypothesis, France will have a nuclear capacity of about thirty megatons around 1975. In other words . . . what one American bomber carries today in its storage tank."[36] Although Isnard fails to acknowledge that one can logically deter with far less than thirty megatons (thousands of times what it took to destroy Hiroshima!), he does raise the critical issue of whether

France's nuclear force was in the long-term national security interest or, instead, an enormous expenditure for the sake of prestige.

In retrospect, it is difficult to see how the sixty-two French bombers deployed between 1964 and 1968 really could have made a serious contribution to nuclear deterrence at that time. French nuclear deterrence theory is discussed in chapter 3. Here, however, it is worth pointing out some of the reasons that, during the 1960s at least, the French deterrent was not very credible. Not only was the Mirage force vulnerable to a preemptive Soviet first strike (for which, unlike for American bombers, very little warning time—from five to seven minutes—would be given), but even if the planes got off the ground, they would have had to evade a growing system of Soviet air defense. Thick nests of SAM III missiles and the Soviet air force, even given the Mirage's supposed capacity for low-altitude flying and evasive maneuvers, would render the delivery onto Russian soil of even a few French bombs, which probably would not be enough to deter, at least highly questionable. Moreover, with a maximum range of 2,500 kilometers, to execute their mission the Mirages would need midair refueling, which would require cooperation from European neighbors and/or indirect flight paths toward the East (over Greek and Turkish or Scandinavian territory), if they were to reach Russian targets successfully and return home. In the *Götterdammerung* of a nuclear war, such a circus trick would have been unlikely to say the least. Finally, even to the extent that the Mirage force could inflict terrible damage on the Soviet Union, without either a sea-based deterrent or significant territorial space, France lacked the second-strike capabilities necessary to make deterrence more credible. Instead of fearing a French deterrent, Soviet leaders probably welcomed the independent nuclear force as an "instrument of blackmail" against NATO, a source of discord within the West, and as a sign of France's "anti-Americanism."[37] Rather than a real or immediate threat to Soviet security, the force de frappe was a pleasant new source of trouble for the Atlantic Alliance.

Consequently, the prevailing explanations for France's nuclear force have been through the years primarily political ones.[38] To the French, even outside of its military considerations (doubtless recognized as, if not admitted to be, marginal), an independent national deterrent had numerous justifications: it could bring France immediate prestige, demonstrate industrial expertise, provide a new and exciting role for a distracted and demoralized army, generate technological spin-offs, prevent domination by the "Anglo-Saxons," convince the French that their country had not lost its former energy, and give France a status not shared by its European neighbors, perhaps thereby compensating for relative economic weakness. Indeed, the French themselves never tried to hide the fact that they saw their nuclear force, for the present at least, primarily as a key to great power status. As François de Rose admitted as early as November 1958 (before the first French nuclear explosion), representing the French Foreign Ministry at the French national war college (IHEDN): "At the general political level, it is probable that the realization of nuclear weapons [will be] exploitable politically before it is exploitable in terms of national defense."[39]

De Gaulle, himself, although he rarely made it explicit (to emphasize the political rather than military role of a nuclear force is to undermine that political role), surely agreed with de Rose. All the talk of French greatness and rightful place as a leader suggested a rather obvious link to the creation of a nuclear force even if this force was most often justified in security terms alone. De Gaulle once went so far as to say that "no country without an atom bomb could consider itself properly independent," and he proclaimed in 1962 (referring to the bomb) that France "does not agree at all to a chronic and gigantic inferiority."[40] On another occasion de Gaulle reasoned that "A great state that does not possess [nuclear weapons], while others have them, does not command its own destiny."[41] France, of course, had to control its own destiny, even if other states did not.

Some of de Gaulle's closest deputies, perhaps less sensitive than the president of France to the potential effects of their rhetoric, went even further. Michel Debré argued in front of the National Assembly that "states without the bomb are satellites" and once even stated that to abandon the nuclear effort would be to "surrender all political autonomy, all influence in international life, all military defense in general."[42] Armed Forces Minister Pierre Messmer wrote in 1963 that "there are two categories of nations: those that have nuclear arms and those that do not. Only the former are capable of defending their liberty and their life, others are reduced to subservience or to satellitization."[43] Perhaps most enthusiastic and imaginative of all in signaling the political role of the nuclear force was Alexandre Sanguinetti, who went to the point of comparing nonnuclear countries to "Moroccan troops in the French army during World War II."[44] The psychological power of being in the small nuclear club had special meaning to a country whose confidence had been put to such a strong test.

Other political explanations for de Gaulle's overriding interest in the force de frappe are, of course, also plausible. Edgar S. Furniss, for example, writing on "civil-military relations" in the wake of the Algerian crisis, suggests that giving the disappointed army leadership a new mission (the nuclear defense of France) was done less for security reasons than for political ones. In his words, "The configurations of the Fifth Republic's military policy in Western Europe [have] been predicated on the need to provide *substitute satisfactions* for the professional army corps." This was like the famous thesis of the *joujou de l'armée de terre* (the army's plaything): France needed a nuclear force to attract the attention of an army that was disgruntled and hostile to the state. By giving nuclear weapons not only to France as a whole but to all three branches of the armed services, de Gaulle was seeking security not only from abroad but also from within.[45]

In any event, even as late as the early 1970s, the major analysts of French security would still quite naturally see the French nuclear force as a diplomatic instrument rather than a military one. In the introduction to his 1971 book, *French Nuclear Diplomacy*, Wilfred Kohl wrote that the force de frappe was inspired "more by political considerations than by concern for military security" and later that "it was a tool which [de Gaulle] employed in the pursuit of his larger foreign policy objectives."[46] Similarly, three years later, Edward Kolodziej wrote that "[the] key importance of the force de frappe was (and is) diplomatic."[47] Indeed, even by the time of the later study, the deterrent quality of French nuclear forces was still highly debatable; its most credible element was to be a fleet of nuclear submarines, but as yet only two ships had become operational, not enough to maintain a secure deterrent.

Although this analysis reflects a widely shared view, and the various political, economic, and industrial rationales for the independent nuclear force obviously all played a role, one can ask in retrospect if the literature describing the nature of the early force de frappe underestimated the deterrent potential it would eventually possess. Surely, it should not be doubted that the *primary* motivating factor behind the nuclear force was a symbolic French place among the world's great powers. Even had he believed, like Aron and other critics, that a French nuclear force could never really deter an aggressor, de Gaulle probably would not have abandoned the project. But was there not also in de Gaulle's mind the possibility that this force could some day form the basis for a genuine French, and possibly even European, deterrent? Was an "independent" nuclear force—even if created at the cost of a French contribution to European defense—not an investment in de Gaulle's "European Europe," a less bipolar future that was already coming about?

Such a proposition cannot be excluded and, in fact, falls rather closely in line with the logic of Gaullist ideas. Indeed, it can be argued that one of de Gaulle's main objectives was to endow Europe with the means—via France, to be sure, but why not?—of providing for its own security long after the prevailing security system had disappeared. That this would have served the French national interest both immediately and over the long term is not enough to discount the European perspective: selfish ends are not in themselves incompatible with ends that are shared.

De Gaulle's worldview included an aversion to the bipolar world of the superpowers, an inherent faith in nuclear deterrence, and the belief that the U.S. guarantee to Europe—because great nations only act in their national interest—was weakened by mutual deterrence. He believed that the military was destined to play a primordial role in national affairs, that Europe should be free from superpower hegemony and based upon the nation-state, and that France was the natural leader of this Europe. What, then, could be more consistent with the Gaullist view than the vision of a powerful French atomic force protecting Europe and freeing it from the chains of dependence? What could be a more logical final target for Gaullist aspirations than a France able to lead a Europe that could stand shoulder to shoulder with the superpowers? Again, the issue of a true European role for the French deterrent could not yet be on the agenda when the French force was still weak, when the American guarantee was still strong, and when European political and defense cooperation were still in their early stages. But the fundamental objectives of Gaullism, along with the General's penchant for looking ahead, make a strong case for the possibility of an eventual European role for the force de frappe.

An analysis of the early French nuclear force must, thus, be put in the context of the configuration of Europe to which de Gaulle aspired; doing so is not in the least incompatible with the recognition of the more immediate goals of political or diplomatic utility but complementary to it. To limit one's consideration of the force de frappe to the decade in which it was created is to neglect the prospects for change and to ignore the significance de Gaulle accorded to circumstance and opportunity. Where the FNS is concerned, indeed, its recent evolution would have to suggest that de Gaulle, or anyone else, would not have been altogether mistaken to have seen the early development of a French nuclear force as having great potential for the future.

Although in the 1960s de Gaulle could obviously neither join his critics and downplay the contemporary utility of the nuclear force nor insist too heavily on its future European role, his deputies were often given the role of making these points. As early as May 1963, that is, before the French nuclear force had even become operational, Armed Forces Minister Pierre Messmer argued in *Défense nationale* that the force de frappe would inevitably play a European role.

> Later, [France's nuclear armament] will come to the fore of European politics, for Europe cannot be built on economic and technical communities alone, however necessary these may be. In order for Europe to exist, it will be necessary that she assume the burden and the responsibility of her defense and that she possess nuclear arms for that purpose. When we reach that

point, we will see that France's possession of national nuclear weapons will be a cornerstone in the construction of Europe.[48]

Soon afterward, Georges Pompidou also began alluding to a potential European role for the force de frappe. As he pointed out to the National Assembly in 1964, using rhetoric more reminiscent of recent years than of the Gaullist period, France's deterrent could be European in a way even the larger American force could not: "[It] must be observed that, by the very fact that France is in Europe, her strength works fully and automatically on behalf of Europe, whose defense is physically and geographically inseparable from her own, which is not the case for powers, even allied, outside of the European continent."[49] The prime minister repeated the point to the same audience even more succinctly two years later, "By defending our own independence, we are defending most of Europe to which we belong, and we are the real Europeans."[50]

Others, both Gaullist and not, also made such arguments about the future French nuclear force. Alexandre Sanguinetti, for example, wrote that "If, one day, this Europe can be created, she will find the French nuclear force in her wedding basket, which will be nothing other than the foundation of the constitution of a European nuclear force, guarantor of the freedom and independence of our old continent."[51] And Michel Habib-Deloncle specifically broached the idea of a common European defense based on a Franco-British nuclear deterrent.[52] Even Raymond Aron, who had derided the military and deterrent capability of the force de frappe and viewed its costs as far out of proportion to its benefits, admitted a potential for a future European role. "The French force," he wrote, "may someday form the nucleus of a European deterrent; in any event it has persuaded our ally, the United States, to enter upon a dialogue with Europe on the subject of strategy. It constitutes an incipient protection against the unpredictability of future diplomacy."[53]

Finally, even some official government statements entertained the idea of an eventual European nuclear role for France. In 1964, while remaining vague, one such statement reasoned that "if a political Europe were formed with real responsibilities, France would be willing to study how this French deterrent could be used within the framework of the Europe of tomorrow."[54]

The European rhetoric of the Gaullists should obviously not be taken too far, and it is important to distinguish oratory from policy. De Gaulle, especially during this period, was concerned first with France, and the force de frappe must be seen primarily in that light. All hyperbole aside, however, logic is inherent in the idea that an independent French nuclear force, once credible in its own right, would "spillover" and contribute to deterrence for all Europe. There would always be a huge disproportion in size between the American force and the French, but there would be an equally important disproportion in the credibility of use, France's survival being threatened in many hypothetical cases in which America's was not. In the words of Georges Pompidou, today difficult to deny, France was "condemned . . . by her geography and by her history . . . to play the role of Europe."[55] As they looked to a multipolar future after the Cold War, in which minimal deterrence for Europe would have to be preserved, de Gaulle and his advisers were surely sincere in their vision of an eventual European role for the French nuclear force.

THE INTERNATIONAL CONTEXT AND THE
FRENCH CONTRIBUTION

The final question to be asked about the French role in European defense during the Gaullist years concerns the international context in which French policies were made. Did France's abiding absence from European defense, for whichever of the reasons discussed, matter at all? De Gaulle, it is often said, was only able to implement the policies he did, only able to pursue his cherished *indépendance*, because he knew that France was still safe under the American guarantee to Europe. Yet at the same time, de Gaulle tirelessly argued that that very guarantee had expired, and he explained his policies as an effort to take this into account. Which is more true, that American protection allowed France to pursue its selfish national goals, or that those national goals were a sensible reaction to the absence of American protection?

The answer is obviously complicated, and in a way, both arguments are correct. No one can pinpoint any one day, year, or event that marks the end of the American security guarantee for Europe. That guarantee was never perfect, nor has it ever been entirely a sham. The credibility of American protection for Europe has always been a question of degree that cannot be measured precisely. What can be said is that the credibility of a protection offered by an invulnerable United States eroded as the invulnerability disappeared, and if U.S. protection was perhaps credible as de Gaulle began his campaign for greater European autonomy, by the end of that period there were clear signs that it could not last forever.

Since the beginning of the Cold War, of course, West European defense was based not on the collective military strength of its individual nation-states but primarily on the military protectorate of the United States. The French role in staving off the threat from the east was limited to one of support. Thus, France, preoccupied or distracted from Europe in the ways discussed, was in the comfortable position of knowing that its contribution was less than vital so long as U.S. troops backed by nuclear weapons were in the Federal Republic of Germany to the east. "For the first time in history," wrote Raymond Aron, underlining the essence of these conditions, "France was no longer on the front lines."[56] De Gaulle could rail all he wanted against the American protectorate and could make a strong case indeed that it would eventually wear thin. But as he well knew, he was arguing from behind the lines, and those lines, at least for the time being, were still rather well entrenched.

Throughout the 1950s, the United States had the capacity—through long-range bombers stationed in the United States and Great Britain, and by the end of the decade IRBMs (Thors and Jupiters) stationed in Britain, Italy, and Turkey—to deliver nuclear weapons onto the home territory of the Soviet Union without risking retaliation on the United States. Even after the Soviets developed such capacity themselves, U.S. nuclear forces remained vastly superior to Russian ones, and if there was any truth to the idea of a "missile gap," by the mid-1960s it was probably on the Soviet side.[57] Although the Soviets had indeed made surprising leaps in their capacity to deliver bombs across the oceans and in their air defenses, the overwhelming U.S. lead in bombers and the advantage of having forward bases kept the Americans in a generally superior position in the nuclear balance. The United States was far from invulnerable, but it was well endowed enough in nuclear delivery capacity to make any aggressive Soviet blackmail effort seem highly unlikely. As late as 1969, the United States had more intercontinental ballistic missiles (ICBMs), more submarine-launched ballistic missiles (SLBMs), and more strategic bombers than the Soviet Union.[58]

Perhaps even more important is the fact that NATO was also less vulnerable at the conventional level than was commonly believed at the time. It had always been assumed that the United States, after its postwar demobilization, could not muster, even with its European allies, the conventional strength to oppose the Red Army in Europe. The Soviets, the argument ran, had some 175 divisions in Europe even without their satellites, and the West had a mere 25 divisions, which were poorly equipped at that. No one in the West had the money to spend or the stomach to meet such a challenge, and the assumption prevailed that the nuclear option was the only possible deterrent. But a closer look revealed some weaknesses in the Soviet position and some of the strengths of the West. NATO, in fact, throughout the 1960s, had more men under arms than did the Warsaw Pact, in 1969 over 6 million for NATO to about 4.5 million for the pact.[59] Soviet divisions may have been more numerous than the West's, but they were smaller, in low states of readiness, and even less well equipped.[60] It was also unclear at best whether or not Russia's East European satellites would fight, how well, and possibly even on which side. The United States was spending far more per division (and overall) than the Soviets, had far more to spend, and, doubtless, were getting "more bang for the buck"; American technology surely compensated for much of the Russian numerical strength in Europe. Finally, realizing that with the growing Sino-Soviet split Moscow would be required to maintain significant forces on its border with China (thus compensating in part for the other global roles of American forces), some analysts concluded, especially after the American military buildup early in the decade, that NATO really was not so badly prepared. According to the U.S. Department of Defense, by the end of the 1960s NATO's conventional forces could stop anything short of an all-out Soviet assault, and the two alliances had "approximate equality on the ground."[61]

None of this is to suggest that Western Europe lived through the 1960s as an impregnable fortress covered by a flawless nuclear guarantee. There was a self-serving aspect to the suddenly optimistic American assessment of the conventional balance in Europe (it was used to justify the flexible response doctrine that Americans in the previous administration had argued was impossible), and if Western Europe was better protected than had been generally admitted, the Soviet threat was still formidable and certainly growing. The point here, instead, is to suggest that throughout the Gaullist years, despite the national revival and rejuvenation of France, French military force and political support were still relatively unimportant to the Western Alliance as a whole. De Gaulle knew that France's potential role in European defense was growing, and he wanted nothing more for France than a leadership role; but he also knew that France was not quite indispensable yet. Perversely, Gaullist policies took advantage of an exceptional geopolitical situation at the same time that they announced its decline.

At the same time, if de Gaulle knew he was protected, he also claimed that such protection could not last, and he did not hesitate to explain out loud why this was so. By the early 1950s the General was already questioning the notion that the Americans would risk the destruction of U.S. cities in response to an attack in Europe. Ten years later, flexible response and the accompanying U.S. rearmament may have resulted in a greater American capacity to help defend Europe, but they were at the same time an implicit admission that the nuclear guarantee proffered in the past was no longer so complete.

From the Soviet's launching of the Sputnik rocket in 1957, in fact, the Americans had reached the same conclusions as de Gaulle: the now-vulnerable United States could no longer be expected with certainty to initiate nuclear war with the Soviets over a conventional conflict in Europe. But whereas U.S. leaders concluded this meant building up nonnuclear forces, de Gaulle believed the only solution was a deterrent for Europe itself. Even if the West had the means to raise the nuclear threshold (which only meant more destruction for the continent), the onset of mutual deterrence meant that "no one alive can say whether, where, how and to what extent American nuclear arms would be used in the defense of Europe."[62] The strategic balance may have remained in American favor, but it was already too close for comfort and tilting the wrong way.

In addition to the waning of extended deterrence, there were a number of other signs that the American protectorate would eventually have to be replaced. The trend implying a greater need for European contributions to Western defense in Europe did not pick up speed rapidly until the 1970s and 1980s when it led to the policy adjustments discussed in part 2 of this book; but its first manifestations appeared well before its consequences took effect.

As early as the 1950s, of course, U.S. leaders would have preferred that France devote to the central front the troops and arms it was squandering overseas. But they were not prepared to make this a major issue as long as European defense depended so largely on extended nuclear deterrence. NATO had never built up the massive conventional force levels deemed necessary for a serious nonnuclear defense. With U.S. nuclear forces still superior to the Soviet Union's, the adequacy of the West's ground forces was not a question of first order. With U.S. budgets and external balance still under control, and European economies not yet fully recovered, pressures on the U.S. role were still rather limited. Washington would, doubtless, have liked the Europeans to do more as their respective "economic miracles" got underway, but it was not prepared to push its allies very hard.

By the 1970s, however, alliance leaders began to see things differently, and France's reluctance to contribute on the central front started to become more of an issue. The Americans, of course, were still not prepared to devolve NATO responsibility to Europeans, which would have been inconsistent with their aspirations to world leadership and incompatible with their operational military plans. But they were becoming increasingly anxious that European states support—both financially and diplomatically—increasingly unsustainable American "burdens" abroad, the most significant of which was in Europe itself. It was becoming clear that the status quo could not endure and that changes on both sides of the Atlantic were making the French military role in Europe more important.

First, the United States, not yet admitting that the immensity of its relative power during the first postwar decades was more likely a historical parenthesis than a fulfillment of national destiny, was beginning to feel the pressures resulting from an inevitable erosion of its means. When the French Fifth Republic was formed in 1959, it was not yet realized in Washington that the just-ending Eisenhower administration would be the last to enjoy consistently balanced budgets, inexpensive nuclear deterrence, and relatively easy and successful interventions abroad. As the Kennedy-Johnson administration paralleled de Gaulle's, the Americans would be confronted with the problems of limits on their power.

The decline of American global preeminence was first manifested not in Vietnam, which became one of its symbols, but in the United States' relationships with its partners and allies, notably in Europe and Japan. The story of America's gradual return toward the status of an "ordinary country," whose implications for American policy may be controversial, is itself well known and difficult to deny.[63] The United States, whose GNP in 1950 was nearly double that of the four biggest European states combined and whose military expenditures were no less than five times as large, could not be expected to maintain such an unnatural international superiority. It was unprecedented in the history of international relations that in such a short time all other great powers collapsed (Germany, France, and Italy all declined rather drastically, with Britain and the Soviet Union suffering severe financial [and for the Soviet Union, population] losses) while one (the United States, whose GNP rose by more than 50 percent in constant dollars from 1939 to 1945) rapidly expanded.[64] With the reconstruction of Europe a priority in American foreign policy planning (for the Europeans, for the world political economy, and as a buffer to Soviet power), it was inevitable and apparently desirable that this exceptional situation come to an end.

Indeed, before long, this changing balance began to manifest itself and to put strains on the hegemonic role to which Americans had become accustomed. Parallel to the familiar strategic-military developments just discussed were some telling economic developments. From one decade to the next, the American balance-of-payments deficits turned from a benign and even necessary source of liquidity for Europe and the Third World to an indication of possible overextension. By 1960, not only was capital flowing out from both private sources and the government as it had been since the war, but the U.S. current account as a whole swung into deficit: Americans were no longer selling enough goods and services abroad to cover the "costs" of their expenditures and investments abroad.[65] At the same time, the dollar, whose value was the pillar of the Bretton Woods system, began to falter both internationally and at home. With American capital flooding world markets, and foreign central banks and corporations accumulating dollars, the U.S. exchange rate required increasing support at the same time American inflation began to rise. Still rising only by 1 percent annually in 1961, the U.S. consumer price index would be increasing at a rate more than five times that by the end of the decade. Inflation averaged 3.8 percent from 1965 to 1969, perhaps low by today's standards but over twice the rate of the previous four years.[66] None of this yet meant that Washington's exclusive leadership of the West was in jeopardy, and the United States began the 1960s brimming with the confidence induced by the Kennedy economic boom and rearmament. But with hindsight, the development of the American economy from the 1950s to the 1960s shows clear signs that adjustment could not forever be postponed.

At the same time that the United States was reaching the inevitable end of its interlude of omnipotence (and obviously not unrelated to this development), Western Europe was beginning to rise at a remarkable pace. The trade liberalization associated with the 1958 formation of the Common Market resulted in unprecedented growth for the continent—an average of 5.5 percent between 1950 and 1970—and in a number of sectors European industrial strength began to challenge American.[67] As a whole, the GNP of the Common Market states had practically equaled that of the United States by 1970, and by 1980 (with the addition of three more states in the meantime) it was clearly well ahead.[68] Moreover, if the "economic miracles" most often discussed were the German and the Italian, France too had embarked on a period of remarkable growth and dynamism known as *"les trente glorieuses."*[69] Europe's military capability lagged far beyond its growing economic prowess, but it seemed likely, as well as necessary, that the one would catch up to the other.

None of this change—the erosion of American omnipotence, Europe's eventual rise, and the gradual withering of the American protectorate—should have been unexpected, and it could even be seen as a rather beneficent development from an American point of view. It is no indictment of American foreign policy to say that it achieved its goal of an economically viable and politically sound Europe, and if this meant an inevitable adjustment in the distribution of Western power, Americans were not necessarily the worse for it. America's loss of invulnerability vis-à-vis its military rival, and its relative economic decline vis-à-vis its European allies did not mean the country had in any way failed but only that the pillars on which Western defense was built would eventually have to be realigned.

De Gaulle's attacks on American hegemony may have been difficult to swallow, and his attempts to resist that hegemony never did much for the cohesion or effectiveness of the Atlantic Alliance. There is even a rather raw element of cynicism in the denunciation of the very conditions on which one's security and foreign policy depend. But de Gaulle, it must be said with hindsight, was also right. As solid as Western defense may have remained throughout the 1960s, there were clear signs that its structures, inherited from the immediate postwar period, would eventually have to be adjusted to a changing geopolitical scene. Like many great figures in history, it could be said of de Gaulle that had he not existed when he did, he would later have had to be invented.

The relationship between the international context and Gaullist security policies in France is, thus, a complicated and dynamic one. No matter how much the French questioned the reliability of the Americans, the geography of Europe and the American role there suggested that France would be defended from its most likely adversary whether it participated in that defense or not. At the same time that de Gaulle claimed the U.S. guarantee was inadequate, that guarantee was the most important factor in allowing France to pursue other goals. At the same time that the Americans maintained their protectorate role in Europe's defense, it was clear that such a role could not endure forever.

CHAPTER THREE

Manipulating Ambiguity

MILITARY DOCTRINES UNDER DE GAULLE
AND POMPIDOU

IT WOULD BE imprudent to try to analyze the evolution, meaning, or fate of Gaullist security policies without at least a basic understanding of the operational military doctrines that were ostensibly behind them. What exactly were the military doctrines that successive French administrations found necessary (and so difficult) to adapt to the requirements of European defense? What were the specific arguments or logic behind the military strategies inherited by French leaders in the late 1970s and 1980s? How did the operational guidelines for the French military of the 1960s become codified into a rigid doctrine that would influence French policymakers for decades to come? Gaullist military doctrine was a brilliant manipulation of particular circumstances to suit France's particular needs but one that caused serious problems in Europe and would become increasingly inappropriate as those circumstances changed.

CONVENTIONAL DOCTRINE THROUGH THE MID-1960S

During the 1950s, with French forces still integrated in NATO's military commands and France possessing no nuclear deterrent, possibilities for French conventional military doctrine were severely circumscribed. Although French divisions never occupied a piece of the Western "layer cake" of forces along the inter-German border, the French troops allocated to NATO were to fall, like other national forces, under Supreme Allied Commander Europe (SACEUR) command in wartime. French conventional forces, however minimal and notwithstanding the Fourth Republic's own desire for independence, were required to take part in an integrated defense according to the war plans of NATO leaders.

As seen in the last two chapters, such a hierarchical scenario had always seemed highly inappropriate to de Gaulle. Throughout the 1950s the General strongly defended the principle of national commands and believed only national defense to be consistent with a country's honor, dignity, and purpose. By the early 1960s, what was already objectionable to de Gaulle in principle was becoming even more so in practice. Not only had Europe greatly changed since the birth of the Atlantic Alliance—the possibilities of conflict there had significantly diminished—but the Americans had begun to adopt just the sort of military doctrine from which de Gaulle wanted to maintain the liberty to abstain. In the face of imminent strategic parity with the Soviet Union, the Americans had begun to believe that their strategy of "massive nuclear retaliation"—in response even to a conventional attack on Europe—was no longer credible, and had announced a new doctrine of "flexible response."[1]

It is not necessary here to undertake a long discussion of that well-known American doctrine, whose main objective was to raise the strategic nuclear threshold by giving U.S. commanders a graduated array of means with which to respond to an attack. Rather, the important point is that for General de Gaulle the new American strategy was a powerful additional reason to regain French control over the conduct of a potential European war, one in which France would inevitably be involved. With the United States developing a military doctrine that might include the use of tactical nuclear weapons on European territory or that might lead to prolonged conventional battles in Europe, de Gaulle found it more necessary than ever to find the means to distance French strategy from that of the alliance.

Almost immediately upon his assumption of the French presidency in 1959, de Gaulle began to do so not only in word but in deed. As early as November 1959 he announced his view that "the system of integration had seen its day," and over the next several years repeated that France intended to "modify profoundly" its relationship with NATO.[2] More concretely, while the Americans were trying to centralize control of allied forces in the hierarchical commands necessary to their new doctrine, France was taking measures to keep its own forces outside those commands. In March 1959, de Gaulle withdrew French ships from NATO's Mediterranean authority on the grounds that France might have military responsibilities or interests in Africa that other allied countries did not share. Later that year, he refused to let NATO maintain stockpiles of nuclear weapons in France, a step that led to the redeployment to Great Britain of the American bombers that were to carry them. When French troops began to return home from Algeria in 1961, de Gaulle decided not to integrate them into NATO and instead created a First Corps, not subordinated to the SACEUR, especially for those units. In 1963, the General decided that France would produce its own tactical nuclear weapons (which would be independent from NATO) and in the same year withdrew French ships from NATO's Atlantic command. By the mid-1960s, the

French had begun to refuse to participate in forward defense exercises with NATO, and it had become obvious that de Gaulle was getting ready to make official the doctrine of France's independent defense.[3] Thus, by the time the withdrawal from NATO's integrated commands was announced in March 1966, it was already clear that French conventional forces would not be subordinated to NATO doctrine and that France would not passively accept the logic of flexible response.

But to what doctrine *would* French forces be subordinated? Was de Gaulle seeking military independence merely to proceed as before (but under the guise of national authority) or did he have an alternative battle plan to that of NATO? As France's nuclear deterrent became operational, the French began to develop their own concept for the role of French conventional forces, and it was very different from the American one. The French formulation was based on the notion that French forces were not to prepare for prolonged battles in Europe but were simply to play a part in setting up the deterrent mechanism of a soon-to-be nuclear France.

Consistent with his practice of avoiding rigid doctrinal formulations and with the principle that the French president not get bogged down in messy policy details, de Gaulle himself was never explicit about how his conventional forces were to be used. (He would be no more loquacious when it came to nuclear doctrines.) He did, however—at a press conference in February 1963—hint at their future role. Without elaborating, de Gaulle suggested that France saw the central front in terms of two potential battles, the first one in Germany and the second one on the Rhine. French nuclear forces (the first operational Mirages were to be deployed within one year) were naturally intended only for use in the battle for France, depending on the outcome of the first one in Germany.[4] If France were invaded, it would be prepared both to use nuclear weapons and to "confront the invader . . . with a national resistance."[5] As will be seen, this was the first, tentative suggestion of what would eventually become a finely tuned doctrine for the employment of French conventional military force.

With the General willing to say little more, it was left up to his deputies to flesh out the emerging strategy. The task in this case fell largely to Armed Forces Chief of Staff General Charles Ailleret, who provided some more details about the "two battles" scenario in a series of articles and statements in the mid-1960s.[6] The role of French conventional forces, Ailleret explained, was primarily to help determine the intentions of an aggressor. He defined two types of aggression, *limited* (*limitée*) and *unmistakable* (*caracterisée*).[7] When an aggression could be considered unmistakable, France would threaten a strategic nuclear response. Less optimistic than the Americans about being able to contain a potential Soviet attack with conventional means alone, the French thus viewed forward-based conventional forces in a fundamentally different way: they were not designed "to stop in its tracks a powerful attack . . . but to measure a minimum level of attack which would define an aggression that would trigger the defensive nuclear strategy."[8] What de Gaulle had referred to as the "first battle" was, thus, only meant as a test to see whether or not France itself would be invaded. If an invasion of France was not likely, it would be up to NATO—with an unspecified amount of French support—to defend the Federal Republic. If such an invasion were imminent, France would prepare a nuclear response. As Ailleret put it, "The conventional forces of infantry, aviation, armor and artillery of a nuclear army [had] no more than the role of covering, exploiting and concluding atomic actions."[9] While NATO and the Americans were making plans to build up conventional forces to be able to avoid an early resort to nuclear weapons, French military doctrine was moving in exactly the opposite direction.

It was clear, then—to simplify only slightly—that French conventional forces under de Gaulle were to be no more than a tripwire for the force de frappe. To be sure, French troops would be expected to fight valiantly at the Rhine against an incoming invasion, but because any such invasion was also supposed to provoke a French nuclear response (and would inevitably have been preceded by an East-West clash in Germany), it was difficult to envisage the scenario in which French conventional forces would actually be called on to fight for very long. And although it was also true that this French doctrine of "nonbattle" depended to a great extent on NATO maintaining significant forward forces, the location, equipment, exercises, and official rationale of French troops all suggested their primary role was that of a link to the French nuclear force. As already seen, French forces were extremely ill-equipped for heavy conventional battle in Central Europe; occupied no space along NATO's forward line of defense; and had ceased to participate fully in the alliance's forward defense exercises in 1963. In short, the "forward battle" was a German-American affair to which France might or might not have something to contribute, and the defense of France, if forward defense failed, was based on a national nuclear threat. In this doctrine, a serious battlefield role for French conventional forces was difficult to find.

This brief description of the role of conventional forces in Gaullist military doctrine obviously leaves out questions of the military context in Europe and the way in which French ground forces would actually conduct their test of enemy intentions. But the French themselves were careful to leave out such considerations as well: de Gaulle wanted no part of elaborate and detailed doctrines, especially when they would betray the extent to which French doctrine was dependent on American force. But even this short description underlines a very simple and important point: in a Europe where defense was primarily left up to NATO—an organization in which the French role was minimal—the French were able to subordinate their conventional forces almost entirely to their own national goals.

EARLY NUCLEAR DOCTRINES

Where nuclear doctrine—by far more important if the above analysis is correct—was concerned, French doctrinal choices under de Gaulle were also greatly influenced, if not altogether determined, by circumstance. Without serious conventional forces, any sort of flexible response, or even a meaningful "pause" or "firebreak," was excluded. Without the second-strike capability afforded by invulnerable nuclear submarines or highly dispersed missiles, any counterforce alternatives to the threatening of Soviet cities were inconceivable. With no tactical nuclear weapons, even a "warning shot" to announce an impending strategic response was not in the range of options for the French. Under these conditions, only a "pure" strategic deterrent, based on the threat of a massive nuclear strike against the Soviet population, was logically possible for France.

This was the very logic manifested in the influential writings of General Pierre Gallois, writings with which de Gaulle seemed to sympathize.[10] The Gallois theory of deterrence is well known and need not be repeated exhaustively here. But as a pure, or even extreme, position, its idealized logic is a useful one with which to compare subsequent attempts to refine it. And the mechanism it describes (what Raymond Aron calls "the fragment of truth that Gallois stretches to absurdity"),[11] by which smaller nuclear powers can deter even much larger ones—by threatening to inflict intolerable damage upon them—has been in one form or another behind all French nuclear strategy ever since. It is indeed upon this "fragment of truth" that all deterrence depends.

For General Gallois, to deter, a country need not possess the capacity to inflict greater damage upon its adversary than the adversary could inflict upon it. Instead, it is only necessary that it be able to inflict damage greater than anything the adversary might hope to gain by attacking it. This was the important asymmetry in Gallois's "proportional deterrence"; if the aggressor's certain losses were out of proportion to its potential gains, it would never attack. What world leader would consciously sacrifice millions of his compatriots to rule the charred remains of defeated enemy territory?

It followed that successful deterrence depended only on the capacity to riposte in turn. Thus, if a "small" country (such as France) could build for itself a "relatively invulnerable" nuclear force (such as 50 Mirage IV bombers, at least according to Gallois), then it would possess just as effective an ultimate deterrent as a larger, more powerful country. To be sure, the large country could destroy the small one many times over. But as long as the small country could threaten to annihilate an unacceptable proportion of the larger's population, the latter could not possibly have anything to gain by aggression. This was why the "weak" could deter even the "strong."[12]

A second important element in Gallois' thinking also played a major role in the official justification of French policy (which it probably mirrored more than it influenced). Because the process—or better yet the threats—just described were based on matters of life and death, human and national, they could only be executed in a national context. In an age of ballistic missiles, when all countries, large and small, are vulnerable to the thermonuclear destruction of their potential adversaries, no country—even the powerful United States—could be expected to engage in nuclear war for another. To defend the integrity, sovereignty, and survival of one's own nation, it was realistic to threaten the use of nuclear weapons; to defend a neighbor, even a friendly one, it was absurd. "The nuclear risk," went the French saying, "cannot be shared."[13]

Gallois followed his early logic to its extreme conclusions over the years and eventually let his theory get ahead of the reality it was supposed to describe. Not only did France, or even Europe, need a deterrent because the U.S. guarantee was on the wane, but so, presumably, did everyone else. In a world "beyond extended deterrence," alliances would be useless except, perhaps, to share the means to keep deterrent forces up to date or to stamp out minor disputes. In a world of ballistic missiles and thermonuclear warheads, tiny Switzerland and mammoth China would essentially be in the same geostrategic boat.[14] And Gallois also spoke out against almost *all* increases in conventional forces, which to him only served as tempting targets for the adversary's nuclear weapons or a drain on resources needed for the nuclear force.[15] Finally, and perhaps most startling, Gallois argued that the anticity threat of the nuclear power—because of the inherent lack of resoluteness of Western democracies—would have to be "virtually automatic," even if this entailed the risk of an unwanted "war of annihilation."[16] This was truly nuclear deterrence in its most pure form.

Such logic, to repeat, was never officially sanctioned as French policy, and General Gallois was less the "close adviser" to General de Gaulle than has sometimes been said. But although de Gaulle rarely delved into the specifics of the nuclear doctrines that were supposed to guide his force de frappe, he did seem to rely heavily on the "fragment of truth" in Gallois's logic that the even minimal threat of destroying enemy populations was itself enough to deter. As de Gaulle described it at one 1963 press conference, it was the very potential to inflict inconceivable disaster on an aggressor that gave the French force its "influence" and enabled it to deter. Because that force had "a certain efficacy . . . even where it did not approach the maximum conceivable" it would have "the somber and terrifying capability of destroying within a few moments millions and millions of people. This cannot help but exert at least some influence upon the intentions of a potential aggressor."[17]

On another occasion, at a 1964 press conference devoted largely to nuclear deterrence, de Gaulle was even more specific about the concept of proportional deterrence: a small country like France could, perhaps, not equal the nuclear might of the superpowers, but given certain conditions it could still deter a potential aggressor.

> Once reaching certain nuclear capability, and with regard to one's own direct defense, the proportion of respective means has no absolute value. Indeed, since a man and people can die only once, the deterrent exists provided that one has the means to wound the possible aggressor mortally, that one is very determined to do it and that the aggressor is convinced of it.[18]

To attack France, de Gaulle reasoned, would mean "frightful destruction" for whomever might contemplate it; that was enough.[19]

In the same press conference de Gaulle reiterated another of his favorite points that Gallois had expounded upon—that true deterrence could only be national. The equilibrium that existed between the United States and Russia only covered them, de Gaulle argued, "and not the other countries of the world, even when they are allied to one or the other colossal powers." Defending the "cause and the integrity" of third states "might not seem worth it to their great ally to see itself destroyed upon destroying its rival."[20]

French deterrence in the mid-1960s, despite its official ambiguity, was, therefore, very specifically and clearly based on the proportional nuclear threat. It was also uniquely "national" deterrence, a characteristic that should have surprised no one in a policy made by Charles de Gaulle. But for all this, deterrence under de Gaulle did not ignore the existence of the alliance, and it recognized, if tacitly, the relationship between the decried American deterrent and the French one. France counted on American nuclear protection while it developed its small force de frappe. But even after that force was built there was another sort of interaction between the two: the French deterrent might be more effective because it could somehow supplement or reinforce the American one. This was the theory associated most closely with General André Beaufre under the name of "multilateral deterrence," and although it was never presented as an official rationale for the French force, its logic does seem to have played a role in French thinking about deterrence.[21]

Beaufre's reasoning, expressed in a number of articles and in two books—*Introduction à la stratégie* (Introduction to Strategy, 1963) and *Dissuasion et stratégie* (Deterrence and Strategy, 1964)—began with an ingredient common to all deterrence theory that had already become a fundamental factor in French military doctrine and declaratory policy: the concept of uncertainty.[22] Now that the Americans had lost their nuclear superiority, Beaufre argued, and could no longer deter as certainly as before because they risked destruction themselves, the American nuclear protection of Western Europe could no longer be counted on with the same assurance. In this new world, one of a "balance of terror," no threat to use nuclear force would be perfectly credible given the potential consequences of such an action. But deterrence was not thereby dead. For although no one could be certain that an adversary would use nuclear weapons, neither could anyone be sure that the adversary would *not* use them. Henceforth, the primary goal of strategy had to be to increase, or at least to maintain, a certain level of uncertainty in the eyes of the potential adversary. Uncertainty had become "the essential factor of deterrence."[23]

So far, the argument was no different than Gallois's: the potential for destruction of the enemy population was still the mechanism that worked to deter aggression. But Beaufre was not as confident as his colleague in the mechanism of pure deterrence. For although a weak country could theoretically deter a strong one, it could only do so if its stakes in the conflict were infinitely greater than those of the larger power. The weak could deter the strong, but "to do so, the stake must be total for the weaker party and minor for the stronger," not at all a certain supposition.[24] Thus, it was not by acting alone, as Gallois had implied, that France's tiny deterrent was most likely to work but only in the context of an alliance with a stronger nuclear partner.

The French force would add to deterrence, Beaufre argued, not so much via a direct threat to the Soviets but through its capacity to initiate a nuclear war in Europe and thereby involve the United States. If the Americans might have been tempted to avoid "going nuclear" now that they were vulnerable, they could no longer do so if France itself could bring about a nuclear war that would threaten even U.S. security. The stable nuclear balance of the superpowers had taken away the uncertainty necessary for effective Western deterrence; France's additional "center of nuclear decision" would bring it back. By "intruding" into a situation of bipolar nuclear equilibrium, the third party could have "strategic consequences out of all proportion to the [its] nuclear strength."[25]

Beaufre himself always avoided the explicit argument that the French nuclear force could act as a "trigger" for the American one, but the notion was implicit in his analysis. Indeed, it was difficult to imagine the mechanism by which multilateral deterrence would work if not via the "nuclear trigger." How could the force de frappe "intrude" on the superpower balance if not in the end by raising the specter of setting off an American nuclear strike? Either small nuclear forces could deter alone (in which case they were proportional, not multilateral, deterrents) or they had to be able to involve one of the superpowers (in which case they were "triggers"). Still, Beaufre thought it unnecessary to conjure up such direct (and implausible) threats: he believed it enough simply to suggest that the Soviets could never know what the relationship between independent centers of decision was and argued that this uncertainty alone complicated their military plans.[26]

"Multilateral deterrence," it should be stressed, was a political rather than military argument. It was an early form of "coupling," the tying together of American interests with European ones. Its goal, like that of deterrence in general, lay "not in the actual employment of nuclear weapons but simply in the utilization of their threat."[27] Thus, the French force need not—indeed, must not—actually be a detonator for an American strategic launch (a rather disastrous "solution" for Europe) but had only to remind the Russians in advance of the possibility of American support for France. As Stanley Hoffmann (one of the few observers defending the force de frappe in the United States at the time) understood it, the mere presence of an independent French nuclear threat would be a sort of "preventive trigger" that would prevent the nuclear trigger from ever having to be pulled.

> In case of extreme Soviet provocation against Western Europe, the French threat of a thermonuclear strike (a threat that the Americans regard themselves as less and less able to brandish except in the most serious circumstances) and the counterthreat of annihilating France, which the Russians will not hesitate to make in return, *would force the U.S. into a manifestation of its solidarity with France*—in other words extend the cover of its nuclear protection to France even if this was precisely the sort of situation it had wanted to avoid. Strategic dissent and France's "disobedience" would not, after all, be sufficient reason to justify abandoning France, the less so since abandoning France to Russian bombs would be a disaster for the United States as well. The manifest purpose, then, is preventive triggering designed to *deter* the Russians ahead of time rather than countering an attack after the fact.[28]

Not surprisingly, de Gaulle remained more circumspect about multilateral deterrence and its implicit trigger concept than he was about Gallois's "equalizing power of the atom." To argue that the French force was valuable primarily as a trigger would be to express doubts about the force's actual deterrent value. And it would have been difficult for de Gaulle to insist on the "independence" of the French force while he admitted its relationship with—or even dependence on—the American one. But the logic of multilateral deterrence was not inconsistent with de Gaulle's other arguments about European defense, and as a way to prevent a superpower agreement to limit war to European soil, it was a primary element in his critique of flexible response. The "trigger" logic probably played a greater part in de Gaulle's own mind than is commonly suggested in France and certainly more than he ever admitted himself.

The General's reasoning probably went something like this: If the French were capable of forcing a nuclear escalation that the Americans would have tried to avoid, then they would obviously have the means to influence the functioning of that doctrine. Flexible response at the strategic nuclear level, of course, meant "counterforce" targeting designed to avoid an automatic holocaust if war broke out. But because deterrence for France was premised precisely on the fear of such a disaster, any such "damage limitation" theory was intolerable. With an independent French force that might trigger more general nuclear war, no one (neither superpower) could be sure to keep war nonnuclear without French cooperation. The French could, thus, be sure to prevent the superpower "condominium" in which the Americans and Russians might agree not to attack each other and, in de Gaulle's words, use Europe as a "battlefield for their expeditionary forces and a target for their exchanges of bombs."[29] If France had its own nuclear bombs, which could be dropped over Russian territory and ensure that the war would become strategic, the superpowers would be denied this possibility.

Beaufre's argument was, thus, in some ways closer to the true French position under de Gaulle than Gallois's because it provided an alternative to the extreme thesis that alliances were useless in the nuclear age. De Gaulle, as noted, never rejected the notion of alliances, and because he always counted on the "insurance" of the American protectorate, he can probably be assumed to have counted in part on the "trigger" effect. The General may have refused Beaufre's contention that successful multilateral deterrence required a closely linked alliance, and he never liked to admit the dependence of French deterrence on the United States. But if the *Soviets* believed the French nuclear force might act as a trigger, then de Gaulle was happy to accept whatever strategic leverage this might imply for France.

The final argument about French nuclear deterrence that must be considered here, the one that forms the most immediate part of the precedent to the Pompidou period (and the one that contrasts most with it), was the famous doctrine of *"défense tous azimuts"* articulated by General Charles Ailleret in 1967. That the concept was never fully implemented does not negate the fact that it did become (albeit briefly) an official part of French doctrine and that it is indicative of a strain of thought inherent in the ideas of General de Gaulle. "Defense in all directions" did not become a lasting part of French defense doctrine like some of the other concepts, such as tripwires, proportional deterrence, and nuclear "triggering," but as an ideal logical conclusion of the project of independence, it cannot be ignored.

Ailleret's argument, published in the *Revue de défense nationale* in December 1967, was that France, rather than remaining dependent on a United States still obsessed with the Soviet threat, had to develop a defense force capable of protecting France from dangers that might threaten it from other parts of the world. France had always in the past concentrated on a single enemy—usually in the East—but with the shrinking of the globe and nuclear proliferation, such a narrow focus would no longer suffice. The necessary force could only be a powerful, thermonuclear, ballistic missile force, capable of "intervening anywhere in the world." If France wanted "to escape the dangers that might threaten her," she had to possess

> significant quantities . . . of global-range megatonic ballistic missiles which would deter anyone, acting in any part of the world, who wanted to make use of us or destroy us in order to assist the achievement of their war aims. . . . To be as strong as possible in an autonomous and individual manner, and to possess in one's own right very long distance and very powerful weapons capable of deterring any aggressor whatever his starting point, is obviously an entirely different formula from that which consists in equipping oneself, at the cost of the same financial effort, with a force that complements that of the principal member of an a priori alliance.[30]

Arguing that it was impossible to know what danger would threaten future generations of the French or whence that danger would come, Ailleret postulated that France had to be able to deter "anyone acting in any part of the world," in other words, "in military jargon, *tous azimuts*."[31]

The concept itself was highly consistent with, and a direct result of, the logic that led to the withdrawal from NATO commands the previous year. Because it was no longer appropriate to be so heavily focused on the outdated notion of a Soviet invasion across Europe, France wanted to reserve for itself the right and endow itself with the means to counter potential threats coming from other parts of the world. It had, of course, always been a French and particularly Gaullist habit to entertain the notion of France as a global power as opposed to a simply European one. What could be more central to grandeur than the capacity to influence war or peace anywhere around the globe? Moreover, a global French ICBM force would further liberate France from the tutelage of the United States, not so much because such a force might one day be used to deter the United States (though this startling suggestion was not excluded) but by reducing the need for U.S. support against potential "third threats" and by allowing France to rely more on its own deterrent and less on the trigger effect. As the Vietnam War and other conflicts caused increasing tension between France and the United States, the idea of triggering was becoming less plausible anyway, and it would apparently be less necessary as well if the French possessed a force great enough to become a fully operational deterrent in its own right.

The Ailleret proposal would not be so interesting had it merely been the case of an overzealous officer trying to show himself to be "more Gaullist than de Gaulle." But as Jean Lacouture and others have pointed out, de Gaulle himself seems to have been the motivating force behind the project: not only did he read the Ailleret article without objection before publication but he apparently asked for it in the first place.[32] Indeed, de Gaulle had reasoned as early as 1959 that "since France can be destroyed, potentially, from anywhere in the world, our force must be capable of acting anywhere in the world."[33] And in January 1968, as observers were wondering if Ailleret's article could be taken to be the official policy of France, de Gaulle announced at the Institut des Hautes Etudes de Défense Nationale (IHEDN) that it was: "By definition," de Gaulle said, "France's atomic forces had to be *tous azimuts*."[34] The doctrine of military independence had reached its ultimate logical end.

THE DIRECT LEGACY: THE FOURQUET DOCTRINE

It has often been debated whether France's adoption of a more "European" or "Atlantic" security role began under Georges Pompidou or not until Valéry Giscard d'Estaing. In fact, however, the adaptation of French security policy actually began under de Gaulle himself.

If the years 1965–1968 were marked by Gaullist displays of hostility or diffidence toward NATO and the United States, the final twelve months of de Gaulle's presidency saw the beginnings of a limited but certain reconciliation. In the mid-1960s, bolstered by the progress of the force de frappe, a rapidly growing French economy, American difficulties in Vietnam, and relative détente in Europe, de Gaulle was able to bargain for French independence from a position of relative strength. It appeared that France and Europe were gaining the means to recover their full sovereignty, that global American hegemony was weakening, and most important to de Gaulle, that the Soviet threat to Western Europe was diminishing and, consequently, reducing the raison d'être of the blocs. By the end of 1968, however, with French society shaken by the events of May and the economy and the franc both in tatters following months of strikes and subsequent wage concessions, de Gaulle was no longer in a position to assert French military independence. Even more importantly, the brutal Warsaw Pact invasion of Czechoslovakia in the summer of that year seemed to have convinced de Gaulle that the Cold War was not yet over and that the risk of conflict in Europe had not yet disappeared. If de Gaulle had had good reason to hope in the mid-1960s that his Europe "from the Atlantic to the Urals" could soon become a reality and that the blocs he so despised might be disbanded or at least loosened, the invasion of Czechoslovakia gave him good reason to pause.

The shift away from the more radical positions of the mid-1960s was discernable in several ways and included the formal extension of the Atlantic Pact for twenty years; French expressions of solidarity with NATO after the invasion of Prague; the postponement of French plans for an autonomous ICBM force; and a warm and promising meeting in Paris between U.S. President Richard Nixon and General de Gaulle.[35] Its first explicit articulation, however, came in a March 1969 speech by General Michel Fourquet, chief of staff of the armed forces, given to the Institut des Hautes Etudes de Défense Nationale.[36] The speech is noteworthy not only because Fourquet was making the final major defense policy statement approved by de Gaulle but because it was the first attempt to express French strategy as the major elements of the nuclear force came onto line. It was also important because its was the first of several highly consistent policy formulations that would emerge during the Pompidou administration, formulations that set a standard for subsequent continuity and change.

As outlined in the preceding section, French conventional and nuclear doctrine as de Gaulle's tenure came to an end can be grossly summarized as follows: conventional forces were essentially reserved for French territory (and even then primarily for France's "nuclear deterrent maneuver") and the force de frappe was not only "independent" but its range and targeting orientation was considered in terms of a global defense. In this context, What was the objective of the policy statement made by General Fourquet in March 1969? What changed in this final articulation of French security policy under de Gaulle?

General Fourquet's speech, given just one month before de Gaulle's resignation, formalized the conclusions that de Gaulle had seemed to reach after the events of the previous year and rejected directly the radical policy broached by Fourquet's predecessor Ailleret; France was not on the road toward armed neutrality or isolation from Europe. In the new formulation, Fourquet dropped two of Ailleret's principal arguments:

that which said France had to be prepared to fight "anyone acting in any part of the world" and that which emphasized France's threat of an all-out nuclear response. Instead, he reaffirmed that the only plausible threat to French territory for the time being still came from the East and that, rather than the almost automatic threat of a massive nuclear response, French conventional forces might be able to play a role in meeting it. "Engaged along the northern and eastern borders against an enemy coming from the East," Fourquet said, "the battle corps will normally operate in close coordination with the forces of our allies."[37]

In an implicit shift away from the logic of "pure deterrence," Fourquet admitted that the participation of French conventional forces had to be more than a simple tripwire for the force de frappe. France, of course, could not build up the significant conventional forces necessary truly to back away from nuclear deterrence; that would not only be too expensive but it might lead governments to "put off the vital decision to use nuclear weapons and so, perhaps, lose all chances of stopping the conflict."[38] If the threatened use of nuclear weapons was wholly incredible to the adversary, all the atom's "compensatory power" was lost. Whereas, on the one hand, "certain military imperatives" made it necessary to stress the primary role of strategic nuclear forces, "on the other hand, one can think of a number of circumstances in which the alternative of 'all or nothing' would make our posture less realistic and less credible."[39] Not quite a French version of flexible response, the new doctrine did admit that some flexibility was required if nuclear deterrence was to work.

It has been suggested—and affirmed by none other than General Fourquet himself[40]—that the 1969 IHEDN speech and the policy it articulated were meant not as a real change in direction but as a mere "clarification" of past formulations. In this view, the Ailleret episode was only intended to "shake the French officer corps out of its mind-set of dependence," and the Fourquet speech sought simply to make French policy more clear as new military means began to come on line.[41] Although this seems a rather liberal—if not altogether misleading—interpretation of the two declarations (misleading because Fourquet's main emphases run directly counter to those of Ailleret), it is true that despite the new emphasis, the fundamental logic of French doctrine remained in place. Notwithstanding the recognition that French forces would "normally" operate in coordination with their allies and that the only serious potential aggressor for the foreseeable future was the Soviet Union, most of the ambiguities of French doctrine survived. In fact, by trying to articulate more clearly just how and when French forces would contribute to the defense of Europe, Fourquet was demonstrating just how ambiguous the French commitment really was. Read closely, the Fourquet speech was not so much an attempt to expand the European function of French defense policy but instead one that underlined its limits.

For Fourquet—elaborating on de Gaulle's 1963 reference to a conceptual "first battle" from which France might abstain—there were still two distinct potential battles in Europe. Fourquet retained and clarified the distinction between participation in the forward battle, which would depend on the French assessment of the situation in Germany, and the "national deterrent maneuver," which concerned only France itself. Although he recognized France's interest in the "first battle," Fourquet stressed that France would not, and could not, contribute much to it. That would be too costly financially, and it would undermine French deterrence.

Instead, the purpose of French conventional forces in this new formulation remained one of "testing" the intentions of an adversary and of threatening nuclear escalation if those intentions proved to be hostile toward France.[42] In opposition to what Fourquet saw as NATO "advocating a force strength which will enable it to defeat any attack at whatever level," France would merely maintain enough force to oblige the aggressor to show its hand (p. 207). After an initial "test" consisting only of contact between French conventional forces and those of the attacker, tactical weapons would be used in a second "test" meant to show French resolve to turn to the strategic nuclear force (p. 209). Because of this discrepancy with NATO doctrine, Fourquet believed that "however improbable such a hypothesis may be . . . one can, indeed must, envisage . . . using the French First Army independently, particularly in the event of there not being complete agreement with our allies as to the point at which nuclear weapons would be used (p. 208)."

Even more problematic for France's role in European defense was the possibility that France, in General Fourquet's words, might determine that "our country is not one of [the enemy's] immediate objectives."[43] This was no less than a suggestion to the West Germans that the French could imagine a situation in which Warsaw Pact troops invaded all or part of the Federal Republic but convinced the French that they would stop at the Rhine. In this case, the logic suggested, the French might decide either to do nothing or to use only their tactical nuclear weapons in West Germany, reserving the First Army for the defense of France. In short, it implied the possibility that in case of attack France would say to the Germans, to borrow Alfred Grosser's sardonic paraphrase: "We will defend you by destroying the enemy the moment [they are] inside your cities."[44] West Germany was still at best a buffer zone and at worst an experimental battlefield for France.

Like the Americans in the late 1950s who denounced "massive retaliation," General Fourquet was groping for an alternative to an increasingly inviable "all or nothing" military doctrine. But unlike the Americans, in control of NATO commands and three thousand miles away, the Frenchman Fourquet did not have the liberty of espousing a doctrine of flexible response, which would have cost too much and which suggested battlefighting on European soil. Thus, he ended up with a caricature of flexible response: France would put off its dubious nuclear retaliation, but only for the time it took to "engage" the enemy or to fire a tactical nuclear salvo. After that France would be back to the original dilemma. By rejecting both "all or nothing" defense and "flexible response," General Fourquet had tried to square the circle. But the circle could not be squared.

POMPIDOU'S INITIAL CHALLENGE

By the time General de Gaulle resigned in April 1969, his grand design of a sovereign, self-confident, and respected France, which had always taken priority over the pros and cons of specific policies, was well on its way to realization. If the final years of the regime were troubled ones, the fact that it survived them and flourished afterward was itself an indication of how far France had come over the past decade. De Gaulle bequeathed some real problems to his successor: a shaken economy and a weak franc, stormy transatlantic and intra-European relations, and a "stalemate society" grumbling for change. But he also passed on what may have been the most unified French nation since before the Great Revolution, strong and fully accepted institutions, and a defense policy that, for all its questions and early controversy, would soon have the support of practically everyone in France.

How did Georges Pompidou face the challenge of succeeding the General in the primordial area of national defense? The first goal of the Pompidou presidency, especially in this area of national defense where his preferences were more suspect, was to ensure the continuity, to show that the faith would be kept. Some of the more traditional—or more nationalistic—Gaullists questioned the "European" sympathies of the former literature professor, and they were careful to make sure he would not betray the cause for which they had worked so hard. But Pompidou was less interested in the high politics of defense and diplomacy than de Gaulle had been, and he was content to concentrate more on his economic and social priorities at home than to implement any great revisions in defense. Thus, arch-Gaullist Michel Debré was named defense minister, and another historic ally of the General, Jacques Chaban-Delmas, prime minister. There would be no reintegration with NATO and no compromise of the independent nuclear force. There would be no "extension" of the deterrent and no new guarantees to neighbors. There was, to be sure, continued pressure on France to do more for European defense, and Pompidou was indeed well disposed toward Europe: he finally approved Great Britain's entry into the Common Market and helped launch a plan for

European economic and monetary union; his first foreign minister (Maurice Schumann) was a former leader of the very "European" Mouvement Républicain Populaire (MRP); and no less than four other ministries were headed by members of Jean Monnet's Action Committee for the United States of Europe.[45] But there were never any plans for "agonizing reappraisals" in the area of defense. France's new relationship with NATO was working just fine, and there was no need to change it yet.

The emphasis on continuity in defense policy was clear not only in the rhetoric and symbols of independence and greatness but in terms of military programs and procurement, budgets, and the composition of forces. Although the military budget for 1969 was abnormally low (only 3.4 percent of GNP) following the 1968 crisis and the devaluation of the franc, all major military equipment programs were kept and the nuclear priority was maintained.[46] Arguing that the 1970 budget was only temporarily austere, Defense Minister Debré insisted that the strategic nuclear force would be "constantly adapted and modernized."[47]

This emphasis on continuity and the irreversibility of Gaullist priorities was written clearly into the military program law of 1970 (for 1971 to 1975), which began with the classic statement that "the major objective of [our] national defense is maintaining the independence of our country in liberty and in peace."[48] What might sound pretentious or self-centered elsewhere (independence rather than security as the *major* objective of national defense) had become practically obligatory in France. More specifically, Pompidou announced that the major military programs begun by de Gaulle and still developing would not be sacrificed to economic rigor or to more collective defense. In fact, the program law stated specifically that past objectives would be pursued: "The statement of [our] intentions explains that the government has not significantly modified those which had inspired previous program laws, and notably the second one which was voted on in 1965. The objective of the third program law is to pursue the realization of already established general objectives."[49] Easily adopted by the absolute Gaullist majority in the National Assembly, the 1970–1974 program law was an early indication of the path the new government intended to follow in the area of military procurement.

It was not enough, however, to proclaim one's fidelity to an independent defense and to confirm the continued construction of major military programs or the nuclear force. Within a few years of Pompidou's election, both the composition of French forces and the context that surrounded them had changed significantly and in a number of ways: the French nuclear force had expanded and was greatly improved, notably with the deployment of tactical nuclear weapons, intermediate-range missiles on the Plateau d'Albion and strategic submarines as mentioned; superpower détente had become practically institutionalized, with strategic arms control stabilized to a point dangerously resembling the "condominium" feared by de Gaulle; and despite arms control, the Soviet Union had gone from a clearly inferior strategic position vis-à-vis the United States to numerical superiority in both ICBMs and strategic submarine launchers.[50] The military situation was scarcely static, and Pompidou, like his predecessor, would have to adapt to change. What logic and operational codes would govern French forces in this context? How would a now more serious nuclear deterrent relate to the restrictive operational guidelines of the First Army? With nuclear retaliatory potential now reasonably ensured, would French nuclear doctrine be able to evolve away from the precarious doctrine of "massive retaliation"?

Answers to all these questions came in a series of pronouncements and actions from 1969 to 1972, fertile years in the development of French security doctrine. The revisions begun with Fourquet and the difficult semantic posturing of the following years were evidence that the adjustment of French military doctrine to the growing demands on France in Europe had begun. But rather than resolving all the dilemmas brought on by earlier French military doctrines, the new formulations made some of them more apparent. By admitting France's interdependence in Europe and interest in the defense of freedom all the way up to the Elbe, the French were making themselves vulnerable to calls that they contribute more to that defense. They were turning away from the notion of national self-sufficiency and the reliance on an all-out nuclear threat that some of their earlier doctrines had implied, but they were not demonstrating the new means or notions that would replace the old. Thus, the Pompidou years were not only the beginning of some major evolutions in French defense doctrine but also of some of the tensions that would confront French policymakers for a long time to come.

CODIFIED AMBIGUITY: THE WHITE PAPER ON NATIONAL DEFENSE

The most complete statement of Gaullist defense doctrine—indeed the only comprehensive and official statement ever attempted—was the *Livre blanc sur la défense nationale* (White paper on national defense) of 1972.[51] The white paper, unprecedented in the Fifth Republic, was a comprehensive statement of the objectives, means, missions, and organization of French forces and, although it did not appear until two years after the General's death, stands as probably the best single official expression of Gaullist principles of national defense. It was based on all the notions of national primacy, esprit de défense, French exceptionalism, and the "exclusively national" character of deterrence that de Gaulle had taught.

It underlined the growing French interest in European defense while it maintained a very national—and more particularly French—point of view, thus setting forth clearly the tensions inherent in the French position. Its language set a precedent that would become a reference point for future policy statements in France, and as such, it, possibly better than any other document or declaration, represents the "Gaullist doctrine" with which subsequent French leaders had to begin. A look at the positions expressed by the white paper in several key areas will both expose its internal contradictions and provide a good understanding of the logic and basic elements of official French military doctrine at the time.

The Defense of Europe

On one hand, the white paper clearly reaffirmed the more European direction of French security policy begun by Fourquet three years before and rejected the more extreme doctrinal manifestations of independence. "[I]t would be illusory," its authors argued, "to claim to ensure the security of our territory without taking interest in the realities that surround it."[52] Some people, they suggested, might be satisfied with the idea that only the "defense of the Hexagon" was essential. But that would be "a narrow and inexact conception of defense that would inevitably lead us to look inward, and to a neutralism that could never really protect the national territory" (p. 7). French "vital interests" were for the first time formally defined as being situated not only on the "national territory" but on its "approaches" (p. 9), and France vowed "to participate as best she can in the defense of Europe" (p. 20). The security of Europe, they admitted, was an integral part of the security of France.

On the other hand, however, the white paper was far from an abandonment of France's particularly national prerogatives and a definitive or unambiguous proclamation of French solidarity with Europe. As openly as its authors recognized the continent's importance as a whole, they reiterated some of the more fundamental Gaullist beliefs about France and about the nation. If France's new leaders were trying to show an intended rapprochement with Europe, they were also confirming the continuity with their Gaullist past. The question was whether the two could be reconciled.

The white paper strongly reasserted the "force of the national idea" and the "unreality" of an integrated European defense "as long as national interests could not be mixed and patriotisms fused."[53] Here, of course, the document's main author, Michel Debré, was reiterating Gaullist arguments with which he was more than slightly familiar. Just as at the time of the EDC twenty years before, when in Debré's view the Fourth

Republic nearly sacrificed French national identity to a supranational defense, national security had to be based on "realities," and these were still the nation-states of Europe. If it were not based on these realities, not only would French forces be inadequate for France—because they would lose their "patriotic conscience" and esprit de défense—but their contribution would be of little value to the alliance as a whole. This was particularly true, according to the white paper, in the state of the alliance as it was, dominated by a huge power that was not even European (p. 5). France "in no way refused" the formation of a truly "European defense," but such an organization depended on the readiness of France's potential partners to accept it, and they were not ready yet (p. 5). The conclusion from all this was simple: Until the hypothetical day when all European states would have the same perspectives, the same interests, and the same goals, "France need[ed] a national defense" (pp. 3–5).

Nuclear Doctrine

In the nuclear domain, fundamental Gaullist precepts were also upheld. Proportional deterrence was the primary means by which France ensured its own defense and avoided war; the American guarantee was not automatic; and the "nuclear risk" could not be shared. The "exclusively national and essentially defensive nature" of nuclear deterrence was reiterated.[54]

But the white paper's authors also followed the more flexible path taken in 1969: they rejected once and for all the idea of a global nuclear defense and further attenuated the French reliance on "pure," or "all-or-nothing" deterrence.[55] Implicitly rejecting the classic logic of Pierre Gallois, they wrote that it was

> inconceivable to think of retaliating to all hostile action, regardless of where it comes from by nuclear threat. Therefore, it is necessary to be able to oppose limited hostile actions either by counteracting directly or by reverting to appropriate retaliation. The notion of deterrence is not absent from this point of view, but when the atomic weapon, because of its very excess, cannot constitute a credible deterrent, conventional and easily deployed means should be available. Crossing the threshold of the atomic threat can only be justified in a really critical situation.[56]

The problem, of course, was to know just how far to move away from exclusive reliance on the nuclear deterrent, knowing that the alternative was a conventional war that could not be won and that would be disastrous to fight.

This capacity for traditional defense must be measured very carefully. Too weak, it could not play its role and the credibility of deterrence would be reduced; too strong, it could suggest that we are ready to accept the risks of an extended war, without resorting to extreme nuclear means, and the credibility of deterrence would similarly be limited.[57]

The questions that remained, then, were the most difficult ones, and they resulted from the two areas just discussed: If French defense could not be exclusively national, how and where would French troops be employed in Europe? And if deterrence could not be exclusively nuclear, to what extent should these conventional forces be used? French strategists had to use conventional doctrine to try to square the circle, to mesh the European objectives with the national ones, and the nuclear with the conventional.

Conventional Defense

French forces were recognized as important to Europe as a whole, and the credibility of even proportional deterrence was admitted to depend on at least some conventional defense. But this retreat from "all-or-nothing" cannot be seen as acceptance of a doctrine of flexible response, which, at least in its American version, was still seen as a "palliative" at best.[58] Although the rigidity of the "two battles" doctrine was somewhat loosened, the idea of fighting a sustained nonnuclear battle that might suggest an unwillingness to "go nuclear" was still anathema.

Instead, the purpose of French nonnuclear forces was, as Fourquet had already explained it, first to make sure their initial reading of an aggression was not mistaken, to "test the intentions of an adversary." If it was determined that the aggression was real and that it was directed at France, French conventional forces would be used to bring the intensity of the conflict up to a level at which nuclear deterrence would be more credible, thus bringing into effect the proportional deterrent.

> We would oblige the adversary, by the vigor of our resistance, to resort to an attack whose intensity would obviously justify in his own eyes, and in the eyes of the world, recourse to a nuclear riposte. . . . It is necessary, in fact, to be able to evaluate by adequate means his determination, that is, to force him to reveal rapidly his profound intentions and thereby oblige him to turn to means whose gathering up would by itself be revealing.[59]

On the surface, the argument seemed perfectly sensible. France's deterrent would not be credible if it was pronounced "usable" from the first moments of conflict. If the Soviets intended a limited "hostage-taking" operation in Hamburg, for example, or if a drunken Russian division commander accidentally carried his war game too far west, it was absurd to think the French would want to risk national annihilation by their response. Nuclear risk could not be bandied about lightly; France needed conventional forces that could react to a crisis at the subnuclear level.

On the other hand, however, those forces could not be so great that they would give the impression that France was ready to fight a long conventional war, detracting from the intended effect of a nuclear doctrine that relied on early first use. Thus, despite the declared interest in helping to quell an early military conflict in Europe, clear limits were placed on the contribution France was prepared to make. The result was the following balancing act: "France, we have said, must be able to participate, to the extent that is possible and with her allies, in the prevention and settlement of a . . . crisis [in Europe]. It is normal that this capacity have certain limits, in time and in space, because it is important not to use up prematurely the forces necessary to the defense of the borders and of their approaches."[60]

Since the NATO withdrawal in 1966, of course, France had quietly signed a number of detailed agreements with NATO concerning how and when French forces would participate in a European conflict.[61] But as extensive as these agreements were, they did nothing to negate the fact that France's official military doctrine formally reserved the right for France to retain its key forces at home if a war in Europe should break out. The white paper's authors made it a point to keep the "option of nonbelligerence" open.

Tactical Nuclear Weapons

These units—the land-based Pluton missiles with a range of approximately 100 km and the more flexible tactical air Jaguar and Mirage IIIE— were to be an integral part of the "national deterrent maneuver" rather than part of the nuclear deterrent itself. In some ways, although they were in no way seen to be instruments of battle, France's tactical nuclear weapons would be given the same role as that of the conventional forces: to raise the level of conflict to one that would "justify a nuclear riposte," thereby showing an aggressor France's determination to defend itself.

In addition to obliging enemy forces to disperse so as to avoid wholesale losses to tactical nuclear weapon (TNW) strikes and, thereby, reducing the effect of Western numerical inferiority, French tactical nuclear forces would have a "great role" to play in the sending of a message to the aggressor: "The very decision to employ tactical nuclear weapons, against an adversary that could not otherwise be contained, gives the government the possibility of letting this adversary know that if the military pressure were to continue, the recourse to strategic nuclear weapons would be ineluctable.[62] Tactical nuclear weapons, then, like conventional defense, were seen as part of a limited "national deterrent maneuver" designed primarily to test the intentions of an aggressor and to signal a readiness to resort to the force de frappe.

What can one conclude from this reading of France's only comprehensive official statement on national defense and military doctrine? In an article he wrote for *Foreign Affairs* called "France's Global Strategy," published one year before the white paper appeared, Michel Debré stated that the "foundations of French defense policy," as "laid down by General de Gaulle," were still valid and that they posed no contradictions for cooperative European defense. On the contrary, argued Debré, France's foreign policy was "based on . . . very simple principles . . . which reconcile the demands of sovereignty and the need for concerted action with other states to advance world peace."[63] This is what the white paper was intended to do. Its authors accepted France's military role and interest in European defense and tried to satisfy them without abandoning what they saw as the requirements of Gaullist defense. Their complicated and sometimes contradictory explanations of the fine lines between the national and the European and between the nuclear and the conventional were meant to harmonize a military doctrine with a defense policy that had largely political goals. How well did they succeed?

Many of the French arguments had considerable logic behind them. French doctrine, nuclear and conventional together, was a doctrine of "nonwar." It was not an attempt to devise plans to prevail in a European conflict but to conceive of a framework that would prevent that conflict from occurring. Its basic principles, expressed first (or at least most forcefully) by de Gaulle himself, were simple and difficult to dispute: (1) American nuclear protection was no longer perfectly effective in the ballistic missile age; and (2) a war fought in Europe along the lines of NATO's plans for flexible response, even if "won," would be an unambiguous disaster for Europe. The obvious strategic goal of France, under these conditions, was to prevent a war from occurring, not by posturing to win it but by making it too risky for the potential aggressor to start. "So that total war should never occur," went Jean Guitton's dictum, "it must be able to occur at any time."[64] The French could scarcely be blamed for trying to deter war, and as their nuclear forces became more and more credible, so did French deterrence became more credible as well.

Granting at least a "fragment of truth" in all this, the real difficulties came over France's contribution to conventional defense. For even the French recognized that nuclear deterrence would not be credible at all levels of threat, and it seemed imperative that France commit some of its significant resources to the cause of raising the nuclear threshold. However, making such a commitment was seen to be incompatible with the principles of national defense and with the requirements of a small national deterrent. The First Army, it was argued, France's conventional "shield" and detonator of the force de frappe, had to be reserved for French territory in case the front line did not hold. How could the French gamble everything by automatically involving their army in a conventional conflict whose initiation they could not control and which NATO, by most indications, would lose if it had to fight? How could French deterrence remain credible if French forces were not reserved for the national territory where their link to French nuclear forces would be more secure? Was it not more credible, and, therefore, more *deterring*, for the bulk of French forces to remain aloof from early incidents that might prevent them from being used for national deterrence?

Although arguable, at the same time something was perverse about this view, if not to say fallacious. The French justification was that if the front line held without the support of the First Army, French forces would not matter, and there would be no cause for complaint. If the front line did not hold, then France would obviously need the First Army stationed in France to protect the national homeland and make credible its deterrent. Why waste such a valuable reserve in a lost cause? The problem, however, was not so much that the five divisions of the First Army, held back in France, would not be very imposing against a Red Army that had just defeated NATO. Rather, it was that the very retention of the First Army for the possibility of a frontline collapse would itself contribute to that collapse. When Debré said that "we will not use up, by resorting to deterrent manoeuvres, the means that would be available to us to halt aggression," he was declaring that France could not in fact be fully counted on by its allies in Europe.[65] In other words, the First Army was ostensibly being held back to deal with a contingency to which the very action of holding it back would clearly contribute. The dangers inherent in such a strategy were poignantly criticized by François de Rose who compared it to the "strategy of the Curiatii." By confronting their enemy (the Horatii) one at a time rather than all together, the Curiatii were defeated.[66]

The French sometimes replied that whatever might have been lost by the absence of a more strict engagement was regained by the measure of uncertainty their posture added. Here, though, was another case of strategic fallacy. Uncertainty, indeed, can be an advantage, but the nature of such advantage should not be confused. Not knowing *how* or *where* a particular opponent might use its forces (while being sure that it would) does pose problems for the operational plans of an attacker; the element of uncertainty can serve to deter, and it can keep the enemy from concentrating its focus and force it to disperse its resources. On the other hand, however, not knowing *if* an opponent will participate in defense and knowing that it does not have the means to do so optimally will not contribute to deterrence but will only reassure the aggressor. The only uncertainty involved in this case is that the allies of the country in question will be obliged to plan their defense without it (for they, too, are uncertain), whereas the enemy will benefit from either the absence of that country's participation or from the disunity of the defending alliance.

The authors of the white paper, then, never managed to escape the seemingly insoluble dilemma of a national defense posture that was meant to meet requirements in Europe as well. De Gaulle, at least, when pulling out of NATO commands, had said only that the conditions in which French forces would participate in a conflict would "have to be determined," and his ambiguity or secrecy on the subject left room for doubt.[67] By trying to be more specific, and with new means on hand that required a doctrine for their employment, de Gaulle's immediate successors only made it clear that the problem had crystallized. No one put the French dilemma better than General Poirier in 1972 when he wrote— about the very strategy he had helped to create—that "the great difficulty with this strategy . . . consists of being able to participate in the interallied settlement of minor affairs without mortgaging the forces that could prove indispensable later, and if the conflict spread, to our autonomous deterrent maneuver."[68] Such a strategy was, in fact, more than difficult, and subsequent policymakers would find that keeping its consequences limited as time went on would be their greatest challenge.

FRENCH MILITARY DOCTRINE IN RETROSPECT

When thinking about French military doctrine during the 1960s and early 1970s—and the apparent incompatibility between France's national military policies and its European political commitments—two general considerations should be kept in mind. First, it is important not to overlook the strong rhetorical element that is often present in official statements about defense and that was particularly critical in the grand design of General de Gaulle. De Gaulle often used policy and language as tools in his effort to restore French self-confidence, and this goal surely played a role in the elaboration of French military doctrine. In France as in the United States, declaratory and operational doctrine have not always been the same thing and should, thus, not be confused.

Second, as a consequence of the first point, it is important not to overstate the significance of the so-called "nonbelligerence option," which has too often been exaggerated by Americans. The real issue has never been whether or not the French would participate in the defense of Western Europe, but *what* they would contribute, and how effective it might be. Those who have studied French relations with NATO know that relations at the military level have, in fact, been quite close and that France has never really imagined that it could avoid participation in a potential war in Europe.[69] Whatever the merits or deficiencies of Gaullist military doctrines, no one should accept the simplistic view that France under de Gaulle and Pompidou was prepared to abstain blithely from European defense.

What is true, on the other hand—and what I have tried to demonstrate here—is that French military doctrines as formulated during the 1960s and 1970s led to dilemmas that would grow steadily over the years, particularly as the French contribution to European defense became more important. Those dilemmas were present from the start of the Gaullist period, and they are exemplified by the contradictions in the white paper on national defense. As hard as they tried, and sometimes because they tried so hard, French statesmen and military leaders through 1974 were simply unable to reconcile basic Gaullist principles with the proclaimed objective of a greater French contribution to European defense. The attempts by French leaders in the 1970s and 1980s to achieve a better record is the subject of part 2.

Part Two

STRUGGLING TO ADAPT

CHAPTER FOUR

Giscard's Balancing Act, 1974–1981

THE "POST-GAULLIST" PERIOD

The seven-year presidency of Valéry Giscard d'Estaing marks the real beginning of France's "post-Gaullist" period and, as such, presents the first opportunity to test the enduring influence of Gaullist military policies and their interaction with subsequent ones. The arrival of Giscard brought with it a new set of premises about French national security and about France's "place in the world," and for several years it seemed that those new premises would bring about a gradual revision of the Gaullist national security model that has been the object of this book. Instead, by the 1981 departure of the Fifth Republic's third president, the fundamental pillars of the Gaullist model had been reinforced and had even become the center of a nebulous "national consensus" on defense. The consensus, as has often been pointed out, never included specifics nor did it descend very far below the level of national elites; but on the whole—and to a far greater degree than in the past—there was agreement about the basics of France's national security policy, and those basics were largely the ones that had been promoted by Charles de Gaulle.

The Giscard years represent the beginning of the post-Gaullist period for several reasons. First, because of a deteriorating East-West military balance and serious policy clashes with the Americans during 1973, they coincide with the beginning of the realization in Western Europe that the American protectorate was on the wane and that the Europeans, including the French, would have to do more for their own defense. The combination of U.S. brinkmanship in the Middle East and the implied condominium of détente and arms control intensified Europe's two historic security fears: that the U.S. would provoke nuclear war in Europe or that it would renounce it. Second, 1974 was the end of Western Europe's (and France's) interlude with rapid economic growth, full employment, and balanced budgets—les trente glorieuses. In the wake of the oil and economic crises Giscard would not have the same resources to devote to national security as de Gaulle had possessed, at least until 1968. Third, this was the Fifth Republic's first experience with a president from outside the Gaullist movement. Although he was one of the few centrists to support de Gaulle during the 1960s, Giscard's attitude toward the Gaullists had gone from one of *"oui, mais"* (his formula for criticism from within the government) in 1967 to an outright *"non"* by 1974, and his overwhelming defeat of the traditional Gaullist candidate for president (Jacques Chaban-Delmas) clearly signalled the first *alternance* in the French political spectrum since 1958.

Finally, and most important, Giscard was simply of a markedly different political and philosophical hue than the General and his loyal associates. To be sure, Giscard had served in the cabinets of both de Gaulle and Pompidou and even held the key post of finance minister during the Gaullist challenge to the world monetary system in the mid-1960s. He was careful during his election campaign to evoke his "hundred and fifty conversations with the General," and to emphasize that there was no great gulf between the two men.[1] But now, France's leader was not only from a different generation—Giscard was only fourteen years old when de Gaulle gave his June 18, 1940 BBC speech—but from a different political "family" as well. To use René Rémond's classic categorization of the French right, Giscard was an "Orléaniste," not a "Bonapartiste" like de Gaulle.[2]

Indeed, Giscard differed from de Gaulle on many of the most basic questions of politics: Giscard was a champion of parliamentary democracy who opposed the "solitary exercise of power"; a political liberal who strongly supported individual and social rights; an economic liberal who claimed to prefer the market to the state; a member of the national elite who felt a mission and duty to lead; and an adept at compromise and conciliation who eschewed confrontation and strong-handed leadership. He had none of de Gaulle's taste for confrontation or struggle, and believed that the aggressive national assertion perhaps necessary under the General had by the 1970s (under Pompidou's foreign minister Michel Jobert) become rather petty and counterproductive. Nor did Giscard, born with manifold social advantages and schooled during a period of postwar peace and prosperity, share de Gaulle's fundamentally pessimistic outlook; as Raymond Aron put it, "Giscard did not know that history was tragic."[3] Finally, and not least important, the new president was much more willing than his predecessors to accept and admit France's relative position in the world.[4]

The arrival of the Giscard administration in 1974 thus marks a major turning point on several levels: international, economic, political, and philosophical. Studying it helps not only to identify the limits to change in post-Gaullist France but to draw some important lessons about those limits. Although the lessons to be drawn about the Gaullist legacy from this period are fundamentally consistent with those drawn from the following ones, the Giscard phase is particularly instructive because it is the one during which the tensions within Gaullist military policies first became acute; the patterns begun during these years would endure and develop right through the end of the Cold War more than one decade later.

The first three years of the Giscard administration (1974–1977) were marked by unprecedented innovation and change whereas the following four years (1977–1981) were marked by an apparent return to caution and a more rigid interpretation of "Gaullist orthodoxy." Why was Giscard, despite his apparently sincere attempts to revise French military doctrine and to restructure French forces, ultimately unable to reconcile France's enduring national imperatives with its growing European ones? This was the first time that a new leader in France deliberately set out to alter the orientation of French defense, and his experience was not without lessons for his successors.

REVISING FRANCE'S MILITARY DOCTRINES

The first years of the Giscard presidency saw a considerable evolution, if not outright revision, of Gaullist military doctrines expressed through the early 1970s. Despite Giscard's 1975 proclamation on French television that he had "reached the same conclusions as General de Gaulle" on the question of national defense,[5] some of the steps he took in that domain seemed to challenge those conclusions and certainly begot the resistance of many who claimed to represent the General's views. The rapid change during the first two years did not, in the end, amount to a lasting revision of French military doctrine, but it did help to define just what that doctrine was and the apparent limits to its evolution.

The innovations in the area of military doctrine were based on three new premises about national security that might be called *European, Atlantic*, and *nonnuclear*. The *European* premise was that France, no matter how securely it might be able to protect its national territory with the force de frappe, could never count on remaining free if the rest of Western Europe did not also remain free. "It would be illusory," the administration argued in the 1976 military program law, "to hope that France could retain more than reduced sovereignty if her neighbors had been occupied by a hostile power or were simply under its control."[6] By allowing even the slightest possibility of indifference to the fate of its neighbors—specifically the Federal Republic of Germany—France was damaging its important European relationships without thereby contributing to "national security" in any meaningful sense.

The second, or *Atlantic* premise, was that in order to prevent such a somber situation (the occupation or foreign control of one of France's neighbors), the Atlantic Alliance, not a putative European alliance, had to remain the primary forum for French defense. Again, as expressed in the program law, "The construction of Europe does not at this point concern defense questions, and it would be premature to anticipate progress in this domain as long as the [necessary] conditions do not prevail. . . . Under the present circumstances, in fact, only the [Atlantic] Alliance is able to . . . guarantee a military balance in Europe."[7] In Giscard's view, European military cooperation had to be reinforced, but within, not at the expense of, the Atlantic Alliance. Any more ambitious sort of "European defense" would have to wait until Europe had its own political structures, and this was not yet the case.

The third, or *nonnuclear* premise, was that a defense posture excessively reliant on nuclear deterrence was not credible, and thus only a more flexible strategy including increased conventional options could contribute adequately to French security. Giscard believed that because an "all or nothing" defense would not be credible, only a "variety of means" could make deterrence work.[8] He criticized past strategists who claimed that France could rely on an exclusively nuclear defense, and argued that the country instead had to acquire the means for conventional battle.[9]

None of the three postulates was entirely new, nor were they ever laid out in a single specific statement or in a new white paper. But together they defined Giscard's conceptual approach to military strategy—both in an absolute sense and vis-à-vis the security premises that came before them—and all had practical consequences for French defense doctrine.

The first consequence—a more forthcoming attitude toward European conventional defense—was a direct result of the *European* and *nonnuclear* premises. Because French security was seen to depend directly on European security as a whole and because an exclusively nuclear defense was not viable, France would have to accept a much greater commitment to participate in the so-called forward battle. In fact, Giscard would soon formally eliminate the conceptual distinction between the "battle for Germany" and the "battle for France"; henceforth, the former would be seen to be part of the latter.

This was a significant departure from past pronouncements. France, of course, had never excluded operational military cooperation and since 1969 had accepted the notion that French troops would "normally participate" (General Fourquet's words) in close coordination with the allies. But even after the publication of the white paper in 1972, many ambiguities remained concerning French participation in European defense, if such participation was not excluded, neither was it automatic. Both Fourquet's statement and those in the white paper allowed for the possibility of an "autonomous engagement" of the First Army and retained the option of an "independent deterrent maneuver"—the resort to an autonomous French nuclear defense if NATO defenses were to fail. In both cases, it was maintained that if NATO were unable to prevent the collapse of the central front along the inter-German border, France would then retreat to the Rhine where its forces, protected by nuclear weapons, would fight to defend the national territory. As argued earlier, this was the equivalent of committing French forces to the alliance only when it was least likely to need them (when forward defense held without them) but retracting them when they were most necessary (when forward defense failed).

The elimination of this contradiction, or at least the attenuation of the ambiguity that surrounded it, was the first major doctrinal step taken under Giscard. In 1975, Prime Minister Jacques Chirac already argued vaguely that France "could not be content to 'sanctuarize' [its] own territory," and Armed Forces Chief of Staff General Guy Méry spoke later that year of the "engagement . . . in all likelihood in cooperation with other countries rather than in an autonomous fashion, of French conventional forces."[10] But it was not until the following year that Méry, with the implicit backing of the president (who seconded him a few months later), came forth with a more explicit revision of past doctrine and announced the clear French intention to prepare for, and if necessary participate in, the "forward battle." The pronouncement initially came forth in the now-famous March 15, 1976, speech by Méry before the IHEDN.[11]

The speech, of course, became famous because of Méry's reference to what he called *"sanctuarisation élargie,"* a concept interpreted by many at the time as an unacceptable break with the principles of French nuclear deterrence, which, thus, set off a major debate. The concept, however, has often been misinterpreted, and the controversy it ignited often obfuscates the speech's more significant doctrinal innovations. These concerned not nuclear deterrence—extended or not—but conventional doctrine.

The confusion arose because by opposing his concept of "extended sanctuary" to what he called "total sanctuarization"—nuclear deterrence for France alone—Méry appeared to be proposing an extended French nuclear guarantee, in effect to the Federal Republic. But although French nuclear deterrence for Germany was not specifically precluded in the speech, it was not the focus of the exposition. Instead, Méry was arguing that because an exclusively nuclear defense of France's borders (and ipso facto of German borders) was not viable, France would have to be prepared to contribute more to German *conventional* defense. Only such an effort could help prevent the disastrous and intractable nuclear dilemma from coming about in the first place. "It was not at all to be excluded," Méry explained, "that France would participate in forward defense. I even think that it would be extremely dangerous for [France] deliberately to hold herself aloof from such a first battle, in the course of which [its] own security would in fact be at stake."[12]

Méry's argument was, thus, based on a certain skepticism about the efficacy of France's proportional deterrent. He doubted that a "merely theoretical" nuclear guarantee could protect the integrity of the national territory. He doubted whether "in an extreme case when everything in Europe had collapsed about us, the national will would survive to have recourse to the threat of massive destruction, even to ensure our continued existence."[13] This, in fact, is where Méry broke most significantly with Gaullist premises—questioning in effect the plausibility of pure deterrence and the concomitant strategy of "massive retaliation" that such a conception implied. The alternative he was proposing, however, was not a direct French nuclear guarantee for Germany (which, according to his own logic, would presumably be even less viable than France's guarantee of its own territory) but a more explicit commitment to conventional defense beyond the French sanctuary. "Extended sanctuary" meant merely that in the case of military aggression in Europe, France would be able to act where that aggression first occurred.[14]

As suggested above, Méry's formulation of French doctrine, like General Ailleret's in 1968 that also caused a great sensation, was not that of a rogue general out ahead of his superiors but one that reflected the wishes of the head of state. This became clear just a few months after Méry's speech when Giscard himself addressed the IHEDN on June 1, 1976.[15] Even less inhibited than his chief of staff, Giscard expounded the view that France could not rely solely on nuclear deterrence, and that French security and European security could not be dissociated from one another.

Like Méry, Giscard argued that an "all-or-nothing" nuclear defense was not credible. He took aim at "a certain number of strategists" who believed that a single means of defense (a strategic nuclear force) was a credible and sufficient form of deterrence, and he claimed to believe just the opposite.[16] He questioned whether a French president, before the outbreak of hostilities in France and, thus, before having called on the population to make sacrifices for its defense, would really resort to a strategic nuclear strike with all the risks that implied for a country the size of France. If no one believed the president would do so, deterrence was not credible and, thereby, was useless; France needed a "variety of means" that would include options other than a strategic nuclear threat. The French, like the Americans more than one decade before, had begun to search more seriously for options in the risky dialectic of nuclear deterrence.

At the substrategic level, Giscard's search for options led him to an explicit rejection of the concept of "two battles." This was a direct departure from French doctrine as understood since the early 1960s and went much further than even that in the white paper, whose authors had been careful to reserve for France any forces it might need were forward defense to fail. Giscard's formulation also surpassed even the statements of General Méry, who although he had already significantly tempered the notion of the "second battle," did not rule out the idea of a "battle on the frontiers" in certain limited circumstances.[17] Giscard, on the other hand, implied that the "battle for France" was to be excluded in any event:

> Some argue that if the conflict were to take place outside of the national zone [*l'espace national*], this zone could remain aloof from the battle. There would thus be, so to speak, two zones: *the conflict zone* between Czechoslovakia and the Rhine, and *the French zone*, totally peaceful and where the only preoccupation would be to support the far-away effort of the belligerents. This concept is not realistic.[18]

Given the speed of communication, transportation, and means of attack in the modern era, Giscard believed the very narrow zone between the central front and the Rhine—at places less than 250 kilometers wide—was militarily insignificant. There would be no distinguishing between "French space" and the general battle that would quickly engulf all of Western Europe. It was of no use to pretend that France could hide behind the forward zone or even behind its nuclear shield; if a conflict were to break out, France would be involved in battle, and it thus had to be better prepared to fight that battle. This may not quite have been the "battle-fighting" doctrine of a Maxwell Taylor, but it was far from the "pure deterrence" of a Pierre Gallois.

Doctrinal change during Giscard's first two years—in the direction of more flexibility and a greater commitment to Europe—was also perceptible where tactical nuclear weapons (TNWs) were concerned. First authorized in the 1965 program law, this new type of armament started to come on line in 1972 with the delivery of free-fall nuclear bombs to France's Mirage IIIE and Jaguar land-based aircraft and was finally completed two years later with the deployment of the land-based Pluton, a solid-fuel missile with a range of 120 km. Tactical nuclear weapons were particularly important in the new conceptions because they were seen as a way to plug the gap, considered increasingly disturbing, between inadequate conventional forces and a potentially devastating (and not always credible) strategic strike.

The primary developments in this area included not only the vague "extension" of tactical nuclear protection broached by Chirac and Méry but a loosening of the view of TNWs as unequivocally bound to the strategic deterrent. By the late 1960s, as noted in chapter 3, French tactical nuclear doctrine had already developed into the rather creative conception of the "warning shot." TNWs were to be part of the "test of enemy intentions" that would let France know what sort of aggression was occurring and how serious it was. If the aggression was found to be serious and if it was directed at France, a TNW strike would signal to the aggressor that a strategic nuclear response was imminent if the attack did not stop.

In other words, TNWs were meant to react to circumstances in which a strategic response would obviously be inappropriate and not credible, but they were still national weapons of deterrence and, in theory at least, given neither a battle-fighting nor a European role.

Under Giscard, this strict interpretation of TNW posture was modified and made more flexible through the relative deemphasis of the "automatic trigger" nature of their role. In 1975 both Chirac and Méry referred, albeit cautiously, to the potential battlefield role of the new weapons. Both excluded the idea of nuclear battle, but Chirac referred to TNWs as "battlefield arms" that could help the First Army to "stop the momentum of an aggressor," and Méry called them "counter-force weapons . . . intended for the battlefield and its surroundings, [whose] possible use must consequently be accompanied by the search for military efficiency."[19] In the 1976 program law, it was further stated that "tactical nuclear weapons . . . offer a wide range of employment possibilities depending on the circumstances. Their presence among conventional forces increases their aptitude to do battle."[20] For Giscard himself, the tactical nuclear arm was "not only an instrument of deterrence" but an "instrument of battle."[21]

The notion of a "test" remained in the official concept as did the concept of the "final warning" meant to demonstrate France's will to use the force de frappe. But at the same time, the quest for greater flexibility and the will to bring more French firepower to forward defense led to a potentially significant change of emphasis: the suggestion was that French TNWs were as much part of European defense as they were part of French deterrence. Under Giscard, the tactical nuclear strike would neither be an abstract nuclear warning shot—a "fireworks display" in the words of some critics—nor part of proportional deterrence but a militarily useful gesture that would force an aggressor to disperse its forces, to prepare them for a nuclear environment, and ultimately, to stop in the face of nuclear fire.

By the end of 1976, then, Giscard and his top military leadership had gone far to move overall French operational strategy out from under the protective ambiguity that had been written into the white paper. Many of the hesitations about when France would consider itself "involved" in a European conflict were gone, the reliability of "deterrence from the weak to the strong" was openly questioned, and the absolute aversion to battle fighting in Europe was attenuated. Although none of these innovations altered entirely or irreversibly the French military posture that had developed since de Gaulle's time, they clearly changed its emphasis and committed France to a greater role in the conventional defense of Western Europe than France had accepted in the past.

REORGANIZING THE ARMY, 1975–1977

Consistent with these verbal commitments to participate in coordination with France's NATO allies were efforts to prepare the French armed forces for such a role. In late 1975 Giscard, along with the newly appointed Méry, undertook a major reorganization of the French army and in 1976 elaborated a military program law that was designed to reflect more closely the premises on which his security policy was based. The thrust of these policies was to create a French army more mobile, more versatile (*polyvalente*) and better equipped with conventional weapons than before—in short, an army better prepared to contribute to the allied defense of Western Europe.[22]

The first requirement was that the army be able to intervene on the central front more quickly, which meant thinning out the relatively immobile divisional arrangement in place since the early 1960s. The structure maintained under de Gaulle and Pompidou of five 1967-type mechanized divisions (of about 19,000 troops each) was transformed into a force of fifteen much smaller 1977-type divisions. The new structure would consist of eight armored divisions (7,000 troops each), four infantry divisions (6,900 troops each), one alpine division (9,800 troops), one airborne division (16,950), and one naval infantry division (9,230).[23] The brigade level was eliminated (in fact, the new divisions were not much bigger than the old brigades), and the overall size of the land army was to be reduced by about 21,000 troops to a new total of 310,000.[24] The drop in size was to be compensated by the rise in quality and mobility of the army.

Next, also in the name of flexibility, the functional distinctions that had existed between *forces de manoeuvre* (the mechanized First Army), *forces d'intervention* (a sort of rapid deployment force for use abroad), and *forces du territoire* (home defense forces), were eliminated. These divisions of labor were seen to be "too specialized," preventing the adaptability of the army to rapidly changing situations, and limiting its capacity to meet the sorts of small "crises" the government believed most probable were armed conflict ever to occur.[25] In the new organization, the former forces du territoire would be reintegrated into the First Army, and all units would be better equipped with the means to fight a conventional battle, especially nonnuclear artillery, antitank (HOT and Milan), and antiaircraft (Roland) weapons.[26] After the completion of the reorganization, all forces—including those formerly reserved for home defense—would be assigned the task of contributing to France's own version of forward defense and (in theory) given the means to do so.

What this meant in practice was the dissolution of the Défense Opera-
tionnelle du Territoire (DOT). A 1963 creation of Armed Forces Minister
Pierre Messmer, the DOT was a relic of the Resistance, a home defense
organization whose mission was to "annihilate enemy elements that
would have managed to implant themselves on the national territory."[27]
Giscard, however, thought that forces assigned to the DOT would be
better used if they were made able to participate in the battle against
invading enemy forces. Indeed, a strong territorial defense—for a country
in France's geographical position and to the extent that it competes for
resources with other functions—is somewhat an isolationist concept; it
suggests that if the allies lose the war, the French will worry about themselves. Giscard believed such a posture to be incompatible with the message he wanted to send both to his allies and to his potential adversaries
and abolished the organization.

Along with the reorganization and relocation of French forces, the new
scheme also called for a restructuring of the military command structure.
Previously deployed in two corps—a First Corps in Nancy consisting of
three divisions and a Second Corps in Baden-Baden (FRG) made up of two
divisions—the army's administrative structure was extensively pruned in
1977 in a process that saw its First Corps headquarters moved to Metz,
100 km to the north. In the new structure, the First Corps would consist
of four armored divisions, and the Second Corps (which remained at
Baden-Baden), three armored divisions. In 1979, a Third Corps was created at Saint-Germain-en-Laye to command the eighth (and final) armored division as well as one Pluton regiment. As part of the push for
flexibility, the new corps was initially not subordinated to the First Army
so that it could act independently under the orders of the armed forces
chief of staff.[28] Finally, the remaining seven divisions were also left out of
any of the First Army's corps in order that they, too, could be used independently either in Europe or abroad, depending on the circumstances.[29]

Giscard's military policies were also consistent with his proclaimed
doctrinal objectives in that they included a relative emphasis of conventional over nuclear forces. (Indeed, the simple fact that the armed forces
were now under the leadership of an army officer, Méry, after having
been dominated for years by the air force, was indicative of the new emphasis on conventional defense.) The administration argued—not without reason—that the successful construction of the independent nuclear
force under de Gaulle had resulted in the relative neglect of conventional
forces. Although the cost overruns of the early force de frappe were partly
compensated in the 1960s by post-Algeria cutbacks, by the end of the
decade French conventional equipment had begun to suffer, and the
army, navy, and air force had to get by on smaller-than-planned amounts
of largely outdated equipment. Even the third program law (1971–1975),

designed to recover some of the lost ground in the conventional field, was modest in its objectives (military spending was reduced as a percentage of Gross Domestic Product [GDP] even if raised slightly in real terms), and increasing inflation after 1972 left many of those objectives unfulfilled. By 1976, then, "the objectives of the three program laws [were] reached where nuclear forces are concerned; but the significant reduction of relative buying power of the armed forces since 1960 permitted only a partial fulfillment of equipment programs, and led as well to particular difficulties in the training of these forces."[30]

To correct these insufficiencies, it was argued not only that overall military spending had to rise significantly—from 17 percent of the overall national budget in 1977 to 20 percent by 1982—but that within that budget spending on nonnuclear forces had to be given greater emphasis.[31]

According to the government, this relative shift in priority from nuclear to conventional forces would not result in the neglect of the former because after years of effort the strategic nuclear force had reached the point of sufficiency and needed only to be maintained. When Yvon Bourges reasoned in 1977 that the FNS was now so advanced that "a more or less constant amount of funds, or a slightly increasing amount, can permit us to attain our objectives," he was echoing what Méry had already argued in his presentation to the IHEDN:

> Where nuclear forces are concerned, we have henceforth an arsenal which is no longer contested by anyone and which places us at the required level. I might say that after a phase of very strong expansion, which was necessary and which has been very productive thanks to the quality and efforts of our engineers, researchers and technicians, we can probably now begin a period at cruising speed, thus permitting us to devote more constant financial means.[32]

To be sure, the nuclear force remained the "absolute priority" of the government whose "primary obligation" was to maintain it at the "necessary" level. But the program law none the less projected a declining proportion of the total defense budget for nuclear programs (from 16.8 percent in 1977 to 15.7 percent in 1982) while it sought to augment significantly the funding of conventional forces. With relative spending on conventional equipment and operations rising for the first time since 1962, the French would dispose of a force capable of contributing more significantly to West European defense and of executing more credibly the "strategic deterrent maneuver."[33]

The new emphases of military doctrine seen in the previous section were, thus, not without a concrete manifestation in military policy. The changes in force structure envisaged by Giscard can surely be criticized as incomplete or insufficient, but it must be said at least that they were con-

sistent with the declared objectives of the administration's military doctrine. That doctrine announced France's intention of fighting in the forward defense of Western Europe if necessary, and French military forces
were indeed designed and reorganized to do so more effectively. By 1977,
with the new priority on conventional forces and the reorganization of
the army, the government had adopted a military posture that seemed a
genuine first step in the direction of a greater French role in European
defense.

NUCLEAR COOPERATION WITH THE UNITED STATES

A final element of innovation under Giscard that must be mentioned here
was the fact, not revealed publicly until 1989, that the new administration engaged in extensive nuclear cooperation with the United States from
the start of its term.[34] In highly secret meetings that had begun tentatively
at the end of Georges Pompidou's tenure, French and American scientists
after 1974 collaborated seriously on a variety of technical aspects of nuclear weaponry—including MIRVs, warhead miniaturization, warhead
safety from accidental explosion, and warhead security against unauthor-
ized use—and military leaders from the two countries discussed jointly
their tactical nuclear targeting plans. Apparently devised by Richard
Nixon and Henry Kissinger, the nuclear cooperation between France and
the United States was meant to help the French nuclear program avoid
wasting time and money; to ensure that in the case of war French tactical
nuclear strikes would not interfere with NATO operations; and, perhaps
most importantly, to establish a relationship of trust and cooperation that
some felt was lacking between Washington and Paris. Whereas the American administrations of the 1950s and 1960s had vehemently opposed the
existence of a French force de frappe, Nixon and Kissinger concluded that
because it was now obvious that the French force would exist regardless
of U.S. policy, it was in the American and overall Western interest that
such a force be as survivable and cost effective as possible.[35]

  This French-American nuclear collaboration is still highly controversial, all its details are not yet known, and many participants on both sides
of the Atlantic still refuse to talk about it. But what is known is enough to
demonstrate both that the Giscard administration had no qualms about
intimate security cooperation with the United States and that Gaullist
taboos were still strong enough to force the president to keep such activity
highly secret. This, of course, could be seen as ironic in that de Gaulle
himself had never opposed technical nuclear cooperation with the Americans and, in fact, had taken advantage of it whenever it was available. (De
Gaulle asked specifically for American nuclear assistance as early as July

1958 only to be flatly refused, overtly bought enriched uranium from the United States while awaiting the production of the Pierrelatte plant, and did not hesitate in 1962 to purchase the American refueling tankers without which French nuclear bombers could not reach their targets.)[36] But Giscard feared—and subsequent events suggest he was probably right—that the revelation of French-American nuclear cooperation would be perceived in France as excessively Atlanticist or as a sign of dependence, and he chose to restrict knowledge of the cooperation to a very small circle of French officials. On the day in May 1981 that he handed power over to François Mitterrand, Giscard briefed his successor on what was taking place, and Mitterrand pursued it—and kept the secret—throughout the decade.

American nuclear aid to France during the 1970s was not essential to the existence of the force de frappe, and no one suggests that the French would not have been able fully to develop that force alone. Indeed, not only had France by 1974 already deployed its first nuclear submarines, IRBMs, and French-made hydrogen bombs, but a number of participants in the nuclear discussions have suggested that they were a two-way street, that the Americans learned as much from the French as the other way around. Most important here, in any event, is the very fact that French-American cooperation was taking place at all—for that fact confirms the Giscard administration's interest in much more extensive and pragmatic military cooperation with the United States than had previously been known.[37]

OPPOSITION TO CHANGE AND ITS LESSONS

If the secret nuclear cooperation between France and the United States was pursued consistently through the end of Giscard's term and into that of his successor, the same could not be said about the other, more public, strategic innovations of 1974–1976. Despite the coherence of the government's position and the widespread approval of France's allies, Giscard's initial reorientations proved to be partial, temporary, and highly controversial in France. If the first three years of the Giscard presidency were marked by innovation and originality in the various domains of security policy, the next four years witnessed much more caution and even conservatism, and the early expectations of radical change proved to be premature.

To be sure, from 1977 to 1981 the government maintained its reinforced interest in forward defense and its search for alternatives to pure deterrence. The program law was not amended or abandoned, and none of the new formulations on military strategy were ever formally retracted or revised. The president's new political organization, the Union pour la Démocratie Française (UDF), even intensified calls for greater participation in the forward battle and greater cooperation with NATO.[38] But after the hostile political reaction to the doctrinal shifts of 1976 and the widespread criticism of the program law, the pace of change in official policy slowed dramatically and little that was new emerged between 1977 and 1981. It was as if the reformer in France's youngest president had explored and discovered the limits to change and had decided not to test them further.

The beginning of the adjustment to the administration's defense program followed the pronouncements of Giscard and Méry about French doctrine in the summer of 1976. Staunch advocates of "pure deterrence" like Generals Gallois and Poirier, orthodox practitioners of indépendance like Michel Debré and Pierre Messmer, conservative analysts like Jean Klein and Jacques Vernant, and even some leftists like Jean-Pierre Chevènement, all found the policy evolution of this period objectionable for one reason or another.[39] The administration's new premises and actions, rather than an adaptation to the present, were seen to be (in Messmer's words) "a leap backward of ten years in French military thought."[40] They would lead not to a more coherent posture for France but to subordination, a loss of national control, and the abandonment of ingredients that had rallied the French people to their republic, brought the French army back behind the nation, and instilled a sense of national pride.

In the wake of these protests, the administration was forced to retreat and to downplay the significance of the proposed changes. Defense Minister Bourges, for example, denied in June 1976 that Giscard had suggested a battlefield role for TNWs, and General Méry made a rather equivocal statement on the question of French participation in the forward battle early the following year.[41] But more concrete proof of a return to "Gaullist orthodoxy" did not come until a speech by the new prime minister, Raymond Barre, in June 1977.[42] Barre had replaced Jacques Chirac as head of government in August 1976, and, ironically, it was thus with the departure of the "Gaullist" leader that France returned to a defense posture (as well as a fiscal policy, for that matter) more in line with what were seen to be Gaullist rules.

The new prime minister's first major speech on the subject of national defense made it clear that the ambitious developments of the administration's first few years would be kept within limits or even reversed. This "turnaround" should not be exaggerated, as Barre upheld the notion of "vital interests" that might extend beyond national borders, and he applauded General Lagarde's efforts to reorganize the army.[43] Barre did not renounce the general trend of the administration's defense policies, and indeed, some purists still found the government's position on deterrence far too lax.[44] But the tone of the speech as well as its content were obvious efforts to "calm the storm" and reassert the fundamentals of the Gaullist model.

As he addressed the Mailly army camp (not coincidentally on June 18, the anniversary of de Gaulle's famous BBC speech), Barre managed to touch upon nearly all of the themes that had come to be seen as central to Gaullist defense. He went out of his way to reassure the administration's opponents—particularly now that the "Gaullists" had become a sort of internal opposition to the government—that the apparent strategic revisions of the previous year would not get out of hand. In this self-described homage to de Gaulle, Barre reminded the country of its "immense debt to the man who saved the honor of France, who restored the Republic . . . who gave our country the institutions and the defense apparatus which are the surest guarantees of its independence." He stressed that "national independence is the law of all French governments" and that although this did not mean isolation or neutralism, it meant that France "has no other goal than to ensure that our country retains the full control of its destiny." He pointed out, in short, that "the defense policy run by the government . . . remains faithful to the fundamental orientations that General de Gaulle traced out in 1958, and which his successors at the top of the State have maintained because they respond to the essential interests of the patrie."[45]

None of these references to the Gaullist heritage were, of course, out of the ordinary in France. By 1977, only seven years after de Gaulle's death, the General had taken on an aura with which no political leader would find it wise to tamper. Even at the beginning of his term, as has already been seen, Giscard found it expedient to stress his loyalty to the founder of the Fifth Republic. But the timing of Barre's speech (following the outcry over Giscard's "betrayal" of national defense) and its specific content (Barre also stressed very forcefully that France would "never reintegrate" with NATO and that tactical nuclear weapons were weapons of deterrence) mark it as a clear indication of a step toward the past rather than into the future.[46] By hailing de Gaulle so conspicuously and by proclaiming the continued validity of the Gaullist doctrines that Giscard had seemed to question, Barre was announcing—it is clear in retrospect—the end of the administration's strategic revisionism. France's new leaders were no longer going to innovate or experiment in the area of national defense.

What explains this turnaround? Why, despite the initial efforts to improve alliance ties and to attenuate the rigidities of independence, did Giscard's "revisionist" program prove so difficult to implement? What were the specific objections to the new doctrines, and why did they prevail? The answers to such questions not only provide observers with some useful insight into French politics in the late 1970s but also taught some useful lessons to French politicians themselves.

It should first be remembered that Giscard was in a precarious political position throughout the late 1970s. Elected by a margin of only 425,000 votes in a country of more than 26 million voters, he was scarcely in a position to implement any radical change in so fundamental an area as national security policy. Allied to the Gaullists and opposed by an increasingly viable "Left alternative," Giscard was squeezed between two hostile forces: a Left that still had its own radically different posture on defense (having yet to adopt Gaullist symbols as its own) and a Right that suspected him of infidelity to Gaullism (and on whose electoral support he depended). With inflation and unemployment rising along with his political opposition, it was not expedient for Giscard to continue to challenge the givens of French defense, especially as the 1978 parliamentary elections approached. In this narrow political situation, it is not difficult to understand why Giscard was obliged to yield to the pressure of his "opposition," an opposition that in this case included his nominal Gaullist "allies" as well.

The main attacks on or objections to the changes in military policy that Giscard proposed came in three related but distinct critiques, two of which concerned military doctrine and one that had to do with alliance strategy. It is worth looking at these points individually and then asking to what extent they were valid.

The first critique—born largely of the 1975–1976 statements by Méry and Giscard that implied much closer operational cooperation with France's allies—was that France was returning to a policy of military integration. Méry's talk of "enlarged sanctuary," participation in the forward battle, and "inter-operability" with allied forces seemed to suggest a willingness to bring France back into NATOs integrated commands and to make peacetime commitments to allies. If it was seen to be so important that France be able to participate with its allies on the central front, it would not be long (so the critics assumed) before the country accepted an integrated position along that front. Indeed, starting in 1974 French forces began annual brigade-size field-training exercises in West Germany, and new agreements—the "Valentin-Ferber Accords"—were signed with NATO on French military cooperation in wartime. Even more alarming in this view was Giscard's conclusion in his IHEDN address that there would be only one battle zone in Europe in the event of war and, particularly, his conclusion that "there must only be one military system in that zone."[47] If there was only "one military system," France, by implication, was in it.

The second critique was that the new policies implied what one critical report called "a progressive alignment with NATO's strategy of flexible response."[48] This critique was different from the first in that military integration and the doctrine of flexible response are not the same thing. France had spent the better part of a decade dissociating itself from this doctrine of graduated response, including nuclear weapons, to a Warsaw Pact attack, and it now appeared that it was moving back in the other direction. The new commitment to participation in the forward battle—and, particularly, the repeated references to the "battlefield role" of tactical nuclear weapons—when combined with the administration's critique of "all or nothing" deterrence, seemed to suggest an adoption of NATO's official doctrine. Indeed, the government was building up French conventional forces, questioning the credibility of the force de frappe, improving relations with NATO allies, and arguing that "the entirety of [France's] defense organization should be designed for battle."[49] And Giscard's calls to "reinforce the credibility of the deterrent" and prepare for "a broad spectrum of possibilities" sounded eerily similar to Robert McNamara's logic of 1962.[50] On the surface, there seemed little separating the goals of the emerging French doctrine from the one NATO had adopted after France left its integrated command.

Third, it was argued that the administration was not only integrating but even worse: it was returning to the "Atlantic fold" and abandoning the French dream of a more independent European defense. The grounds for this critique were seen in what at the beginning of this chapter was called the "Atlantic premise"—Giscard's view that only NATO for the time being could ensure Western European security. Indeed, from the very start of his term, Giscard abandoned the attempts of his predecessors (most recently by Pompidou's foreign minister Michel Jobert) to foster a distinct European defense entity and sought to improve France's ties to the United States and NATO. He criticized Jobert for trying to move too quickly toward an "independent" European defense, and he studiously avoided specific discussions of new structures.[51] Even to an unbiased American observer, Giscard's European policy was "devoid of emphasis on the formation of a separate or identifiable European identity in the defense arena."[52] Whereas one of de Gaulle's primary objectives for Europe had been the creation of a more independent European security system, Giscard seemed content to rely on the existing Atlantic arrangement.

How well do these critiques hold up? On one hand, the arguments that Giscard was abandoning the Gaullist model and seeking to return to the past were not without merit; France was indeed seeking to integrate further into the existing framework for European defense, and an Atlantic organization was preferred to the creation of a European one. However, when the objections to those policies are reconsidered and the changing context taken into account, a somewhat more nuanced judgment seems more appropriate. It is debatable both whether the French were really on their way down these forbidden paths and whether this should have been seen as a "betrayal of the General" to the extent that they were. Rather than a venture outside the limits of the Gaullist model, Giscard's policies were primarily an effort to redefine French policy within that model and to bring it up to date. Giscard's security policies were not judged on the criterion of how best to ensure French security given a certain context but by a set of criteria developed from a set of specific military policies made in the past. Nothing, of course, automatically requires policies to become outdated over time, but nothing suggests they should forever be appropriate to one's goals, either.

Where military strategy is concerned, it would be a great exaggeration to say that France from one day to the next abandoned massive retaliation in favor of flexible response. The two doctrines have never existed in pure form in any national strategy and—rather than absolute and mutually exclusive alternatives—should be seen as idealized poles on a wide spectrum of options. The difference between the French doctrine and the American one had always been less a question of nature than of degree, and during these years that degree of difference was simply reduced. The dilemma faced by the French as they confronted the problem of nuclear credibility was the same that the Americans had faced in the early 1960s, and the set of alternatives for dealing with it was limited. The revisions under Giscard were a step toward the rapprochement of French military doctrine with NATO's, but the step was along a continuum, not a jump from one extreme to the other.

Furthermore, Giscard's logic did not mean that France would occupy an assigned space on the central front or would reenter NATO's integrated military command. To prepare a nation's armed forces to intervene more effectively in a conflict whose stake was vital to its security (and in which participation had never been excluded in the first place) was not to abandon the right to decide when and if it would be necessary to take action. Méry, in fact, despite his emphasis on participation in the forward battle, stated clearly in 1976 that occupying a space along the front was "completely out of the question" and that the principle of independence of decision would be maintained.[53] When Raymond Barre emphasized in June 1977 that France would not occupy a forward slot on the central front, rejoin NATO's integrated military command, or relinquish control over the possible French logistic support to the allies, he was in no way reversing official policies, only reemphasizing their abiding foundations. Among Giscard's military critics there seems to have been a confusion of "independence of decision" and "independence of action," two fundamentally different concepts whose distinction had always been maintained in the original Gaullist strategy.

The description of Giscard's attitude as Atlanticist (a pejorative term in France), if literally correct, also seems to have been somewhat misplaced or misunderstood. As suggested earlier, Giscard's position was not so much that "European defense" was undesirable but only that given present circumstances it had to be a part of a more effective and still necessary Atlantic Alliance. Giscard's argument—one made frequently by Méry as well—was that there could be no true European defense without a true political Europe. How could there be a European defense system without a European political structure for running it? Without that structure, it would be nothing but an interstate alliance like NATO, only a weaker one. What was necessary in Giscard's view was to seek present security through the Atlantic Alliance while striving to create a true European political organization that would help make possible a more European defense in the future.[54]

To be sure, rather than seeking to oppose American and European objectives and interests, Giscard sought to bring them together. But the context in which he was seeking to do so was vastly different from one or two decades before. Giscard was operating under a rather more questionable American protectorate; the Russian conventional military threat had grown immensely; France's own proportional deterrent was now worthy of being taken much more seriously; French national self-confidence had been restored; and, finally, the Europeans were starting to seek more actively the creation of political structures around which a more autonomous defense could be built. Because the French had come so far since the late 1950s in recovering their sense of national sovereignty, it was no longer as necessary as in the past that they aggressively reassert their particular security interests. And because of the changing European balance of power in favor of the Warsaw Pact, it was no longer as safe to do so. There was now reason to believe that France had more to gain by cooperating with its allies, including the Americans, and a lot more to lose by failing to cooperate with them.

Finally, to the extent that Europe really could only have its own defense once it had its own political structures, Giscard arguably did more than any of his predecessors to create those structures. His role in building European institutions and practices—the European Council (periodic meetings of European heads of state or government not too far removed from de Gaulle's Fouchet Plan), the European Monetary System, a directly elected European Parliament, and European Political Cooperation (EPC)—was not insignificant in the path toward the creation of the political union prerequisite to any true European security organization. Thus, Giscard was not, as Michel Tatu has argued, "always against a European defense."[55] He merely believed that the unfortunate combination during the late 1970s of Soviet military power, American vulnerability, and still-embryonic European political structures required France to do more within the Atlantic Alliance while it sought to bring about the day when a more independent Europe could emerge.

The innovative security measures taken by Giscard and his military leadership before the 1976–1977 turnaround were not so much direct challenges to past French military doctrine but attempts to clarify that doctrine and to make it more effective in a changing context. Nothing done during the Giscard years fell squarely outside the very wide parameters traced by the white paper, and there was little contradiction with the amorphous body of military doctrine that had prevailed under de Gaulle. One French analyst at the time (Jean Klein) even went so far as to argue that the pragmatic cooperation under Giscard was "not fundamentally any different from that which had been practised between 1966 and 1969."[56] The present analysis has found the differences between the two periods rather more significant than this, but that a well-respected observer of French security policy could make such a statement attests to the limited nature of the change. New parameters were not drawn, but new lines were drawn within those parameters, and some of the ambiguity surrounding French security policy was correspondingly reduced. It was this attack on ambiguity, rather than any attack on Gaullist principles, that resulted in such intense opposition.

If there is a lesson to be learned from the experience of the mid-1970s, it is that by assailing ambiguity, consensus, too, was put at risk. After 1977, it was only by returning to vague general principles of independence and slowing the pace of change that the administration was able to obtain the support of the Left, retain that of the Right, and achieve a relative consensus on French national defense.

DEFENSE POLICY AND THE ECONOMIC CONSTRAINT

The Giscard era is noted for its redoubled efforts to increase overall military spending and for the increased attention it paid to French conventional defense. The administration, as noted, had claimed that it would redress defense spending after years of decline, and it promised to create an army that would be better prepared to participate with its allies along the central front, that is, a more mobile and more heavily armed force equipped with modern weapons. It argued, moreover, that it could increase the strength and improve the quality of French conventional forces without detracting from the viability of the strategic deterrent force. When reconsidered, however, one must conclude that although French spending on the armed forces in this period was an improvement on preceding years—and should even be considered impressive given the overall economic context—it was ultimately not commensurate with the expanding tasks assigned to those forces. French defense policy came under strain in the late 1970s not only because of the political factors discussed above but because of a growing incompatibility between rising demands and limited resources.

Military spending under Giscard d'Estaing rose substantially—by 16 percent in real terms during the first four years of the program law—and redressed a steady relative decline in the share of the French economy allocated to defense.[57] Whereas the French defense budget had fallen from 6.3 percent of GNP in 1960 to 3.7 percent by 1970 and was down as low as 3.4 percent in 1975, it would rise back to nearly 4 percent by the end of Giscard's term.[58] Although the ambitious spending goals outlined in the program law of 1977–1982 were never met (a consistent pattern for French program laws), a 4 percent real annual increase in defense spending is rather significant, particularly given the economic context of the time. The problem for the French defense budget during the late 1970s was not that means were not increased but that commitments were increased to an even greater extent.

The Gaullist years, as already observed, had been a period of diminishing military roles rather than expanding ones. To be sure, the creation of the force de frappe was a new and obviously very costly role, but France was able to compensate for it by cutting back significantly on its expensive land army after 1962. Under an American nuclear umbrella still considered viable and with a military doctrine that deemphasized conventional forces, the French could neglect their land army as well as their navy with little serious consequence and instead concentrate their military resources on the nuclear force. Nor should it be forgotten that the French economy during the 1960s was growing at a pace close to 6 percent per year, nearly twice the rate of growth from 1974–1979.[59]

The Giscard years, on the other hand, saw the number of roles for the military expand without any concomitant increase in resources—on the contrary. The strategic deterrent force had grown up and had to be maintained (even if it was not to be developed with the previous vigor), tactical nuclear weapons were added to the French arsenal, the overseas intervention role became more important (as the United States turned inward and left Africa to the French), and most importantly, the conventional military role in Europe was given much greater substance. Calls for an army capable of "battle fighting" in central Europe implied a considerable accompanying price tag. Without a rapidly growing economy and with the added costs of the economic slowdown, not to mention the new costs of Giscard's generous social policies, the government was led to the same sorts of "cutbacks, delays, and cancellations" that Giscard had decried in past programming periods. Indeed, the last two years under the 1977–1982 program law were so underfunded that the Socialists had to "skip" a year in order to catch up (just as Giscard had done in 1976 because of the spending shortfalls of the Pompidou administration). According to a report by the Cour des Comptes, the 1977–1982 program law was underfunded (vis-à-vis its own projections) by a total of FFr48 bn.[60]

This is not the place to examine in detail the orders, deliveries, and modernization of French military forces in the 1970s. What can be said, however, is that the ambitious goals laid out in the program law—1,200 AMX-30 tanks and 450 combat aircraft (Mirage F1 and Mirage 2000) by 1982; of 930 Milan (antitank) and 110 Roland (antiair) deliveries; of twelve new minesweepers and eighty Super-Etendard aircraft; and of increased research and development for conventional forces—were not all met by the end of the programming period. Indeed, as David Yost points out, there were significant delays in the new tank program, in the delivery of new automatic rifles and 155-mm guns to the army, and in the procurement of engineering equipment, mortars, munitions, and armored and tactical vehicles.[61] No one could deny that the administration was serious about augmenting the French capacity for conventional defense, but it also seems clear that it overestimated its own capacity to fund the programs needed.

Where nuclear programs were concerned, the balance sheet was similarly mixed. Most observers, of course, have stressed the new priority placed on conventional forces, and it was widely argued at the time that this would inevitably lead to the relative deemphasis of the FNS; throughout its term the government was obliged constantly to defend itself against charges of neglecting France's nuclear deterrent. Indeed, as the 1981 elections approached, the "Gaullists" chose Giscard's "neglect" of the force de frappe as a favorite area of criticism. Jacques Chirac, for example (though prime minister when the program law was written and from 1974–1976 a leading defender of the administration's military policies), argued that "in the area of deterrence, despite the declarations of principle or spectacular claims . . . from 1974 to 1981 nothing was undertaken that had not been decided previously, whether it is a question of modernizing the Plateau d'Albion or [building] SLBMs.[62] By 1980, Chirac and the RPR, which had criticized Giscard's slowness in approving construction of France's sixth submarine (and whose pressure finally brought about the decision to build it in 1979), were talking about nine French SLBMs by 1992, fifteen by 2010, and criticizing the government for its lack of support for the FNS.[63] Giscard could not, it seems, emphasize France's responsibilities toward the conventional defense of Western Europe without threatening a Gaullist "doctrine" whose priority had always been nuclear deterrence.

When looked at closely, however, Giscard did sustain the priority accorded to nuclear deterrence, and if no new nuclear programs were initiated, the modernization and improvement of old ones did go ahead. Although the share of the French defense budget apportioned to the nuclear force had been programmed to fall during the Giscard years, it actually rose from its 1977 level of 16.8 percent to 19 percent in 1981.[64] Indeed, during Giscard's tenure numerous improvements in the nuclear force were made. Two new nuclear submarines were deployed, and all five (including the two new ones) were refitted with 3,000 km-range M-20 missiles (replacing the M-1 and M-2); the Plateau d'Albion silos were hardened and the IRBM force refitted with S-3 missiles and warheads of greater yield (1 megaton compared to 150 kilotons for the S-2) and greater range (3,500 km to 3,000); the Mirage IV force was maintained as part of the strategic force and modernized to last until 1985; the air-delivered tactical nuclear force of Jaguar, Mirage III, and Super-Etendard was improved and expanded; studies were undertaken on a mobile missile that could reach the Soviet Union and on the neutron bomb; and finally, the decision was taken to replace the M-20 SLBMs with M-4 multiple-warhead missiles on all the submarines but the aging *Redoubtable*. Total nuclear firepower increased under Giscard from 20 megatons in 1974 to 70 megatons in 1981, scarcely the "neglect" of the nuclear force that Giscard's opponents claimed.

Giscard's record in the domain of military funding was thus not altogether unimpressive, particularly when economic and other constraints are taken into account. Despite the president's abiding passion for détente, France's capacity for battle was improved. Overall military spending rose in real terms from 1975 to 1981 despite a struggling economy and the high costs of an expanding welfare state, and not even the unyielding austerity of the Barre Plan after 1976 prevented the continued funding and modernization of the force de frappe.

Yet, intentions and efforts notwithstanding, the goals set by the administration itself proved too ambitious. Even if it is conceded that the FNS had reached a sufficient plateau, it must be recognized that conventional cutbacks kept the French army from playing the sort of major role assigned to it by the government. Even with a reorganized force structure and new operational doctrines, military forces without adequate equipment cannot credibly contribute to the capacity for battle that Giscard deemed necessary to French and European defense. Tactical nuclear weapons could not replace a big army. France seemed to want to have it both ways—taking on new roles in Europe's conventional defense while maintaining the old advantages of independence and nuclear status—but it was unable to foot the bill. Even had it not been opposed for political reasons, Giscard's military program would still have proved very difficult to implement for economic ones.

CONCLUSIONS ON THE GISCARDIAN EXPERIENCE

By the time Giscard's presidential term came to an end in 1981, France was clearly better able to contribute to the defense of Western Europe than it had been in 1974. The army was more mobile, better equipped and organized for conventional battle, and—despite the remaining ambiguities and gaps in official military doctrine—France's commitment to its neighbors was also more forthright (and, thereby, more deterring). The country was more solidly anchored in the Western Alliance than at any time since the Fourth Republic, and few could doubt that France would play a full role were a military crisis ever to erupt in Europe. But there were limits to how fully that role could be expressed or, at least, to how explicit it could be made. The requirements of domestic politics along with significant economic constraints—both of which would reappear in later years—prevented those who made French security policy from making an adaptation to Europe as completely as they might have wished.

The internal opposition to Giscard's supposed "violation" of Gaullist doctrines was not surprising—it was associated with a constant fear that France would be taken back down the path of subordination, Atlantic integration, and national abandon that de Gaulle had risked so much to fight. That which is gained through struggle is always defended more forcefully than something achieved with ease. But the fact that it was seen to be "Gaullist requirements" that ruled out the implementation of Giscard's original defense program is not without irony. For Giscard's efforts to give France a more prominent military role in Europe were not incompatible with Gaullist principles but only with a static interpretation of them. Somehow, by the late 1970s the military doctrines that had been elaborated around an embryonic nuclear force and post-Algerian army during the 1960s had come to be taken as inviolable parts of a indissoluble whole. As long as ambiguity could allow for a flexible interpretation of those doctrines, nearly everybody could be satisfied. But as Giscard attempted to do away with the ambiguity in order to reassure neighbors and reinforce French deterrence, he raised questions on whose answers the French could not agree.

"Gaullist" vigilance was perhaps necessary, and it was important to protect the gains of the struggle for independence. But it was surely overdone. Despite some changes in particular military doctrines, French security policy during the Giscard years remained Gaullist. Giscard maintained the priority of the force de frappe, upheld the principle of autonomy of decision, and continued to pursue the objectives of French primacy and national grandeur. The fact that he tried to do all of this while adapting French security policy to a situation that was obviously evolving—tried, in other words, to prevent France's defense from becoming outmoded—should scarcely have been seen as a betrayal of the fundamental principles embodied by General de Gaulle.

This first experience with "post-Gaullist" leadership in the Fifth Republic was an important period of transition. Giscard's tenure was situated between the Gaullist period, when the French contribution to European security was relatively expendable and purely national objectives could be given priority, and a hypothetical later period in which a revitalized France would be able to play a greater, or even leading, role in a more autonomous European defense. Giscard tried to manage that transition and to help bring it about but for the reasons discussed ultimately failed to do so. The tensions inherent in Gaullist military policy had started to become acute.

CHAPTER FIVE

Mitterrand's Adaptations, 1981–1986

ANY ANALYSIS of the first five years of Socialist government in the Fifth Republic must describe two important "adaptations" of French security policy. First, it must account for the French Left's adaptation to the Gaullist model for defense, the acceptance of a set of fundamentals that the Socialist party (PS) and its leader had long rejected as unrealistic and pernicious. President François Mitterrand had for decades been General de Gaulle's most severe and most persistent critic, yet by 1981 he was implementing a security policy that was firmly in the Gaullist tradition. Second, it must assess the Socialists' adaptation of that same Gaullist model to the changing demands of European defense. The French contribution to the defense of Western Europe became more imperative in the early 1980s than it had been throughout the entire postwar period, and even while they held onto pretensions of national independence, the French realized that they had to act. The great challenge faced by the Mitterrand administration was to reconcile the demands of the Gaullist model (at least as interpreted in France) with those of a greater French contribution to a stronger European defense.

THE SOCIALISTS' TURNAROUND AND ITS EXPLANATIONS

Historians and observers of politics often seek to discover continuities and to trace the roots of what otherwise seems like radical change. In the French Socialists' adoption of basic Gaullist principles and policies on national defense, however, such an effort should probably not be taken too far. The PS's turnaround on defense policy was as complete as it was rapid. Opposed to Gaullist policies on Atlanticist and European grounds throughout the 1960s (as the Section Française de l'Internationale Ouvrière [SFIO]), the French Socialist movement of the 1970s was even more hostile albeit for different reasons. A majority of the "new" Socialists—at least until the later part of the decade—had strong reservations about both France's membership in the Atlantic Alliance and about the nuclear force on which French defense was based.

The party formed in 1971 with the fusion of the main elements of the non-Communist Left—Alain Savary's Nouveau Parti Socialiste (NPS) and

François Mitterrand's Convention des Institutions Républicaines (CIR)—was highly radical, fervently anticapitalist, and openly hostile to the Atlantic Alliance. It embraced a Marxist analysis of the international system that downplayed the notion of a Soviet military threat and instead claimed to feel most threatened by the capitalist world and its "imperialist" leader, the United States. The party's 1972 program of government, *Changer la vie*, called for the "renunciation" of the strategic nuclear force and denounced the NATO Alliance, which "[ties] all signatories to American imperialism and . . . exposes them to preventive attacks."[1] For the party's leader, François Mitterrand, membership in the Atlantic Alliance only facilitated France's "economic colonization by the United States."[2]

It was difficult to see how this party, allied since 1972 with the French Communist party (PCF) and led by a man who had failed in twenty-three years in the National Assembly to approve a single military budget, could ever have come to power without bringing about a radical reorientation of French defense. Indeed, had the Socialists come to power in 1974 under the 1972 PS-PCF Common Program of Government (and their candidate was only 425,000 votes away in the presidential elections that year)—or even in 1978 (when they barely lost a legislative majority)—it cannot be excluded that they would have fundamentally altered French security policy and jettisoned much of the Gaullist model that had taken over a decade to implement. As late as 1980, the Socialist party's official platform warned that although it accepted the Atlantic Alliance, it was firmly against an alignment with "imperialist positions" in the world, that is, those of the United States.[3]

And yet, after 1981, Gaullist doctrines and practices were consistently applied, and the great tremors feared on the one hand by NATO, and on the other by the Gaullists, never came about. As will be seen, the French Socialists ardently supported the policies they once even more ardently refused, and they defended and refined with remarkable talent and vigor the very doctrines they had once ridiculed. The mocking tones heard on the subject of Gaullist defense principles throughout the 1950s, 1960s, and 1970s had, by the early 1980s, become eloquent justifications of many of those same principles. In this sense, the Socialists' turnaround on national security issues in the late 1970s—and their adoption of apparently very Gaullist policies in the 1980s—would leave a legacy in France whose importance comes close to rivaling de Gaulle's own.

What explains this remarkable turnaround? The simplest explanation has always focused on domestic politics. In this view, the Socialists' primary goal was to come to power, and the party's leaders saw electoral advantages in adopting a defense policy that had begun to win the loyalty and esteem of most of their compatriots. Just as Pompidou and Giscard—whose loyalties to the General and his heritage were suspect—were obliged to fall into line on questions of foreign policy and defense, so, obviously, was Mitterrand, even more so given his "heretical" past. The Socialists ended their opposition to Gaullist defense policy in the late 1970s, the story goes, simply because that policy had become a vote-getter, and the PS needed all the votes it could get.

As will be seen, this analysis is incomplete in a number of ways: it does not explain why the Socialists would have been more attentive to security issues in the early 1980s than they had been in the past, why they actually became even *more* "Gaullist" once in power, or why French voters would have suddenly begun to pay attention to military affairs that they had long ignored. However, it must be recognized that political factors played their part. By the mid-1970s, de Gaulle's defense policies had become something of a rallying point for the French, and as Giscard's experience proved, they were already sacred to the political elite. It would have been a gamble for a politician on either the Left or the Right to tamper with a doctrine that had apparently come to be accepted by such a large major-ity, especially a doctrine so flattering to national sensibilities and so closely linked with the idea of national grandeur. The French people had been looking for something of which they could be proud after two de-cades of travail and distress, and now with the "third largest nuclear force in the world" and the impression that their defense was "independent," they seemed to have found it.

Indeed, once highly contested, both in terms of military logic and avail-able means, the basic premises of de Gaulle's defense policies had by the mid-1970s become a fundamental part of what might be called a French military ethos. Gaullist ideas, largely responsible for restoring a sense of self-respect among French people who had lost it, were now well-an-chored in public opinion and would have been difficult to uproot. Some of their practical manifestations, like the withdrawal from NATO's inte-grated command structure or the ousting of foreign troops from French soil, were by now so widely accepted and had been so successfully exe-cuted that they were probably irreversible. Could anyone have imagined calling for a reinstallation of foreign troops in France after years of Gaull-ist association of military integration with political subordination? Or could anyone seriously propose abandoning the nuclear force, symbol of French independence and grandeur and key to the exclusive club open only to *les grands?* The Gaullist "lesson" that integration in NATO and nonnuclear status meant national dependence and foreign hegemony could no longer be ignored.

Still, the Socialists' reversal cannot be seen solely as a vote-getting tac-tic, and they were not obliged to accept Gaullist principles merely to win an election; indeed they won the election before their defense policies became altogether clear. Other factors—including the internal makeup of the Socialist party, the development of the French nuclear force, and a changing international political climate—seem more significant than the simple electoral explanation of the Socialists' adaptation to Gaullist defense.

Within the Socialist party, pressure for change had come from a small number of individuals who had never accepted the French Left's antimilitary tradition. The steady work and growing influence of Charles Hernu, Jean-Pierre Chevènement, and Robert Pontillon over time led the party to accept at least the foundations of France's existing defense and alliance positions. By 1976, the party's Executive Committee had concluded that the nuclear force was necessary to the independence of a Socialist France in a capitalist world, and by January 1978 the party as a whole finally agreed to "maintain" the FNS while it pursued international disarmament.[4] This was far from a rousing endorsement of French nuclear policy or of the Gaullist legacy as a whole, but it was also a long way from the rhetoric of 1972.

Although the party was thus able to agree on the broad lines of a more "realistic" security policy, its leaders—foreshadowing the factionalism that would mark the PS in years to come—were still far from a common view on ultimate goals. Each of the individual Socialist leaders mentioned here, for example, had different motives for their efforts to get the party to abandon its "leftist" security policy and, in particular, for their support of the FNS. Hernu, a member of Mitterrand's inner circle and concerned about the party's electoral fortunes, believed that the Socialists could never come to power as long as they embraced pacifist and antimilitary policies that were associated with defeatism in France and by now out of touch with public opinion. He also believed, like de Gaulle, that the nuclear force would give France greater status than France's neighbors in Europe and thereby compensate for an economy seen to be in relative decline. Chevènement, on the other hand, leader of the leftist Centre d'Etudes, de Recherches, et d'Education Socialiste (CERES) and antipathetic toward the United States, saw the advantages of a military posture that emphasized France's independence and saw the force de frappe as a way to limit the excesses of U.S. capitalist hegemony in Europe. Chevènement claimed not only that independent nuclear weapons could give France more autonomy within the Atlantic Alliance but that they would allow France to withdraw from it altogether, which CERES had proposed to the party in 1972. Finally, for Pontillon—friend and adviser to former SFIO leader Guy Mollet (and like his mentor an Atlanticist from the Fourth Republic)—the logic was different again, this time just the opposite of that of Chevènement. By abandoning the Left's traditional hostility toward the alliance, Pontillon reasoned, and by accepting a nuclear deterrent that NATO had by now come to accept (and which

Pontillon himself had once opposed on the grounds that it would disrupt alliance relations), France would enhance both its position within the Atlantic Alliance and the alliance itself. The FNS in this view would reinforce NATO, not undermine it. The different factions of the French Socialist movement could, thus, not agree on just why France had to maintain both its military ties with the West and its independent nuclear stance, but at least they agreed on what had to be done. Mitterrand, ever the chameleon, let his henchmen convince the party and then went along.[5]

Another important element in explaining the Socialist turnaround, perhaps even more critical than those mentioned so far, was the actual *material* state of the Gaullist defense program and specifically of the nuclear force. The force de frappe that the Socialists had opposed in the 1960s was little more than an embryo, a project for the future that few believed would develop fully. It was perfectly conceivable to oppose it not only on strategic grounds but on technical and financial ones: nobody was sure it would work and, if it did, how much it would cost. As late as 1970, France had deployed no land-based missiles or operational nuclear submarines, and arguments could still be made that they should never be deployed.

By the mid-1970s, however, this was no longer the case. The French nuclear force had developed too far, and too much money had been spent on it, for anyone to think realistically of canceling major programs. As Mitterrand himself explained in 1974: "I am hostile to the development of nuclear forces. But . . . you are asking me the question in 1974, and I am a realistic man. . . . The force de frappe has existed for fifteen years, it has become real, it exists."[6] By the time the Socialists came to power, France had no less than five operational nuclear-fueled ballistic missile submarines (SSBNs), eighteen IRBMs, thirty-four modernized Mirage IV bombers, forty-two Plutons, thrity-six Super-Etendards, forty-five Jaguars, thirty Mirage IIIs, M-20, M-4, S-2, and S-3 missiles, and an extensive infrastructure of command, control, and communication facilities. Although there is no absolute reason that all these programs could not have been canceled—sunk costs, after all, are sunk—it would have been enormously difficult to jettison a nuclear force upon which so much pride had been staked and so much money spent. De Gaulle's technological, financial, and diplomatic gambles had all been won, and it was no longer realistic to suggest turning back.

The most critical factor of all in bringing about the Socialist turnaround may have been the evolution of the international situation—the deterioration of détente—and the French reaction to it. At the beginning of the 1970s, it was not surprising that the Socialists stuck to the anti-NATO line of their ideology and the antimilitary line of their political roots. Détente was popular on both the Left and the Right, the United

States was demonstrating military "imperialism" in Vietnam (and economic "imperialism" by manipulating the dollar), the Soviets seemed to be less interested in ideology than in trade with the West, and even the Americans were negotiating arms treaties with the Russians. At home, the PS was still outflanked on the Left by a pro-Soviet PCF, and to reach its goal of "rebalancing the Left" (by stealing votes from the Communists), it had to play up its "peace-loving" credentials. With even the center-Right government optimistic about better relations with Moscow and convinced that increased trade would open up the Communist system, it was neither urgent nor politically necessary for the Socialists to adopt a firmer stand on questions of defense.

Beginning in about 1975, however, Soviet actions at home and abroad and the changing mood in East-West relations began to bring about a change in the French attitude, and the so-called Gulag effect took hold. A massive Soviet military buildup (including the deployment of SS-20s targeted at Western Europe), Moscow's interference in the Third World (in Angola, Ethiopia, and Vietnam) and widely publicized Soviet human rights abuses (underlined by the exposure given to these issues in the 1975 Helsinki Accords), led by the end of the decade to a sharp erosion of the historic French good will toward the Soviets. While President Giscard d'Estaing clung sometimes carelessly to what was left of détente, it was the Socialists who began to comprehend the new mood in France, and it was François Mitterrand who best took advantage of it. Communists had made advances in the Third World, were acting aggressively (and even murderously) in the former French territories of Vietnam and Cambodia, and were even "threatening" Western Europe via a growing Euro-Communist movement. By the time the Soviets invaded Afghanistan in December 1979—the last straw—it had become clear that the geopolitical situation had changed. The Cold War was back on, and the French wanted to help fight it.

This changing international environment, of course, explains the Socialist abandonment of their leftist security platform more than it does their adoption of a Gaullist one. Indeed, a hard line toward the Soviet Union can even be seen as distinctly un-Gaullist if one compares it to de Gaulle's use of the "Soviet card" and pursuit of détente in the mid-1960s. But de Gaulle, too, took a firm stance vis-à-vis Moscow when prospects for change seemed to him less propitious—as between 1959 and 1965, to say nothing of 1947–1952. (Had de Gaulle lost the 1965 election, it is doubtful that he would be remembered among the founders of détente.) And with the Soviets of the early 1980s behaving in a more consistently aggressive manner than they had since at least the early 1960s, it was not surprising that the PS abandoned its former pacifism. The transition from the heady détente of the early 1970s to the new Cold War by the end of the decade did not by itself drive the Socialist conversion, but it clearly facilitated it.

The Socialists' abandonment of their leftist defense ideals and subsequent espousal of Gaullist policies and premises was, thus, not as surprising, or as superficial, as it might have seemed. It was not only a political strategy designed to reassure voters but the natural result of several simultaneous and interrelated evolutions. The impact of the Gaullist model on French strategic culture, the Socialist party's changing internal makeup, the success of de Gaulle's nuclear ambitions and the international atmosphere had all greatly changed since the days in which François Mitterrand and his allies were denouncing the force de frappe and the Atlantic Alliance alike. By the time Mitterrand and his party came to power in May 1981, they had accepted nearly all of the basic premises of Gaullist defense. But even then, nobody yet knew just how faithful to the General's legacy the Socialists would prove to be.

SECURITY POLICY UNDER THE SOCIALISTS: ADAPTING TO DE GAULLE

The Socialist adoption of Gaullist defense policies and practices is seen here as one of the outstanding themes of the Left's five-year stint in power. This view, however, is scarcely the object of consensus among scholars on France. If Mitterrand has been seen by one analyst (Dominique Moïsi) as the "most Gaullist of de Gaulle's successors"[7] and by another (Stanley Hoffmann) as having practiced "Gaullism by any other name,"[8] a number of other observers have found the early Mitterrand years to have marked a significant break with the past. In 1984 Anton DePorte called Mitterrand's policies toward the superpowers "remarkably un-Gaullist in style as well as substance" and argued that overall, the label "'Gaullist' does not fit."[9] Similarly, Robert S. Rudney, writing of "Mitterrand's New Atlanticism" also in 1984, claimed to see "a historic reorientation of French security policy vis-à-vis the Atlantic Alliance."[10] For Jolyon Howorth that same year, the consensus around Gaullist rhetoric remained in place, but French security policies and attitudes had significantly changed.[11] Perhaps most insistent of all, Jean-François Révél has argued that French defense policy in the 1980s in no way reflected de Gaulle's policies and that France's "new defense policy . . . might be good, it might be bad . . . [but] one thing is certain, it is not Gaullist."[12]

With a few years of hindsight, one can now look back at the first five Mitterrand years, place them in a broader context, and see how this latter view misses the point. One does not have to find that the specific policies and doctrines made in the 1960s were implemented without alteration in the 1980s to argue that fundamental Gaullist principles were upheld. (A defense policy that failed to change at all after twenty years, after all, would scarcely be Gaullist.) The point here is not that these were years of stagnation or that nothing changed in the military domain between 1981 and 1986. Rather, the point is that far from replacing the Gaullist paradigm for French defense policy, the evolving policies of the Mitterrand administration took place within it. Mitterrand did not opt either for the untried leftist defense he had previously supported or for a return to the integrated, nonnuclear defense that prevailed in France before 1958. Instead, he relied on the Gaullist model and brought it up to date. When compared either to the Socialist policy platform of the previous decade or to the security policies of neighboring states in Europe, the defense policies of the Mitterrand government might even be called "more Gaullist than de Gaulle."

The General's influence was manifested in a number of ways during Mitterrand's first five years in office. First, of course, continuity might be noted in the new president's style and foreign policy practices. For example, the former parliamentarian Mitterrand was nothing other than Gaullist in his assertion of supreme or even exclusive presidential control over foreign policy and defense. Although he had long criticized de Gaulle's "authoritarian" rule (once characterizing it as no less than a "permanent coup d'état"), Mitterrand, too, proved to have a taste for strong personalized policy making out of the Elysée.[13] As already noted, Defense Minister Hernu was a friend and close ally of the president, and if the first foreign minister (Claude Cheysson) asserted some autonomy, the second (Mitterrand's friend Roland Dumas) clearly represented the president alone. Mitterrand, like his predecessors, also used "personal envoys" like Dumas, Jacques Attali, or Charles Salzmann to conduct foreign policy in his name. And in marked contrast to domestic and economic policy making, in matters of defense the Socialist party played no role at all.[14]

As in the past, presidential authority was also asserted when it came to nuclear deterrence policy. Although Mitterrand had long argued that presidential control over the decision to use nuclear weapons amounted to an antidemocratic "supreme authority held by one man alone,"[15] by 1983 he was announcing on French television that the "key element" of deterrence strategy in France was himself (best summed up by the quip "*la dissuasion, c'est moi*").[16] Throughout his tenure, he would state repeatedly the position that "the responsibility of [nuclear] decision lies with the president of the Republic, and with the president alone" and that "the possible use of the deterrent force could only come about with the decision of the head of state."[17] Defense—and, particularly, nuclear—policy thus remained, with all the caveats or qualifications one might wish to add about the influence of the bureaucracy, the military establishment, or the government, a presidential *domaine privilégié*.

More consequential than these questions of practice or style, however—and more pertinent to this book—was the adoption by the Socialists of a relatively orthodox set of military policies and doctrines. This is not to say that there were no significant developments in France's military posture during the early 1980s, but those changes were highly circumscribed and clearly influenced by the policies and logic of the past. Socialist military policies and doctrines are telling both for what they say about Gaullist influences and for what they say about the objectives of the Mitterrand government itself.

The area of Socialist military policy where continuity stands out most is the absolute priority that Mitterrand and his military planners gave to the national nuclear force. In fact, this aspect of de Gaulle's legacy is now so firmly embedded in French strategic culture and is so taken for granted that it is sometimes forgotten how singular the nuclear policy once was. When it is remembered, however, that the creation of the force de frappe under de Gaulle was vehemently opposed by the center, the Left, and even by some Gaullists, that in 1960 it provoked two censure motions (one of which garnered 215 votes), and that François Mitterrand himself was for years its most vociferous opponent, it becomes apparent how significant a change had taken place in so short a time. A highly controversial and uniquely Gaullist policy just two decades before had become a fundamental pillar of French defense.

Mitterrand's nuclear policy, though, was not Gaullist simply because it existed. It was Gaullist because of the priority accorded to it, the force structure adopted for it, and the employment doctrine with which it was governed. From the very start of his term, the new president confirmed that Socialist acceptance of the French nuclear force was real and that the nuclear priority would not be abandoned. On the contrary, among Mitterrand's very first decisions as president of the Republic were the construction of a seventh strategic submarine by 1994 and the continuation of nuclear tests in the South Pacific.[18] Later in 1981, Mitterrand authorized the continuation of plans to develop a longer-range tactical nuclear weapon (the Hadès), to build a land-based intermediate-range missile (the sx, since canceled), and to modernize part of the aging Mirage IV force and equip it with a new air-to-ground nuclear missile (the ASMP). In the 1984–1988 program law, funding was approved for the seventh submarine as well as for a retrofitting of four out of the five existing subs with new M-4 missiles capable of carrying six 150-kiloton warheads each. This program would increase the planned number of warheads on the *force océanique stratégique* (FOST) from 80 in 1983 to 592 by 1994. The program law also set aside funds for the transformation of eighteen Mirage IVs which would receive the ASMP, the hardening of the communications network to protect it from nuclear attack, studies on new materials for both the sx and the M-5 missile, and the tactical nuclear-capable Mirage 2000-N and Super-Etendard, which would both be equipped to carry the ASMP.[19] Under Mitterrand, more than 30 percent of all spending on military equipment would go to nuclear forces. By the time the Mitterrand strategic modernization would be complete in the mid-1990s, France would have a total of more than nine hundred deployable nuclear warheads, more than a threefold increase from the force available when Mitterrand came to power in 1981.[20]

It was, thus, already clear after just a few years that Mitterrand's nuclear policy would go well beyond the 1978 Socialist party decision merely to "maintain" the nuclear force. Whereas his predecessor had sought merely to maintain the FNS as conventional forces were revamped, Mitterrand presided over an accomplishment in the nuclear domain that even the creators of the force de frappe would have had to admit was impressive, perhaps even beyond their own hopes and ambitions at the time. Defense Minister Hernu—in a phrase that might just as well stand as an epithet for the Gaullist era—summed up the administration's new attitude best: "Anyone who tells me he would prefer an armored division to a nuclear submarine has got his eras all mixed up."[21]

The continued influence of Gaullist traditions was also apparent in the doctrines that governed the nuclear force. In contrast to Giscard's early experiments with an implicit extension of the French deterrent, the Mitterrand administration began much more cautiously. To be sure, the Socialists continued to emphasize the principles of "uncertainty" and "vital interests" that had become part of the French strategic landscape since the early 1970s. They recognized as well as anyone that a gap existed between the concept of a national nuclear sanctuary and the expression of solidarity in Europe, and that the gap was growing as the American nuclear guarantee became less and less credible. But at the same time, the Mitterrand team insisted, publicly at least, that the "rules" governing France's nuclear force had not fundamentally changed.

In a famous speech before the United Nations General Assembly in 1983, Mitterrand laid out the conditions that would have to be met before France would even consider any participation in nuclear disarmament. France would only take part in nuclear negotiations (such as those the superpowers had undertaken in Geneva) if: (1) the United States and the Soviet Union reduced their own atomic arsenals to a level comparable to that of France; (2) the disequilibrium in conventional forces in Europe was reduced; and (3) the antimissile, antisubmarine, and antisatellite arms race would stop.[22] In other words, for the foreseeable future France would maintain and develop its independent nuclear force.

More important than this, however, was the maintenance of the orthodox argument that the force de frappe was independent and that authority over it could not be shared. General Jeannou Lacaze emphasized this point in his speech to the IHEDN, stating that military cooperation with the Atlantic Alliance would only involve conventional forces and "therefore excludes all nuclear force employment planning."[23] And the president himself put it even more directly when he spoke at the Hague in February 1984: "Aside from the protection of the national sanctuary and the 'vital interests' attached to it, it is out of the question that France take charge of European security. . . . Both for strategic reasons and for reasons of international politics which are a result of [World War II], the decision on using French nuclear weapons cannot be shared."[24] The president and his advisers continually stressed that there could be no question of extending the nuclear guarantee to West Germany, that the Germans were not asking for it anyway, and that the French deterrent was a "proportional" one that could not be credible as the guarantor of the security of any country other than France. In short, according to François Heisbourg, a Defense Ministry official from 1981–1985, there were certain "factual limitations" that continued to govern the French nuclear force: "A medium-sized power cannot give an explicit nuclear guarantee to third countries without, at best, appearing ridiculous; Paris will not try to do what already does not seem to be sufficiently credible coming from Washington; [and] deterrence between the weak and the strong has its rules."[25] The Gaullist nuclear catechism had obviously been learned.

In the area of conventional forces, there was admittedly somewhat greater innovation. In 1983, the Mitterrand government reorganized the army for a greater European role, created a Rapid Action Force that could intervene far forward in Germany, and even began to participate in maneuvers meant to show France's willingness to take part in forward defense if necessary. The specifics of these force adaptations—the sine qua non of a genuine French commitment to European defense in the early 1980s—will be examined in more detail in the context of Franco-German relations later in this chapter. Here, however, it is important to note that even these sometimes far-reaching modifications did not depart too greatly (if at all) from the original Gaullist model. France continued to refuse all of the following: participation in NATO's integrated military commands; the deployment of foreign forces on French territory; automatic access of allied air forces to French airspace; the automatic engagement of French troops in case of conflict; and the occupation of a "space" on the central front. Indeed, this conservative view of France's conventional military role in Europe was made explicit as early as 1981 by Lacaze in the same IHEDN speech previously cited. Lacaze stated that

1. military cooperation would only involve conventional forces, and would therefore exclude all nuclear force employment planning;

2. France would make no automatic commitment of its forces, and excluded in particular France receiving any peacetime responsibility for ground, sea or air zones and participating in what is called the "forward battle"; and

3. In the case of a commitment at NATO's side, French forces would remain grouped under national command and in directions or zones covering national territory.[26]

Moreover, the justifications for all these relatively restrictive policies were the same ones that had guided French policy in the past. In July 1981, for example, Defense Minister Hernu made it a point to emphasize that the Gaullist principle of national autonomy over the use of French forces would be maintained: "We have to preserve our freedom of decision," Hernu said to Le Monde, "to avoid becoming automatically engaged in a conflict that we would not want to pursue."[27] Similarly, General Lacaze declared in 1981 that the "prime aim" of French policy was "to safeguard, in all circumstances, our complete freedom of decision and assessment so that our country cannot be automatically engaged in a conflict in which we would not feel implicated."[28] And Prime Minister Pierre Mauroy echoed these themes, stating that "France does not intend to risk undergoing the consequences of conflicts that would be foreign to her."[29] The notion that NATO might be involved in conflicts that would not concern France was a step back from the positions taken by Giscard and Méry a few years before and was more reminiscent of an era during which de Gaulle was worried about American actions in Vietnam provoking unwanted conflict in Europe.

Finally, the influence of Gaullist doctrines on Socialist military policy—once again to a greater degree than under the previous administration—was also apparent in tactical nuclear doctrine. Whereas Giscard had announced that tactical nuclear weapons were "battlefield weapons as well as weapons of deterrence," Mitterrand made it explicit that they would not be used "like some sort of battlefield superartillery."[30] One year later, the administration defined its position on tactical nuclear arms even more clearly by changing their official name to armes préstratégiques (prestrategic weapons) thus emphasizing their direct link to the strategic nuclear force.[31] This "new" concept was, in fact, a return to the "old" one as written into the white paper in 1972. France's short-range nuclear weapons would be given no battlefield role whatsoever, and their sole purpose was to signal to a potential adversary France's willingness to use its nuclear arms. To emphasize this point even further, Mitterrand ordered that the new longer-range Hadès missiles be grouped in separate units directly subordinate to the chief of staff of the armed forces, thereby to the head of state. French tactical nuclear weapons were to remain entirely distinct, in theory and in practice, from NATO's flexible response.

The adaptation of François Mitterrand after May 1981 to the habits, doctrines, theories, and force postures put in place by General de Gaulle was, thus, remarkable, and it could scarcely be argued that the early 1980s saw a fundamental break with traditional Gaullist practices and principles where national defense was concerned. A system in which the head of state was the dominant force in the making of defense and foreign policy, in which national independence remained the primordial theme of security policy, in which independent nuclear weapons functioned as a source of both deterrence and national prestige, in which deterrence was based on concepts of "proportionality" and "uncertainty," and in which NATO's doctrine of "flexible response" was formally refused was by any standard a Gaullist system. One need only compare French security policy at this time to the security policies of any of France's neighbors, where *none* of the aforementioned characteristics apply, to see that Mitterrand's policies were still far more Gaullist than they were anything else.

Within the Gaullist approach, of course, was much room for maneuver, and no policy directed by the wily Mitterrand has ever lacked maneuver. Throughout his long career, Mitterrand, a "man of seven faces" to one of his biographers, has proven willing and able to adapt to the most diverse circumstances.[32] Having established that the guiding principles and basic doctrines of French security policy would not be changed, Mitterrand was also driven to adapt certain aspects of that policy to a military and political balance that *was* changing. This brings the discussion to the second major theme of this chapter: the adaptation of the Gaullist model to Europe.

The most important aspects of this adaptation were a more conciliatory policy toward the Atlantic Alliance and the pursuit of a better relationship with the Federal Republic of Germany, which included a reorganization of French conventional forces for a greater European role. Arguably, however, even these major new trends were not inconsistent with the patterns of the past.

MITTERRAND'S ATLANTIC RAPPROCHEMENT: ADAPTING TO NATO

Perhaps the most striking feature of President Mitterrand's management of defense policy, after the accommodation of Gaullist traditions, was the accommodation to the Atlantic Alliance. Mitterrand and the Socialists, sharp critics of American "economic imperialism" and highly suspicious of NATO, not only accepted the basic premises of Gaullist defense but they ironically departed from Gaullism most in the one area in which logic suggested they might have agreed with it—relations with the United States. Instead of rejecting the NATO relationship or even maintaining France's aloofness from it, the Mitterrand government went further to cooperate with NATO than any French administration had for more than twenty years, including that of the so-called Atlanticist, Giscard d'Estaing.

The *Atlanticization* of French security policy began from the very start of the new administration. Whereas many expected or feared that the Socialist president of France—bent on ridding his country of capitalism and whose government included ministers from the Communist party—would have great difficulties getting along with his more conservative allies (like Ronald Reagan, Margaret Thatcher, and Helmut Schmidt), just the opposite occurred. Beginning with the 1981 Western summit in Ottawa, Mitterrand began a surprisingly cordial working relationship with most of his alliance partners, and in the following years French-Atlantic cooperation flourished. In June 1982 the French president attended an Atlantic Alliance dinner in Bonn, had Prime Minister Mauroy attend a working meeting of heads of state or government, and broke with precedent to invite alliance leaders back to Paris for the annual summit the following year.[33] The June 1983 Atlantic Council meeting was the first in Paris since 1966, and after that meeting NATO's Secretary General Joseph Luns declared not only that "France was a full-fledged member of NATO" but that President Mitterrand's positions on security issues "[were] rather more favorable than those of his predecessor."[34] France, of course, maintained its refusal to participate in NATO's Nuclear Planning Group or its Defense Planning Committee (let alone its integrated military commands), but it was more prepared than ever to consult, cooperate with, and discuss military contingencies with NATO. For Mitterrand, the Atlantic Alliance was now to be considered, with the nuclear force, one of the "two pillars of security" for France.[35]

The new alliance relationship also included extensive direct military cooperation. Contacts and communication between NATO headquarters and the French military were said to be more extensive than at any time during the Fifth Republic (they were "extremely close" according to NATO SACEUR Bernard Rogers) and new command and logistics arrangements between France and NATO were worked out.[36] Plans were developed for French forces to serve under NATO commands in central Germany, for French airfields to be used as potential dispersion bases for NATO's airborne early warning system, for French and NATO tactical air forces to coordinate flight plans, and for French hospitals to serve as wartime treatment centers for American casualties.[37] Numerous joint maneuvers even took place between the alliance and France, including a large-scale air-sea exercise in June 1983 in which France participated fully and during which U.S. bombers were permitted to refuel in French airspace for the first time since 1966. The French-American nuclear cooperation that had begun in the early 1970s was also pursued, and Mitterrand apparently went "further in the direction of [nuclear] coordination with NATO than even Giscard had gone."[38] Whereas the popular perception on both sides of the Atlantic was that France was "not in NATO" and that its defense policy was "independent," the reality was that behind the scenes French and U.S. military cooperation was very extensive and highly fruitful.

Another spectacular, if still ambiguous, manifestation of France's new Atlantic role was the speech made by François Mitterrand before the West German Bundestag on January 20, 1983. To the Americans and to Germans in the governing Christian Democratic Union/Christian Social Union (CDU/CSU) coalition, this unprecedented step—a French president overtly calling on the Germans to reaffirm their loyalty to NATO—was a highly favorable watershed that signaled France's own commitment to the alliance. The French, of course, could place the Bundestag speech in a European context, depicting it as an affirmation of Franco-German rather than Atlantic solidarity. (The occasion of the speech, after all, was the commemoration of the 1963 Elysée treaty). But it was lost on no one that Mitterrand was taking a very American line on an issue of great importance to the alliance. In marked contrast to Giscard's public silence on the question of the Euromissiles (on the shaky grounds that France was not concerned because there were no American missiles in France), Mitterrand warned of the dangers of nuclear "decoupling" and of Soviet "conventional superiority" as he emphasized the need for the U.S. missiles in Europe.[39]

Indeed, the Bundestag speech seemed to mark not only a diplomatic rapprochement but an apparent coming together of French and American views on the requirements of Western security. No longer did French leaders have the luxury of denouncing the American protectorate at the same time as they relied on it; now they were affirming its worth. One month after Mitterrand's speech, Foreign Minister Cheysson (scarcely an uncritical Atlanticist) argued for the deployment of the American missiles on the grounds that "the guarantee of European territories that do not have nuclear weapons . . . can come only from the integrated command of NATO, that is to say, in fact, the [United States]."[40] The French view, like the American, was that the European commitment to NATO—and at the same time the NATO commitment to Europe—had to be reaffirmed.

French and American views also coincided where the Soviet Union was concerned. France, like its European neighbors, had traditionally sought to counterbalance superpower tensions by maintaining a certain détente with the Soviet Union during East-West conflicts so that the Cold War would not get out of hand. This remained the case during the early 1980s, as evidenced, for example, by the French and European tenacity in pursuing the creation of a natural gas pipeline between Western Europe and the USSR. France even went ahead with the agreement, which provided government-guaranteed export credits to Moscow, after the Soviet-sponsored military crackdown in Poland in December 1981.

This exception notwithstanding, the first five years of the Mitterrand presidency were marked more by hostility toward Moscow than by détente. In 1983, for example, a French military program law for the first time explicitly named the Soviet Union as a threat to Western Europe. Using rhetoric markedly similar to that coming out of Washington, it referred to the "mounting disequilibrium in the balance of conventional forces in Europe," the "considerable advantage in favor of the Warsaw Pact," and the "risk of a decoupling between Europe and the United States."[41] From a country that had always insisted on the weakness of that coupling in the first place, this was a rather fundamental change of emphasis. In 1983 also, the French expelled forty-seven Soviet "diplomats" and "journalists" for industrial espionage and later that year responded in uncommonly sharp terms to the Soviet shooting-down of a civilian Korean airliner, Cheysson denouncing it as a "brutal, shocking act."[42] During the first three years of his term, moreover, Mitterrand refused to hold summit meetings with Soviet leaders until the situations in Poland and in Afghanistan had changed. He wanted to remind the Soviets that good relations with France would not be automatic and at the same time to show his Western partners that France would be a solid European anchor in the West as long as the Russians misbehaved. Even when the president finally went back on this promise by visiting the Kremlin in 1984, he compensated by boldly pressing Afghanistan, Poland, and the issue of Soviet dissident André Sakharov with the Soviet leaders. The days of "playing the Russian card" to gain leverage within the alliance were over, at least for the time being.

By the mid-1980s, the American and the French views of security questions in Europe had at least superficially converged, and their policies were remarkably similar in orientation. To be sure, policy differences remained (such as over the United States' Strategic Defense Initiative [SDI]), and the fact that France was calling for a tightening of the Atlantic Alliance and deployment of American missiles—but abstaining from the consequences—was not lost on many (particularly German) observers. Still, a French president who had recently expressed great hostility toward U.S. and NATO policies and whose country had always been among the least cooperative in Europe was now joining the Americans on a common security policy stance. The same François Mitterrand who had written as late as 1980 that he felt "no more attached to the Atlantic Alliance than a Rumanian or a Pole to the Warsaw Pact" was now insisting that "the determination and the solidarity of the members of NATO must be clearly confirmed."[43]

Why did the French come back to the Atlantic fold to the extent that they did? The first and most obvious factor has already been discussed. By the early 1980s—after the Soviet invasion of Afghanistan, the crackdown in Poland, deployment of the SS-20s, the Soviet conventional buildup, and the shooting down of KAL 007—the French had not surprisingly (even if belatedly) lost their enthusiasm for détente and come to the conclusion that NATO had to be reinforced. In the past, the French had always resented and resisted the United States when it was overwhelmingly powerful and meddled in the affairs of Europe, but after a period of perceived American weakness and introspection, a greater degree of support for Washington became both tolerable and necessary. Second, there was the fear that the West Germans, unsure about their security in the face of this Soviet onslaught, were for the first time in many years seriously courting neutralism. As the nightmare of nuclear decoupling began to become a reality, a reinforcement of the Atlantic link seemed to the French the only way to reassure fully their neighbors to the East. (The Germans, after all, had always looked first to Washington for their defense, and if a Franco-German rapprochement could help, it had to take place within an Atlantic context.) Third, there were domestic political reasons for Mitterrand's Atlantic policy. Contrary to what logic might suggest, the presence of Communist ministers in the second Mauroy government led not to increased criticism of Washington and better relations with Moscow but just the opposite. Without the suspicions raised by the Communist presence—to which the United States had reacted with some consternation—Mitterrand might have been freer to take a less hostile position vis-à-vis the Soviets and to distance himself somewhat from the West. In the event, however, the government was particularly careful to reassure its Western allies that it would "behave." Perversely, the presence of government ministers from a party whose foreign policy was totally subordinated to the Soviet Union helped ensure that the government would have good relations with the West.

Finally, Mitterrand was able to seek an Atlantic rapprochement with limited political risk. His leftist orientation and self-proclaimed "Third Worldism" shielded him from the accusations of subordinate Atlanticism that had proved so damaging and so constraining to his predecessor. The president's fervent critique of American "economic imperialism," his vocal opposition to American policies like SDI, and his party's recent indifference to the Atlantic Alliance made it much easier for him to align with Washington on defense questions than it would have been for a more openly Atlanticist leader like Giscard.

Whatever the causes, it is clear that an extensive rapprochement between France and the United States took place in the early 1980s despite the French Socialist experiment, despite diverging views on economic and Third World issues, and despite traditional French-American differences over issues of security in Europe. By 1986, French and American views about the military balance in Europe for once coincided, and the French were more willing than ever before in the Fifth Republic to cooperate in the political and military domains. France was still far from a NATO member "like any other," but it was closer to the alliance than it had been for two decades, and ironically, it was the once quasi-neutralist Parti Socialiste that was responsible.

It remains to be explained, of course, how it can be argued here that Mitterrand's security policies were Atlanticist and Gaullist at the same time. Was not one of de Gaulle's main objectives to pry Europe away from the Atlantic grip? The question makes obvious sense, but when put into context, France's extensive rapprochement with the Atlantic Alliance was not the great break with continuity that has sometimes been claimed.

To be sure, de Gaulle never let his interest in a military balance in Europe drive him too closely into the Atlantic fold. Nor did he ever pursue as anti-Soviet a foreign policy as did Mitterrand during the period 1981–1984 (although the de Gaulle of the early 1960s was scarcely indulgent vis-à-vis the Russians). Even when de Gaulle admitted the necessity of the alliance, he maintained France's distance from it and was fortunate enough to be able to depend for security on NATO's superior military strength. But when military tensions rose between East and West, de Gaulle, too, closed ranks with the alliance. This was evident at the time of the Paris summit in 1960 (when Khrushchev sought to intimidate the West), the Berlin crisis of 1961, the Cuban missile crisis in October 1962, and again after August 1968 when Soviet and Warsaw Pact troops crushed the Prague Spring. After all these incidents, de Gaulle reaffirmed his ties to the West and after the last one even seemed to embrace a new relationship with Washington and allow an inflection in French military doctrine. Even more importantly, none of these crises took place in the same sort of context as the cumulative one which Western Europe faced in 1981. Throughout the 1960s, American military superiority—or at the very least, parity—was clearly adequate to deter the Soviets from nuclear or even conventional diplomatic blackmail. When de Gaulle retired in 1969 there was at worst a general conventional balance in Europe, and the United States still had strategic superiority vis-à-vis the Soviet Union. But by the late 1970s, after a decade and a half of relentless Soviet buildup and an American "decade of neglect," the balance had shifted, and the margin of maneuver was reduced. Just as de Gaulle's policies toward the Atlantic Alliance were a function of the East-West climate, the rebirth of the Cold War in the early 1980s drove Mitterrand to move closer to the United States.

Finally, de Gaulle's NATO policy took place not only while France's security was assured from abroad but when its domestic priorities had yet to be achieved. Still pursuing his project of national restoration and trying to build an "independent" nuclear force, General de Gaulle could have embraced the Atlantic Alliance only at the expense of his goals at home. Embedded in an integrated command structure and tightly tied to the hegemonic leader of the alliance, France could never have become the independent world power of which de Gaulle dreamed. Mitterrand, on the other hand, wielding the force de frappe and with both the French army's and public's morale more firmly ensured, could pursue closer ties with NATO from a position of greater strength. A self-confident, nuclear-armed, and politically stable France, whose resources were now becoming vital to the alliance, was no longer merely a demandeur.

In short, even in times of military tension, de Gaulle never believed like Mitterrand that "the worst danger for [the French], as for our Western European neighbors, would be if the United States were now to stray away from the borders of our continent."[44] For all sorts of historic and personal reasons, the General was much less inclined than the Socialist leader to cooperate closely with the United States. But in de Gaulle's time, the danger was that the Americans would domineer the alliance, not that they would leave it. No one can say what de Gaulle's Atlantic policy would have been given the circumstances of 1981–1986.

THE GERMAN ROLE: ADAPTING TO EUROPE

The adaptation of the Mitterrand administration to changes going on in Europe was not limited to a more cooperative policy toward the Atlantic Alliance. France realized that even if the changing military balance in Europe suggested the need to reinforce NATO, at the same time it empha-sized the limits of the Atlantic link and demonstrated Western Europe's continued dependence on the United States. Indeed, Mitterrand was well aware that while "[it] would be dangerous to reinforce European solidar-ity under the illusion that it could be a substitute for the present alliance . . . it would be just as dangerous for Europe to abandon itself to the protection of a country outside of our own continent."[45] Thus, French efforts to improve Atlantic solidarity did not preclude—but made even more imperative—the perceived French need to build a closer relationship with their neighbors across the Rhine. It is sometimes difficult to separate the Atlantic and European aspects of French security policy in Europe; the two do not have to be mutually exclusive. But it is also clear that if Mitterrand's short-term security priority was NATO—and that he believed that under the circumstances at the time only NATO could match the Soviet threat—he had not abandoned the longstanding French desire for a more "European Europe," one which would eventually be responsible for its own defense. Such a "European pillar," moreover, would also be useful as a means of better "burden sharing," seen as necessary to maintaining U.S. support for the alliance.

This is obviously not the place for an exhaustive treatment of Franco-German security relations in the early 1980s, a subject that deserves an entire study itself. But even looked at as an aspect of France's own security policies and choices, the role of the Federal Republic is critical. In fact, the *Deutschlandpolitik* of the Mitterrand administration is not only pertinent to this book because of what it says about France's adaptation to changes in the European security situation but because it, like much that has been seen here already, was profoundly influenced by the precedents set during the Gaullist years. That it developed along highly personal lines (the Mitterrand-Kohl couple picking up where de Gaulle–Adenauer and Giscard–Schmidt left off); that it consisted of ministerial consultation rather than integrated institutions; that each country retained ultimate decision-making power; that it dealt with foreign policy and defense and not just economics; and indeed that the 1963 Elysée treaty served as its acknowledged inspiration were all indications that France was successfully returning to a policy that had stalled under de Gaulle. Now that France was no longer offering a Franco-German alliance as an *alternative* to NATO and now that the Germans too were beginning to question the durability of the Atlantic link, de Gaulle's policy of Franco-German cooperation seemed to be getting a second chance.

That the Franco-German couple would be a priority of the new administration was manifested from the start of Mitterrand's term. As early as July 1981, the French president met with German Chancellor Helmut Schmidt to reaffirm France's interest in close cooperation, and in February of the following year he and Schmidt agreed to "thorough exchanges of views on security problems."[46] Although the change of government in Bonn delayed the process for several months, in October 1982 Mitterrand used his first meeting with new German Chancellor Helmut Kohl (with whom his relationship would prove much better than with fellow "Socialist" Schmidt) to discuss bilateral military questions.[47] And although the French president reasserted France's independence and refused German participation in French nuclear planning (eternal French prerequisites) and the German leader reaffirmed the Federal Republic's primary tie to NATO and the U.S. (eternal German prerequisites), the meeting produced some significant results, including the commitment to implement the long-dormant and far-reaching defense clauses of the 1963 Elysée treaty. That treaty, never fully implemented because of the German fear of offending NATO by flirting with France, called for no less than the rapprochement of military doctrines, regular meetings of defense ministers (every three months) and chiefs of staff (every two months), personnel exchanges between the each country's armed forces, armaments cooperation, and cooperation in civil defense.[48]

To expedite the treaty's implementation, the two leaders also decided to create a Franco-German Commission on Security and Defense, which would meet regularly with the objective of institutionalizing the exchange of views between the Germans and the French on security policy. Defense and foreign ministers of the two countries would meet at least twice per year, and the commission's three specialized working groups—on arms collaboration, military cooperation, and politicostrategic issues—would meet even more often in small groups just below the ministerial level.[49] The success of the treaty's revival should not be exaggerated, but the fact that French and German officials were now meeting regularly at the highest of levels to discuss security—and that they finally managed to agree on the coproduction of a combat helicopter—did lend a certain amount of momentum and credibility to the relationship.[50]

Indeed, by 1984, the momentum of the "Franco-German couple" was strong enough to act as the motor for the relaunching of another long-dormant institution of European defense cooperation, the Western European Union. Such a move had, of course, been tried ten years before under Michel Jobert during the fateful American "Year of Europe," but German suspicions of French motives at that time made progress impossible. This time, however, with the French having shown a real interest in European cooperation (and having ceased to portray such cooperation as a means to undermine NATO), and with the Germans themselves finally accepting the need for a more European "pillar," the proponents of the WEU were able to give it new life. After France pushed to have the remaining restrictions on German conventional armament removed from the original WEU treaty, the Germans agreed to reactivate the organization.[51] In October 1984 European defense and foreign ministers met in Rome to seek new ways for the seven members of this thirty-year-old alliance to cooperate.

Even more important to Franco-German defense cooperation than these diplomatic acts were the changes made in French conventional force structures, intended to enhance France's capacity to contribute to European defense. These included the redeployment of France's Third Army Corps from Saint-Germain-en-Laye near Paris to Lille in the northeast (where it might better support NATO's Northern Army Group, NORTHAG); an enhanced role for the Gendarmerie in territorial defense (which would liberate more of the regular army for possible action on the central front); the separation of French tactical nuclear forces from the First Army command (which made the army's engagement in Europe more likely by enabling it to fight independently of the nuclear threat); a new structure for France's reserves (which would have to be mobilized quickly and massively for France to play the role of "second echelon" in Western Europe); and, finally, the creation of a 47,000-man Force d'Action Rapide (FAR) (which could intervene quickly in Central Europe).

Of all these changes, the most significant, and surely the most talked about, was the last. In many ways, the FAR was a microcosm of the entire French defense effort during these years: it was a classic example of France's desire to show concrete interest in European solidarity while holding onto the pretense as well as the reality of national autonomy. Whether the FAR should be seen more as an expression of the former (European solidarity) or of the latter (the French will to independence) is a debate that depends on the analyst's perspective and one that will probably never be resolved.

On one hand, the FAR was a major step in the direction of European defense. Consisting of five divisions (the 11th parachute division, the 27th alpine division, the 9th marine infantry division, the 4th aeromobile division, and the 6th light-armored division), and to be endowed by 1985 with five hundred Milan anti-tank missiles, 180 armored vehicles and two hundred helicopters, the new mobile force would give France unprecedented flexibility in terms of its conventional engagement in Europe. According to Charles Hernu, the FAR was designed to "permit [France], infinitely better than today, to commit ourselves at the side of our allies, as soon as we would have taken the decision, at the place and time that we would have chosen, should the occasion arise."[52] Whereas France had in the past been susceptible to the charge that French forces (deployed in France and in Germany just over the Rhine) were physically unable to participate in the "first battle," the FAR's combination of mobility and capacity for antitank warfare rendered it capable of combat on the front lines.

On the other hand, however, the message of the FAR was still ambiguous, and its impact was limited in a number of ways. First, it was unclear whether this force, designed to intervene in conflicts abroad as well as in Europe, would be able to perform both missions adequately, given the very different conditions that would prevail. The requirements of doing battle against Third World forces in the open deserts of Africa or the Middle East (to say nothing of getting to those places) were obviously not the same ones that would be required on the crowded, cloud-covered central front with its concentration of tanks, heavy armor, and chemical and atomic weapons.

Second, because of the perceived need to keep French forces from being too closely identified with NATO, Paris refused to give a clear answer to the question of whether the FAR would be used independent from, or in coordination with, NATO forces. On one hand, Hernu professed that "the autonomy of the government is complete" and that "the independence of the FAR with regard to the integrated military structure of NATO is total."[53] Yet, at the same time, he admitted that any FAR operation in Europe would automatically come under SACEUR's command and that its forward engagement would depend on NATO air support and logistics to be successful.[54] He emphasized that the FAR was "capable of inserting itself in the Allied deployment in Europe" and even allowed one of the FAR's commanders to suggest that the unit would fit into the controversial Rogers Plan to attack the second-echelon forces of the Warsaw Pact.[55] Such contradictions were evidence of the enduring struggle in French doctrine—not eliminated by the FAR—between Allied and independent military operations.

Third, there were ambiguities about the link between the FAR and the French nuclear force. Whereas Hernu made it quite clear on one hand that "the FAR is a conventional force [whose] action is not tied to our nuclear means," he also affirmed on several occasions that "a potential aggressor [faced with the FAR] would have to hesitate before confronting physically the forces of a nuclear power," thus implying that the nuclear link might indeed be made.[56] Seizing on this ambiguity, some observers urged that the nonnuclear FAR be kept not only physically but conceptually distinct from the First Army so that the latter could retain its nuclear role while the former could contribute to forward defense.[57] The idea would be to have two different kinds of forces: one (the FAR) free to show France's solidarity in Europe and the other (the First Army) reserved for the *sanctuaire national.*

The government, however, not wanting to limit the FAR's importance by unequivocally delinking it from the French deterrent—but at the same time unable credibly to make that link—sought to maintain a position somewhere in-between. General Lacaze used all his powers of rhetorical subtlety to square this circle but in the end only highlighted the inherent contradictions in it:

> In fact, to emphasize our strategy for intervention on behalf of the Allies could harm the operational credibility of our forces which cover our territory, and thus diminish our national deterrent. On the other hand, to minimize our initial engagement could incite the adversary to doubt our determination. The fair balance seems to me to lie in the absolute necessity of giving our capability for intervention at the side of the Allies a sufficient dimension

to increase the deterrent character of the alliance's forces, it being understood that our possibility of participation would signify to the adversary that it henceforth runs the risk of confronting very early on the forces of a nuclear country which has, moreover, independence over its decisions.[58]

But Lacaze's "fair balance" was an elusive one, and in the end perhaps impossible to find. Either the FAR's use would imply the possible triggering of the nuclear force, or it would not. If it did, then France was extending its deterrent to West Germany via the FAR—sanctuarisation élargie. If it did not, then the FAR was little more than a token force for Europe while the First Army guarded the French sanctuary. There was not much ground in-between.

Finally, it must also be said that however significant the FAR's political message, militarily it was rather weak. Its helicopter forces were unproven and vulnerable to Soviet combat aircraft, there were serious questions about how it would be resupplied on the front, and some of its heterogeneous five divisions were more mobile than others (which raised questions about just how much of the FAR would show up and when). Most importantly, its land forces were so lightly armored—and of the much vaunted helicopter force only ninety were equipped with antitank weaponry—that some defense experts wondered just what the FAR would do on the central front if and when it arrived. Separated from the rest of the First Army—itself accused of being too lightly armed—the FAR was at best capable of highly localized and relatively minor actions.

The FAR was not the resolution of the French strategic dilemma that some of its more enthusiastic proponents liked to suggest. And although it did help to support the claim that "France [was] ready to participate in the common defense from the start of a conflict,"[59] it was not yet clear how meaningful that participation would be. Still, for all its limits and ambiguities, the FAR was not the mere "publicity stunt" that its detractors argued, and it is an exaggeration to say that it "added nothing to the French capacity for external action."[60] The organization of a mobile force of nearly fifty thousand men and grouping of nearly two hundred helicopters able to respond rapidly to a surprise attack in Europe—and, thereby, unequivocally to implicate France in a European battle from the start—was not an insignificant endeavor. Along with the other force reorganizations previously mentioned, the FAR was at least one more symbolic step toward the manifestation of French solidarity with their German neighbors. And as the French themselves liked so much to point out, ambiguity and deterrence are in the eyes of the beholder.

After 1985, Franco-German military cooperation slowed somewhat as the Euromissile crisis receded, the superpower confrontation cooled, and French fears of German "drift" eased, but the French relationship with Germany under the first Socialist administration ended on a positive note

none the less. In February 1986—just one month before the widely foreseen legislative victory of the opposition—President Mitterrand met with
Chancellor Kohl (for no less than the twelfth time since the beginning of
the previous year) and reached a number of significant agreements. The
two leaders announced studies on the use of the FAR in Germany, expanded joint maneuvers, a telephone hot line that would enable Bonn and
Paris to communicate immediately in case of crises, and most importantly, a French commitment to consult with the Germans before using
tactical nuclear weapons on German territory. A statement released by
Mitterrand following the meetings announced that

> Within the limits imposed by the extreme rapidity of such decisions, the
> president of the Republic declares himself disposed to consult the chancellor
> of the FRG on the possible employment of prestrategic French weapons on
> German territory. He notes that the decision cannot be shared in this matter.
> The president of the Republic indicates that he has decided, with the chan-
> cellor of the FRG, to equip himself with technical means for immediate and
> reliable consultation in time of crisis.[61]

As the declaration clearly affirms, the French were still not going to give
up their independence. But at the same time they had taken one more step
toward proving what Hernu had announced six months before in an attempt to sum up the French view of the relationship: "[The Federal Re-
public] is the closest of our allies, from all viewpoints, and we maintain
with it the most intense relations in the domain of defense and security.
France and Federal Germany share security interests in common."[62]

What drove the renewed French desire for this Franco-German "alliance within the alliance"? Why did it seem even more imperative under
Mitterrand to reach security agreements with the Federal Republic than
it had under Pompidou and Giscard? and Why were those agreements
now easier to achieve? As with the Atlantic rapprochement, several different factors can be identified that pushed the French to adapt.

The first was the same one that led to the closer French ties with
NATO—an unfavorably evolving military balance in Europe. With tensions rising across the continent, the Soviets deploying multiple-warhead
nuclear missiles targeted at Western Europe, and a growing conventional
force imbalance between East and West, the French reached the obvious
conclusion that Western defense had to be bolstered. But they also realized that the United States and NATO in its current form would not be
around forever (a view reinforced by fears of American isolationism and
the possibility that U.S. deficits would lead to troop reductions in Europe)
and that French security was increasingly tied to German security. As
Hernu put it: "It is clear that a grave threat to European security would
deeply affect the security of France. Our sphere of action would be considerably reduced if France were surrounded by countries who were en-

slaved or plunged into uncertainty about their own future."[63] By trying to develop a Franco-German core for European defense, the French were hoping to protect their own longer-term security interests.

At the same time, the French were also driven to pursue security cooperation with the Germans by political developments within the FRG itself. Mitterrand, like many others in France, saw the Federal Republic of the early 1980s as dangerously poised on a crest between the Western alliance and what was called at the time "neutralist drift." During the late 1970s and early 1980s, the governing German Social Democratic Party (SPD) underwent a transformation the very opposite of that of the French Socialists on questions of security. Staunchly Atlanticist and pronuclear under Chancellor Helmut Schmidt (who had called for the deployment of Euromissiles in the first place), by 1982 a large number of German Social Democrats had joined the pacifist and antinuclear camp and begun to support nuclear disarmament and to oppose the deployment of American missiles in Germany. In addition, the SPD was now outflanked on its left by a new "Green" party—strong enough to enter the Bundestag for the first time by winning more than 5 percent of the votes in the 1983 elections—which was even more opposed to the military and to the Atlantic Alliance. For the French, the slogan "Germany out of NATO and NATO out of Germany" was not an encouraging prospect, and it prompted Mitterrand's own poignant quip: "The missiles are in the East, but the pacifists are in the West."[64]

The reason these internal German developments were so disquieting in France was that Germany, France's postwar *glacis* within NATO, now appeared in real danger of leaving France on the hypothetical "front line." Under de Gaulle it had always been (rightly) assumed that the Federal Republic—under Adenauer, Ludwig Erhard, and then Georg Kiesinger—was firmly embedded in the Western Alliance and that if France had an interest in affecting this relationship at all, it was in prying the Germans away from the Atlantic pillar rather than helping solder them more tightly to it. De Gaulle could try to get the FRG to buy into a more European arrangement for European security—as he did try in 1962–1963—and the most he had to worry about was that Bonn would refuse, which it did. By the early 1980s, however, after a decade of *Ostpolitik* had led many Germans to forget their original enthusiasm for the Atlantic Alliance and when Cold War tensions were frightening others into downright rejection of it, the French had to take stock. No longer was the problem that the Federal Republic's preoccupation with security and with Ostpolitik would drive it into too close an alliance with Washington, but just the opposite: without a stable Atlantic pillar on which to rest, the Germans might seek their security through compromise with Moscow.

German Ostpolitik, in fact, had always forced the French to respond in some way, which usually meant seeking a certain rapprochement with the rest of the Atlantic Alliance. This was perhaps not so true under de Gaulle (who sought instead to Europeanize Germany's Eastern policy by pursuing his own relations with the Soviet Union), but it was certainly the case under the General's successors, who turned to Washington and even London as counterweights to Bonn's successes in the East. Mitterrand, however, knew that this time, NATO alone would not be enough to reassure the Germans, particularly those who had begun to see NATO as the problem in the first place. For the same reasons as many in France—the new isolationism on the American Right, the implications of U.S. budget deficits, the pursuit of SDI, and the massive Soviet military buildup—some Germans were now beginning to doubt the American commitment (and ability) to defend Western Europe. It appeared to Mitterrand that a European anchor—even if attached to an Atlantic ship—was necessary to keep the Germans from drifting away.

Finally, there was also an economic component to the French pursuit of cooperation with the Germans: French economic choices were influenced by security issues, and French security choices were influenced by economic needs. The battles over the Euromissiles and European security were going on at the same time as the internal battle in France over Europe and economic cooperation. After two years of frantic economic expansion in France (while the Germans were growing slowly in the name of disinflation) had led to enormous French trade and balance of payments deficits, an increasingly feeble French franc, and two French devaluations (in October 1981 and June 1982), France's economic dependence on Bonn had become manifest. By 1982 the French trade deficit with Germany had already more than doubled since 1979, the current account balance had fallen to a deficit of FFr79 bn (from a surplus in the late 1970s), and the still-weakening franc was headed toward an inevitable third devaluation.[65] By 1983—the year Mitterrand went to Bonn to call on the Germans to deploy American missiles—France was faced with a very clear choice: to drop out of the European Monetary System (EMS), erect tariff barriers, and continue its economic expansion (the "Albanian solution"), or to reverse its Socialist experiment, cut its budget deficit, and seek to cooperate with the Germans.[66]

Although a number of Mitterrand's economic advisers and the left wing of his party (with the apparent sympathy of the president himself) favored the former solution, in the end geopolitics prevailed. The costs of "Socialism in one country" went far beyond balance of payments issues or inflation and entered into the realm of the future of Western Europe. With the Germans going through a period of national elections, social unrest, and uncertainty about their place in Europe, nothing seemed more important than for the French to extend a hand of solidarity. The French could not ask the Germans to put all of their marbles in the European basket while they refused to do the same. Mitterrand never came out and said that the domestic policy reversal was tied to the broader question of Franco-German security, but as Patrick McCarthy has argued: "The link [between security and] economic issues is clear. In choosing *rigueur* in April 1983, Mitterrand was choosing internationalism. . . . He could hardly have exhorted the Germans to accept the Pershing missiles in January 1983 and then withdrawn from the EMS three months later."[67] McCarthy, in fact, could have also put it the other way around: Mitterrand could scarcely have asked for German support of the franc after having left the Germans to bear the security burden in Europe alone.

Clearly, by the mid-1980s Franco-German security relations were as good as they had ever been, and the Germans were not unhappy to see changes taking place in Paris. Germany was not given a formal say in French nuclear policy, but the issue was at least confronted and discussed. The French nuclear force was not extended to German territory as some Germans might have hoped, but that force was expanded and made more credible. France's interest in a more autonomous European defense distinct from the Atlantic Alliance that the Germans preferred was not abandoned, but it was no longer presented as an alternative to NATO. French conventional forces were not built up to the levels the Germans might have liked, but they were better organized for participation in Europe. And the French commitment to intervene on the central front with those forces was not made automatic, but it was given more substance.

Yet for all this, it could scarcely be said that the Franco-German military "couple" entered the second half of the 1980s without problems. First, it should not be forgotten that one of the main catalysts on the French side of the relationship was the French suspicion of German intentions—not the best grounds on which to build a close and enduring relationship. Second, the two countries continued to have fundamentally different views about nuclear weapons and about armed forces in general. In France both were symbols of power, independence, prestige, and "victor status," whereas in Germany they were reminders of foreign dominance, national dependence, and the potential for destruction of their homeland. Third, as long as Germany was divided, different French and German attitudes toward the Soviet Union were inevitable: whereas France had no territorial or minority rights disputes with the Soviet bloc and no major role to play in the East-West military confrontation, Germany had vital national interests—like Ostpolitik—at stake. France had become a status quo power, whereas the Germans retained an underlying and growing desire for change. Finally, despite the increased Paris-Bonn dialogue and frequent high-level meetings, a number of conflicting perspectives remained: to the French, Bonn was still seen as more interested in the GDR, Ostpolitik, and the United States than in France (which it probably was), and to the Germans, the French remained more concerned with their national independence and international prestige than with Franco-German relations (which they probably were).

One of the greatest lingering problems was that whereas the French believed they had made great strides toward a full commitment to German and European defense—and congratulated themselves for their efforts—the Germans saw how much further the French had yet to go. Many in the Federal Republic found France's European defense policies under Mitterrand *mehr Schein als Sein*—long on symbolism but woefully short on substance. Indeed, reflecting on the Socialists' many "adaptations" discussed in this chapter, it is striking how little was concrete. From the Atlantic rapprochement (cordial Western summits, Atlantic Council meetings in France, cooperation with NATO) to the Franco-German couple (good relations with Helmut Kohl, Commission on Security and Defense, increased ministerial contacts) to the reorganization of the army (a FAR with no new equipment or troops, the redeployment of the Third Corps, the new Hadès command), nearly all of the changes made in the interests of European defense were symbolic, political, organizational, or rhetorical. This is not to say that politics, symbols, or organizations are not important to defense and security. But it does suggest that although Mitterrand's France may have "adapted" its defense policies to Europe, it may not have adapted them enough.

DEFENSE POLICY AND THE ECONOMIC CONSTRAINT REVISITED

The description and analysis of French security policies from 1981 to 1986, and the growing tensions in them, would be incomplete if it did not at least mention something already familiar to our story—the economic constraint. For the claim that France did not come FAR enough in its attempts to Europeanize its defense policies stemmed not only from the French unwillingness to compromise national independence but from the government's not surprising inability to afford everything at once. It has already been argued that one of the most difficult aspects of the Gaullist military legacy is that it left France in a position of having to fund a global role, an independent nuclear force, and an independent national armaments industry at the same time it had to contribute to conventional defense in Western Europe. Funding such diversified forces may have been possible while the French economy was booming and the Americans were largely responsible for the defense of Europe, but it was increasingly difficult as both of those conditions disappeared. How well did the Socialists deal with the economic constraint?

It should first be said that the new administration's record was not nearly as bad as its critics suggested.[68] To be sure, between 1981 and

1986 the real French defense budget rose only by 1.1 percent per year, was barely maintained as a share of GDP, and declined significantly as a share of overall government spending. Thus, members of the opposition and some military analysts could argue that "the figures speak for themselves,"[69] and on the surface they appeared to do just that. As indicated in tables 5.1, 5.2, and 5.3, the figures do not seem very impressive.

TABLE 5.1

Annual Percent Change in Real French Defense Spending, 1981–1986

1981	1982	1983	1984	1985	1986
	2.3	1.7	−0.4	0.1	1.7

TABLE 5.2

Defense Budget as Percentage of PIBm (Market GDP) under Giscard and Mitterrand, 1974–1986

Giscard		Mitterrand	
Year	Percent PIBm[a]	Year	Percent PIBm[a]
1974	3.37	1982	3.88
1975	3.42	1983	3.92
1976	3.39	1984	3.84
1977	3.54	1985	3.87
1978	3.61	1986	3.72
1979	3.61		
1980	3.67		
1981	3.87		

[a]PIBm = *Produit intérieure brut marchand* (market gross domestic product), a subset of GDP.

TABLE 5.3

Defense Budget as Percent Share of Overall Government Spending 1960–1986

Year	Percent Share	Year	Percent Share	Year	Percent Share
1960	28.5	1970	17.6	1980	16.9
1961	26.8	1971	17.9	1981	16.9
1962	24.7	1972	17.7	1982	15.5
1963	23.9	1973	17.7	1983	15.1
1964	23.0	1974	17.4	1984	15.1
1965	22.5	1975	16.9	1985	15.1
1966	21.8	1976	17.1	1986	15.4
1967	20.7	1977	17.4		
1968	20.1	1978	16.9		
1969	17.8	1979	16.8		

Sources: Ministère de la Défense, *Regards sur la défense: 1981–1986* (Paris, 1986), p. 18; Frédéric Tiberghien, "L'effort de défense depuis 1981," *Défense nationale* (November 1985): 32; and Ministère de la Défense Nationale, *Livre blanc sur la défense nationale* (Paris, 1972), 1: 58.

Numbers alone can be misleading, however, and to be properly understood they must be put into perspective. First, the early 1980s were years of very slow economic growth and budgetary austerity not only in France, where the recession was particularly severe, but throughout Europe; West German defense spending during the same period, it might be noted, grew at an even slower rate than France's (under 1 percent).[70] Second, although it is true that military spending as a share of GDP rose under Giscard and stagnated under Mitterrand (table 5.2), the more important points are that as great a share of the overall economy went to defense under the Socialists as it ever did under their opponents and that the average share (3.8 percent) under the Left was the highest proportion spent on defense since the late 1960s. Finally, the Right's lament that defense spending as a share of the overall government budget (table 5.3) had fallen from nearly 30 percent in 1960 to just over 15 percent by 1986 was also true, but again misleading. The critics failed to take into account that during the 1960s France was fighting or drawing down from a major conventional war in Algeria; that military inflation during the 1970s and 1980s was significantly greater than overall inflation; and (most importantly) that government spending as a whole rose rapidly not only under Mitterrand but under Giscard as well (from 19.4 percent of GDP in 1974 to 24.5 percent in 1986).[71] With the expansionary social program of the Left, including, in particular, greater unemployment benefits for rising numbers of unemployed and interest on skyrocketing government debt (made even worse by high interest rates), it is not surprising that the share of state spending allocated to defense declined.

In short, the highly critical and often repeated charges of the opposition that there was a "constant decline" in the French defense effort were often exaggerated. When compared either to France's neighbors or to the Socialist government's predecessors, the general pattern of French defense spending in the early 1980s held up rather well.

What may be more true, on the other hand—and more important—is that even if the Socialists *maintained* patterns of defense spending that had developed under Giscard, those patterns were increasingly out of step with the new administration's expanding goals and with France's security needs.[72] Even if one admits that defense spending under the Socialists did not fall below previous levels (and that cutbacks, delays, and cancellations were no worse under Mitterrand than under Giscard), one could still criticize the government because its means were not commensurate with its announced ends. The Socialists resumed an extensive nuclear expansion that Giscard had curbed; they chose not to reduce France's costly global role (and even intervened militarily in Africa just as the "neocolonialist" Giscard had done); they sought to increase France's conventional contribution to Europe as a sign of their European and Atlantic commitments; their overall ability to spend was severely constrained by budgetary austerity, "double deficits," and a weak franc; and, finally, the cost of both nuclear and conventional weaponry was rising much more quickly than overall inflation, which was itself near 10 percent. Continuity, in other words, was not enough.

Most important where the French contribution to Europe was concerned, the nuclear priority within a defense budget that was not growing meant that conventional forces would bear the brunt of the austerity measures after 1982. In that year some FFr16 bn (about 30 percent of military equipment purchases) were cut from the defense budget, delaying or canceling orders of tanks, helicopters, armored vehicles, Mirage jets, and artillery batteries. Troops were scheduled to be reduced by thirty-five thousand in the program law of 1983 (with twenty-two thousand coming from the army alone), and by the time that law was implemented it was not only the Germans who were complaining about French conventional spending cuts. The French army itself, supposedly *"la Grande Muette,"* was increasingly vocal in its opposition to conventional force cuts beginning in 1982.[73] The army believed that delays in the purchases and delivery of equipment along with the troop cuts would severely undermine France's capacity for anything other than a "nuclear sanctuary" defense—the very sort of defense the government was trying to avoid.

By 1985, the equipment and maintenance of French conventional forces in Germany was so bad or behind schedule that the commander of the First Tank Division in the Federal Republic (General Philippe Arnold) risked official sanctions (and was, in fact, fired) when he decried the French AMX-30 tank as up to two generations behind its American or West German counterparts. He also lamented the limited number of French tanks, the delays in deploying their modernized version (the AMX-30 B-2), and the "major political failure" of the projected Franco-German tank.[74] General Guy Méry, always an advocate of a greater French capacity for nonnuclear defense, supported Arnold's view and himself denounced the "significant weakening of the operational capacities of the First Army." Méry cited in particular the same lacunas as his colleagues: a successor to the AMX-30 tank, a new nuclear-powered aircraft carrier, and an observation satellite.[75] Even as loyal a supporter of the government's defense program as Armed Forces Chief of Staff General Jeannou Lacaze was arguing by 1985 that if spending cuts continued they could "compromise the operational capacity of the armed forces."[76] That Lacaze should have eventually reached this position was not surprising if one goes back to his views about French security and military budgets as early as 1981, "If our budget . . . continues to remain below 4 percent of PIBm . . . there would be incompatibility between the missions fixed and the means provided."[77]

The point, then, is that such an incompatibility existed. It was nothing new that France's nuclear priority starved its conventional armies of equipment and funding they would have liked to have had. Nor was it new that many observers found French nonnuclear forces inadequate given the missions they were supposed to assume. What *was* new was that these old budgetary problems were becoming acute as the French role in European security necessarily grew. The government obviously knew this, but that was not enough.

THE SOCIALISTS IN RETROSPECT

French security policies under François Mitterrand from 1981 to 1986 fell well within the Gaullist model for national security that was elaborated during the 1960s. Although the Socialists innovated in a number of areas—their policies were more Atlanticist than those of any administration since the Fourth Republic, their rhetoric accepted more explicitly than ever the need for Franco-German military cooperation, and their conventional force reorganizations were clearly in the interests of European defense—the extent to which they adapted to Gaullist precedents was even more remarkable.

There is no question that France under Mitterrand continued on the path toward greater cooperation in Europe that had begun after 1968 and that had increased with each successive administration. But it is easy to exaggerate the French adaptation to Europe simply because France had come from so far away to start with. The white light of relative change should not blind observers to the fact that even during the years considered in this chapter French policies were still quintessentially French, that is to say, very Gaullist. Of the Socialists' two adaptations—to Gaullist policies and to European defense—it seems obvious that the first was the more consequential.

Perhaps because of this very continuity, the Socialists did not manage to resolve all the tensions that had been building in French defense policy since the Gaullist years. Into the mid-1980s, there were still strategic disputes with the Federal Republic, there were still budgetary dilemmas, and there were new tensions arising within a supposed defense "consensus" that had always depended on a margin of maneuver that was rapidly diminishing. These strategic, budgetary, and political tensions would all peak during the following three years.

CHAPTER SIX

Tensions in the Consensus, 1986–1989

NEARLY FIVE YEARS after the Left's celebrated victory of May and June 1981, French politics took another historic turn. On March 16, 1986—for the first time in the history of the Fifth Republic—a coalition of opposition parties won national legislative elections before the completion of the president of the republic's seven-year term. With the president unwilling to abandon the office that he was given a popular mandate to hold until May 1988, an unprecedented period of political "cohabitation" began—a Socialist, François Mitterrand, would preside over a politically conservative and economically neoliberal government led by Jacques Chirac.

Cohabitation was a curious experiment in many ways and—because it may well one day be repeated—will doubtless be studied by French constitutional scholars for years to come. Most important here, however, is what this experience meant for French security policy during a period of incipient but manifest change. Cohabitation raised questions not only about the Fifth Republic's still-young institutions and practices but also about its vaunted "consensus" on national defense. How would the new "Gaullist" government try to make its mark on French defense policies and distinguish itself from the Socialist government that preceded it? How would the supposed presidential *domaine réservé* in foreign policy and defense hold up under the new arrangements? How would France's two-headed leadership react to changes as potentially great as American disengagement, superpower disarmament, or Soviet reform? All of this was uncharted territory for France.

In fact, this was a critical period for French security policy not only because of what was happening inside France itself but because the mid-1980s also saw a significant increase in the pressures on West Europeans to augment their contribution to European defense. With new questions being raised about the American role in Europe and with the Soviet Union continuing its massive military buildup despite its new leadership, it was becoming more and more clear that the arrangements that had governed European defense for so long were in need of some adjustment.

A CHANGING MILITARY CONTEXT AND
ITS IMPACT ON FRANCE

The growing need for a stronger European pillar in the Atlantic Alliance, of course, was as old as the alliance itself, and the implications of this trend were clear to French leaders long before March 1986. As noted, Presidents Pompidou, Giscard d'Estaing, and Mitterrand had all taken meaningful steps throughout the 1970s and 1980s to move France toward a greater military role in Europe. Still, if these trends had long been in motion, it might be argued that in the mid-1980s they reached a peak. At the time the cohabitation experiment in France began, the two main elements of postwar European security—extended nuclear deterrence and the U.S. presence in Europe—were arguably weaker than they had ever been before. Western Europe's denuclearization and American disengagement were no longer merely risks for the future but now very real and possibly immediate prospects.

The first of these twin specters that preoccupied security-conscious Europeans was the possibility of denuclearization, the withdrawal of all or part of the American nuclear weapons that were seen to have kept the peace in Europe for forty years. It is difficult to say just when the long-questioned concept of extended deterrence acquired a "critical mass" of doubt, but it could easily be argued that the early- to mid-1980s represent a watershed. Indeed, after the massive American strategic buildup of 1981 and the subsequent Euromissile deployment appeared to suggest a desire to reinforce extended deterrence, signs instead began to emerge portending an American desire to replace it.

Already in 1982, for example, several prominent Americans began calling for the adoption of a policy of nuclear "no first use," a policy that implied a high-level recognition of the implausibility of American nuclear doctrine.[1] By abandoning the threat to use nuclear weapons to defend against a conventional attack—long a pillar of NATO strategy—the new doctrine suggested that Americans would sooner retreat to their "national sanctuary" and see Europe collapse than risk nuclear war. "No first use" was never adopted as official American policy, but the fact that serious, influential Americans were promoting it caused great concern in a number of European minds.[2] For many in Europe, a policy of "no first use" was a disconcerting first step toward a nondeterring policy of "no use at all."

One year later, Ronald Reagan's March 23, 1983, speech announcing the Strategic Defense Initiative and at the same time calling for an end to "mutually assured destruction" seemed to give official backing to the notion that extended deterrence was being replaced. At the very least, this expensive program would draw badly needed funds away from the American contribution to conventional European defense. More ominously, by making the United States theoretically "invulnerable" to Soviet ballistic missiles while leaving Europe open to attack, SDI made possible an American retreat from Europe in the face of nuclear war. It was obviously difficult for West European leaders to affirm their faith in the American resolve to use nuclear weapons to defend Europe when the American administration itself had begun to denounce those same weapons as immoral and to call for their eventual elimination.

Next, after an apparent lull during which Europeans digested the INF deployment and watched SDI lose steam, the apparently inexorable march away from the era of deterrence received a sudden boost at the Reykjavík "presummit" of late 1986. When Europeans realized that the Reagan administration was inches away from concluding an agreement "over their heads" on the elimination of ballistic missiles within ten years—and even of nuclear weapons altogether by the turn of the century—their somewhat abstract anxieties became more immediate concerns. Was Ronald Reagan really prepared to negotiate away the foundation of their defense for forty years without consulting them? Reykjavík, in the words of Valéry Giscard d'Estaing—scarcely known for his anti-Americanism—reflected the United States' "indifference or quasi-indifference" to Europe's security interests.[3] Along with the Iran-Contra scandal of the same period, it confirmed what Dominique Moïsi called "an old, and rather negative, image [that] not only were the Americans unpredictable and adventuristic, their diplomacy was unreliable and probably incompetent."[4] These were not the people to whom Europeans could trust their ultimate defense.

Finally, in 1987, the symbolic and rhetorical steps mentioned above suddenly took on real substance with the U.S.-Soviet agreement to eliminate all intermediate-range ballistic missiles. For many Europeans, the INF treaty confirmed de Gaulle's old warnings about the Americans looking after their own interests while leaving Europeans to their own devices. To be sure, European support for the treaty was widespread, and it was difficult to oppose the first incidence ever of superpower nuclear disarmament. But no matter how hard the U.S. administration tried, it had difficulties convincing everyone that the removal of missiles deployed specifically to "couple" Europe to the United States, was not, in turn, a sign of "decoupling." After the elimination of "an entire class of nuclear weapons," with promises of more reductions to come (and memories of Reykjavík still fresh in everyone's minds), who could credibly tell Europeans not to worry about denuclearization? At the end of the year, strategists such as Edward Luttwak began announcing the "end of the nuclear era," and for many Europeans they were probably not exaggerating.[5]

The second transatlantic security trend that caused anxiety in Europe was American "disengagement," the partial or even total withdrawal of

U.S. forces from Western Europe. Like denuclearization, an American troop withdrawal had been a concern in Europe for years, but in the mid-1980s it seemed to become much more realistic. After annual U.S. government budget deficits of over $150 billion became the norm, it seemed only a matter of time before the defense budget would start to feel the strain. Indeed, starting in 1984 U.S. military spending leveled off, and by 1987 Defense Secretary Frank Carlucci was announcing cuts in projected spending of $33 billion for 1988 and a further reduction of $200 billion for the next three years.[6] With U.S. government debt building up and many domestic needs going seriously underfunded, the days of indulgence for the U.S. military in Europe seemed bound to end.

Inevitably, such budgetary pressures not only led to unilateral U.S. cuts but to increases in the traditional calls for greater "burden-sharing" within the alliance. Protecting Europe was said to cost the United States somewhere around $150 billion per year, and with the government budget deficit hovering around the same figure, the link between the two was easy for some to make.[7] Influential members of Congress began to propose that American troops in Europe be cut; a neoisolationist movement started to call for a unilateral American withdrawal; and even high-level members of the administration were asserting that the United States "can't be expected to carry as large a share of the defense burden as in the past."[8] With American demographic trends putting a strain on all-volunteer forces, moreover, and with popular pressures growing in some European Allied countries to reduce the U.S. presence there, it could not be excluded that the large numbers of American troops that had been in Europe since the early 1950s might finally be reduced.

The mood prevailing in Europe at the time was summed up by French Defense Minister André Giraud, who in the summer of 1987 reasoned that "It cannot be excluded that the United States, in debt, one day will find itself obliged to conduct an economic policy that would lead it to reduce the part of its military budget that concerns Europe. . . . American consciousness about the problem of European security might not always be so acute."[9] Anyone looking soberly at the situation could not help but notice that the old pillars of the NATO edifice were becoming strained.

One obvious consequence of these two putative trends—denuclearization and de-Americanization—was that Europe's conventional defense would have to be built up and rendered more autonomous. As strategic deterrence became not only less credible but potentially more cataclysmic—with new theories like "nuclear winter" accompanying the development of ever more destructive weapons—conventional forces came to play a greater role. Nonnuclear arms were now being seen as much more than the tripwire for massive retaliation that they were in the 1950s, and even more than the time-buying device of flexible response; they were now becoming a necessary cog in NATO's operational military plans. Indeed, by the middle of the decade, it was appropriate to speak of a "new and broadening consensus [within Europe] on the desirability of enhancing conventional defenses."[10]

Such a "new consensus" had an obvious impact in France because it was also obvious that if NATO were going to augment its conventional defense, a greater French contribution to it was indispensable. The crux of the problem, as David Calleo stated it, was that "without France, NATO's defense must soon collapse or else turn to nuclear weapons."[11] For a number of reasons, the serious conventional defense that NATO never had could only be achieved if France were to play a greater role in it.

First, the troop shortages that had always put Western conventional forces at a disadvantage against the numerically superior Warsaw Pact were now becoming acute. With the birthrate in the Federal Republic of Germany down to a near postwar low, and with the possibility of an American troop *buildup* out of the question given budgetary and political considerations in Washington, it was only to France that NATO could turn for compensation, at least for the large operational reserves a serious conventional defense would need. The British were already spending nearly one-half of their defense budget on their British Army of the Rhine, the Italian army was geared more toward the South than toward the East, and the smaller countries had few potential forces to offer; it was only France—with its large but not fully Europe-oriented army—that could give NATO the men in arms it needed.

Second, American schemes for achieving conventional parity with the Soviets by relying on new military strategies and superior technology (rather than on increased troop strength) raised a number of questions about cost, arms control, stability, feasibility, and the Western ability to maintain a technological lead. How could NATO governments be expected to foot the bill for advanced, or "smart" weapons—a 4 percent annual defense spending increase according to SACEUR Bernard Rogers—when they had never even met their 3 percent pledge of 1977?[12] Americans have always had more faith in technology than the more skeptical Europeans, but in this case the evidence seemed to suggest that some pessimism was warranted.[13]

A third difficulty for NATO without France was the recurring issue of logistics and support. NATO's access to French territory, communication, and supply routes was never indispensable so long as the alliance's military strategy was one of forward defense and relatively early recourse to nuclear weapons. If the West were going to be defended at the Elbe or else turn to nuclear weapons, there was no real need to envisage a retreat across France or even the use of French territory to supply a protracted war on the front. However, as Western war plans began to consider more seriously the prospects of fighting a sustained conventional battle, French airspace, territory, and logistical support became more important. The concept of forward defense remained, of course, but it was now one that meant delaying the recourse to nuclear weapons as long as possible, a feat that required NATO to be able to supply, manage, and communicate with a huge forward-based army. It could not do this for long without French ports, airspace, lines of communication, and other logistical assets. In short, the French could tag along passively while credible extended deterrence precluded the need for nonnuclear defense; as the American protectorate eroded, however, active French support became vital.

Finally, it is also important to note that NATO in the mid-1980s had to meet not a static Soviet military threat but one that was growing at a fast and steady pace. The Soviet buildup that had begun during the mid-1960s lasted throughout the 1970s and did not slow significantly even during détente. It went, moreover, well beyond the highly publicized issues of the SS-20 missiles and backfire bombers and included a similar augmentation and modernization of conventional and short-range nuclear forces (SNF). During the 1970s, the Soviets increased their forces in central Europe by five divisions and increased military spending by at least 4–5 percent annually in real terms.[14] Thus, for NATO to bolster its conventional defense, its forces would not only have to be improved in an absolute sense but would have to be improved at a faster pace than the already superior conventional forces of the Warsaw Pact. For all these reasons, military analyst Robert Komer's conclusion seemed particularly apt: "Whether NATO can achieve a credible nonnuclear initial defense posture . . . will depend on the key role played by France."[15]

COHABITATION AND THE FRENCH DEFENSE DEBATE

It was this changing military context that set the stage for the defense debate under cohabitation. Because of the pressing need for a French response to the new situation and because of the gravity of that situation, many observers were concerned that France would be unprepared to act given its political instability at home. They wondered if France, in this period of flux, would not be paralyzed by its divided government and its need for consensus and whether it would be able to cope with its emerging new responsibilities in Europe. Cohabitation was not only a theoretical test of French institutions or decision-making processes but an important test of whether a "defense consensus" really existed and, if it did, whether the French would be able to adapt it in the face of change. With a president and prime minister from different ends of the political spectrum, who would decide when critical defense decisions would have to be made?

The Fifth Republic furnished little useful precedent in such a matter. De Gaulle and his successors, of course, had run security policy out of the

Elysée; but they had each had a loyal government, a parliamentary majority, and ministers whom they had appointed themselves; during cohabitation none of this was the case. Furthermore, not even the Constitution was much help: If its Article 15 states that the president of the republic is the "leader of the armed forces" and that he "presides over the councils and high committees of national defense," Articles 20 and 21 go on to say that the government "disposes of the armed forces" and that the prime minister is "responsible for national defense." Whereas a decree (*ordonnance*) of January 7, 1959 states that "decisions concerning the general direction of defense" are to be taken under the Conseil de Défense—presided over by the president—that same decree puts "the general direction ... of defense" in the hands of the government.[16]

Even in the prime minister's own mind, the question was ambiguous and difficult to resolve. On one hand, with his strong new mandate, Chirac seemed to have the right as well as the intention to take the lead in security policy making. Early in his term he argued that as "prime minister, and as such responsible for national defense, I intend ... to exercise fully the role that is mine."[17] On the other hand, however, the "Gaullist" leader—with no greater ambition than to become president of the Republic himself—had no interest in undermining the authority of the institution created by the General. Hoping one day to wield the power of the Fifth Republic's imperial presidency, Chirac was willing to leave some of that power in Mitterrand's hands. He believed that "national defense should remain a domain of national unity" and that there should be no open divergence between Matignon and the Elysée: "Because it is an essential element of our force of our trustworthiness, and of our dignity in the world ... our defense policy [must not be] the object of any polemics. I should not, it goes without saying, be counted on to start one."[18] The prime minister would do his best to play a leading role in the making of security policy, but he would be careful not to damage irreparably the presidential domaine réservé.

Rather than an all-out battle for power, then, cohabitation became a sort of nonlethal duel, a sparring match in which both participants had to use guile and subtlety to score points rather than ruthlessness to go for the kill. Neither leader questioned outright the decisions or actions of the other; neither sought openly to embarrass his adversary; and both perceived it to be in their interests not to be seen as the spoiler of consensus.

Thus, although there were a number of fundamental disagreements between the majority and the president, it is important not to exaggerate the "end of the defense consensus" that many observers at the time professed to have perceived.[19] France doubtless remained the country in Western Europe with the broadest national agreement on questions of national security, and the two heads of its leadership even supported jointly a number of initiatives in the area of European defense. Whereas many had feared that the diffusion of power would stifle major initiatives on the part of France—and some even claimed to see this happen—in fact, these two years saw an impressive array of steps taken toward a greater French military role in Europe.

Between 1986 and 1988, Mitterrand and Chirac both sought to augment the French commitment to German security, to maintain France's nuclear priority, and to improve the French relationship with NATO. Both supported the new military program law, the continued implementation of the defense clauses of the 1963 Elysée treaty, and the development of a joint military brigade with the Germans. When Chirac took the initiative to relaunch the Western European Union in 1987 and to sponsor a "European security charter," Mitterrand backed him, and when Mitterrand approved French military maneuvers deep inside the Federal Republic, Chirac gladly signed on. Both leaders celebrated the 25th anniversary of the Elysée treaty in January 1988, both supported the creation of a Franco-German Council for Security and Defense, and both broke with precedent to attend the March 1988 NATO summit. It may be true, as some critics have argued, that this was all more show than substance and that Chirac and Mitterrand often had diverging motives for their common actions; but it would be an exaggeration to see cohabitation as a head-to-head clash of fundamentally different national security conceptions.

The most notable thing about the debates between Mitterrand and Chirac, in fact, was that they were usually not over ends but over means. Both leaders believed France had an interest in bolstering European defense in the face of possible American cutbacks and German insecurities, both recognized that it was becoming more difficult for France to maintain the nuclear status quo, and both held the view that it was more imperative than ever that France augment its European role. What they disagreed about was the nature of that role and how best to strengthen it. In this light, it may be instructive to look more closely at some of the main issues in the French security policy debate during and after cohabitation. Doing so reveals clearly that cracks were starting to appear in the previously uniform French policy facade and that the enduring dilemmas of the post-Gaullist period were becoming increasingly difficult to resolve.

THE DEBATES OF COHABITATION

The New Military Program Law

The first national security issue that had to be settled under cohabitation concerned the presentation of a new five-year military program law. As seen in chapter 5, the Right had criticized the Socialists' 1984–1988 defense program law as insufficient and underfunded and had made the issue a theme of its 1986 election campaign. As in previous instances when program laws had fallen behind schedule, the new government could have chosen to let the Socialists' law run its course until 1988 and then to "skip" a year before presenting a new law. Chirac, however, seeking to play a role in defense policy from the start and having made stronger defense one of his primary campaign issues, opted to put forth his own five-year military plan.[20]

The new law, which reverted to the old practice of excluding military operations and programming only for military equipment, was notable mostly for the marked increase in the credits allocated to equipment. Over the five-year period in question, it foresaw spending FFr474 bn on equipment, an average annual increase of 7 percent.[21] The new law did not give specific figures for the cost of operations, but a Defense Ministry estimate projected that the total defense budget would rise from a 3.72 percent share of PIBm to 3.99 percent by 1991, restoring a progression not seen since the beginning of the decade.[22]

Aside from these increases in planned spending, however, little distinguished the Right's new program law from the one that it replaced. None of the most important weapons or weapons systems to be developed over the coming decade were new, and all but one—the S-4 "mobile missile"—were the source of consensus between Matignon and the Elysée. The new law left in place the organization of the army that had been implemented after 1983 (including the much-maligned FAR); it maintained the same balance between nuclear and conventional forces as in the previous law (64 percent of credits for conventional forces, 34 percent for nuclear); and its articulation of French defense policy's "fundamental principles" ("national independence, solidarity with our allies, presence and *rayonnement* in the world") remained largely unchanged.[23] Comparing closely the 1987 program law with the one it replaced, one can only agree with former Socialist Defense Minister Paul Quilès as he put it during the parliamentary debates: "Your law adds little, if not to say nothing, to the one that preceded it."[24] After having criticized so severely the Left for its management of defense, the new government could scarcely claim to have changed it.

Not surprisingly, the Socialists believed the content of the new program law vindicated their own defense policy of the previous five years. They voted for the law in Parliament (it passed by an unprecedented majority of 537 to 35 with only the PCF voting against), and President Mitterrand issued a statement calling it "serious," "reasonable," and "coherent."[25] The president played no active role in the drafting of the new law, but even had he done so it is doubtful that the text would have looked much different. As an Elysée statement described it, the Right's program law was "in line with the fundamental orientations that [the president] himself had established."[26]

In one sense, then, it was no exaggeration to say that a general defense consensus still existed in France and that neither cohabitation nor a changing context damaged it. The Left and the Right could debate the precise amounts to be spent on certain weapons systems, they could argue over the methodology of the five-year plan, and they could disagree about whether a certain missile was necessary or not. But they continued to agree on the basics—the primacy of strategic nuclear forces, the maintenance of the means for a global military role, and the continuity of French military principles—and they managed largely to hide their main disputes. Few countries in Western Europe have seen their long-term defense plans approved by 94 percent of the parliament.

In another sense, however, the debate over the program law (or lack thereof) was not a sign of clear national consensus but the result of neither the Left nor the Right wanting to spoil cohabitation and of the fact that the costly law was generous enough to satisfy nearly everyone's desires. By ordering modern, expensive equipment for all French forces, nuclear and conventional, land, sea, and air, the government was not really agreeing but was putting off choices that would eventually have to be made. As the following two years would demonstrate, by unanimously supporting the new program law, French leaders were papering over increasingly serious disagreements that were emerging, not only over French strategy itself but over American and NATO strategy as well.

France and the INF Debate

The second great issue to confront French decision makers during cohabitation had to do not so much with France's own military policy but, ostensibly, with that of the United States. Cohabitation coincided with the second "Euromissile debate" of the 1980s, a debate that this time was not over the deployment of American missiles in Europe but over their anticipated withdrawal. The September 1987 "agreement in principle" between the superpowers to eliminate all intermediate-range nuclear forces from Europe (the "double-zero option") and the growing possibility that this would be followed by the departure of short-range nuclear forces as well (the "triple-zero option") raised serious questions in France about the future of deterrence in Europe. And although French leaders liked to repeat that they were not "directly concerned" by these superpower negotiations, in fact they knew that they were very much concerned and—remembering Giscard's awkward abstinence from the first Euromissile debate—that they had a political interest in taking a stand.

As would soon become clear, however, the two leaders differed over just what stand to take.

It should, perhaps, be said that French leaders in general were much cooler to the idea of an INF withdrawal than were their European neighbors, who for various reasons all officially supported it. The Germans, Italians, Belgians, Dutch, and even British were happy to see the removal of foreign missiles from their soil (and with them the source of protest movements and national divisions), to say nothing of the removal of Soviet missiles pointed at their homelands. They could only welcome the new progress toward disarmament and the new climate in superpower relations. The French, on the other hand, were understandably less enthusiastic. In contrast to its neighbors, France had little to gain by an eventual withdrawal of the Euromissiles (because the missiles were not deployed in France anyway and because the country had no significant peace movement) and much to lose (because the presence of American nuclear missiles on European soil not only coupled France to the United States but also protected the French somewhat from calls for their own disarmament). The Euromissiles symbolized a long-standing arrangement that suited the French rather well: American nuclear power would be deployed in Germany, protecting all of France but at no cost to the French.

In the most often-quoted example of French reservations about an INF deal, Defense Minister Giraud described the zero option as a "nuclear Munich," but this was only the most forthright statement of what a number of other French officials were thinking.[27] Many in France believed that an INF "zero option" would weaken deterrence and agreed with the assessment of the French army's official public relations service that "the zero options could suggest the beginning of an American disengagement and especially the denuclearization of Europe, which would leave it exposed to the devastating conventional and nuclear superiority and considerable chemical threat of the forces of the Warsaw Pact."[28] Although some of the more vehement defenders of Gaullist nuclear orthodoxy took this logic to its extremes in their condemnation of the INF withdrawal (General Gallois called the deal a "negotiation of the deceived"[29]), these French concerns about the treaty were not without some justification. The U.S. INF had been deployed not only to counter the SS-20s that would be dismantled but also to replace aging NATO aircraft; to compensate for a significant Soviet SNF buildup; and as a means of coupling the United States to Europe in the wake of strategic arms limitations. Moreover, critics of the accord pointed out, even if it was a good thing to take out one rung from the escalation ladder of flexible response, the INF took out the "wrong" one. By leaving short-range nuclear systems in place but removing intermediate-range ones, the United States was left with the perverse result that its only means of nuclear response based in Western Europe would be those that would explode in Western Europe itself.

While members of the center-Right majority were making these arguably valid points, however, and raising concerns about what they saw as the progressive denuclearization of Western Europe, François Mitterrand and his supporters came out strongly behind the accord. The president overcame whatever personal reservations he may have had about the removal of the Euromissiles and argued that France should support the "double zero" option along with everyone else. He took up most of the American arguments about other sources of deterrence remaining in place, reasserted the traditional French view that "pure deterrence" was preferable to flexible response anyway, and argued that "it would be paradoxical to claim that European security had only been assured for four years, from 1983 to 1987, thanks only to the Pershing IIs."[30] For Mitterrand, France without question should stand behind the INF treaty.

Several different reasons for Mitterrand's position can be discerned and are worth illuminating. First, however logical the Right's opposition to the INF treaty may have been, Mitterrand was wise enough to see that for France to oppose the first real step ever taken in the direction of superpower disarmament, which it had always claimed to support, would be a mistake. Later, once the Washington treaty was signed and accepted, Mitterrand was able to take political advantage of having supported the INF withdrawal while the Right had dragged its feet. In his *Lettre à tous les Français* (Letter to all the French) written before the 1988 presidential election, the president wrote of the "Reagan-Gorbachev agreement which I supported but which was criticized in public or in private by the principal spokesmen for the majority."[31] In short, Mitterrand had a sense that the outcome of this issue had already been decided, and he wanted to be on the winning side.

Second, Mitterrand believed that relations with the Federal Republic—whose government had come out strongly in favor of an INF withdrawal—were more important than the physical presence of missiles in Europe. Because the Euromissiles had been deployed primarily on political and symbolic grounds in the first place, it made little sense to oppose their withdrawal on military grounds. Mitterrand's famous Bundestag speech in 1983 was a sign of support for his allies in Bonn, and to oppose their withdrawal now for whatever reason would have been a sign of just the opposite. It was far more important to be seen as siding with the Germans than to keep the militarily redundant missiles in place.

Third, Mitterrand was well aware that French public opinion—long the most skeptical in Europe about Gorbachev and his reforms (perhaps to compensate for their tardy acceptance of the nature of the Brezhnev regime)—was becoming increasingly favorable to disarmament and détente. This was particularly true among the left wing voters whose support Mitterrand knew he would have to obtain in the coming presidential election. In this sense, too, it would not have been wise to oppose the withdrawal of missiles that neither the Russians nor the Americans wanted to keep.

Finally, and perhaps most importantly, the president's acceptance of the INF withdrawal was consistent with the military strategy of "pure deterrence" that he (and France) had long claimed to uphold. As "theater" nuclear weapons, the Euromissiles were part of NATO's flexible response, which implied gradual nuclear escalation in response to a conventional attack that could not be stopped. Rejecting that doctrine, Mitterrand argued that "[the INF Accord] permits us to come back to the true deterrence, the one of long-range nuclear arms which can strike the territory of the adversary."[32] Mitterrand did not admit or seem to care that France's "pure deterrence" had always depended to a certain degree on NATO's flexible response; more importantly he appeared consistent with the strategy he had long claimed to accept.

During what remained of cohabitation—only six months as it turned out—the positions of the president and the majority on alliance nuclear issues became even more clear and their differences even more pronounced. As NATO debated what to do with its short-range nuclear forces after the agreement on the intermediate-range ones, Mitterrand and Chirac once again found themselves in opposing camps. Whereas Chirac argued that it was essential for NATO to reiterate its commitment to nuclear deterrence and to avoid negotiations that might lead to the denuclearization of Europe, Mitterrand sided with the Germans in the view that modernization should not procced before conventional force negotiations were given a chance.[33] Once again, France's two leaders continued their attempts to keep up a common front—neither forgetting that the presidential election was only two months away—but it was now apparent that their "agreement" was coming under increasing strain.

The Russians, the Germans, and French Military Doctrine

The cases just discussed—the military program law and the INF debate—suggest that significant divisions were beginning to emerge within France over national security questions and that these divisions fell primarily along lines of Right and Left. To be sure, this breach was not comprehensive, and although the Left generally lined up behind President Mitterrand and the Right behind Prime Minister Chirac, there were exceptions to both of these "rules." On the Right, for example, some "old Gaullists" opposed the government's new commitments to the Federal Republic and its rapprochement with NATO, and on the Left, prodefense nationalists like Jean-Pierre Chevènement opposed the Socialists' enthusiasm for disarmament and détente. Still, the main elements of a Right/Left, government/opposition debate over French strategy were easy to discern. And when it came time to make choices about France's own overall political and military strategy in Europe, the contrast between the two competing approaches became even more clear.

The Right's approach, articulated primarily by Chirac and Giraud and supported by the majority of the Rassemblement pour la République (RPR) and UDF, was to augment the French capacity to contribute to the defense of Western Europe in the wake of perceived denuclearization and incipient American withdrawal. This meant endowing French forces with the means and the doctrine to intervene early in the "forward battle" alongside NATO and German allies and, if necessary, to use tactical nuclear weapons in that battle. It meant much closer European and Atlantic cooperation and emphasized the concept of the "single military space" as opposed to the "national sanctuary." Such a strategy had its roots in the positions taken by Giscard d'Estaing in the mid-1970s, when Chirac was prime minister, and might fairly be described as a French version of Atlanticism and flexible response.

In contrast, the Left, primarily in the person of Mitterrand himself, sought to take advantage of the changing international environment and to emphasize disarmament, détente, and arms control. It sought to distinguish itself from the government's implied policies of "battle fighting" and further integration with NATO and instead emphasized its continued commitment to the doctrines of pure deterrence and "nonwar." The Left's new strategy was an interesting combination of traditional Socialism, with its themes of lower defense spending and opposition to the arms race, and traditional Gaullism, which stressed French military independence, better relations with the Russians, and a strict opposition to flexible response.

The first area in which these Right/Left differences were evident was in terms of policy toward the Soviet Union. The Right's approach was based on the premise that whereas the United States' role in Europe's defense was weakening, the Soviet Union remained a significant military threat. Whereas the Socialists might be "duped" into turning back to their pacifist roots, the government would stand up firmly against the Soviet Union's new peace campaign. Whereas Mitterrand was expressing faith in Gorbachev and an enthusiasm to disarm, Chirac vowed his intention "to be very vigilant, for the temptation to play Gorbachev's game might seduce some others."[34] Such a view was also articulated by Giraud, who argued strongly for a more concerted French defense effort, and even by Raymond Barre (far from an anti-Soviet hard-liner while Giscard's prime minister), who warned in late 1987 that "Gorbachev has essentially taken up where his predecessors left off."[35]

Thus, the situation of the previous decade, when the Socialists began to mock the government's naïveté, was being reversed, and it was now the Right that sought to emphasize firmness toward Moscow and to claim the prodefense terrain. The irony of such a development was articulated in a trenchant quip by Barrist deputy Philippe Mestre, who turned what Mitterrand had once said about Giscard and Brezhnev around: It was now Mitterrand, Mestre said, who was the Kremlin's "little messenger boy."[36]

Mitterrand, of course, was not having second thoughts about the Left's adoption of a more positive attitude toward defense and nuclear deterrence. But he felt that the situation of the early 1980s that had required those policies was changing. Mitterrand believed that Gorbachev was "for real," that France's allies were taking him to be real, and that the French should not be seen as failing to keep up with the times. As before, the masterful French political leader was able to understand and follow a public opinion that seemed to be shifting now just as sharply as it had in the late 1970s when it tired of Giscard's détente. By late 1987, only 17 percent of French people surveyed saw the Soviet Union as the most threatening country to France (in fifth place behind four Muslim countries), and more than half those questioned believed that France should follow the superpowers' path toward disarmament.[37] Another poll showed that 31 percent of the French believed that France should reduce defense spending—still a relatively low figure but the highest ever recorded in France.[38] Just as the Mitterrand of 1981–1984 knew that political mileage could be gained by taking a hard line against Moscow and supporting the deployment of American missiles, the Mitterrand of 1986–1988 knew that just the opposite had become the case.[39] In short, the "Solzhenitsyn effect" (French anti-Sovietism in the late 1970s) was being replaced by the "Gorbachev effect," and Mitterrand was the first to pick up on the latter change just as he had been first to take advantage of the former.[40]

The Chirac government and the Mitterrand Elysée also differed over French policy toward Germany. As already mentioned, both Right and Left agreed that relations with the Federal Republic were of the utmost importance, and a certain amount of competition even took place between the president and the prime minister to see who could be the Germans' "best friend." But although the Deutschlandpolitik of both Mitterrand and Chirac can be characterized as favorable toward Germany, there were significant differences in nature and emphasis between the two.

Chirac, along with Giraud, took the view that some sort of true European pillar had to be built up to replace the declining American role in European defense and in the face of a Soviet Union that still posed a threat to Western Europe.[41] They believed that nuclear deterrence remained the only viable means of offsetting Soviet conventional power and that if the U.S. deterrent were becoming less credible, then Europe itself had to make up the difference. Thus, the Franco-German relationship had to be seen as "a necessary and irreplaceable contribution to the security of all of Western Europe."[42] More concretely, Chirac went further than any previous French prime minister in his statements about France's role in the defense of Germany. He repeated often the formula that "if France's survival began at her borders, France's security began at the borders of her neighbors" and announced that "France would never consider the territory of her neighbors as a glacis."[43] In a speech to the IHEDN in late 1987, he pledged that if Germany were attacked, France's military response would be "immediate and without reservation." He implied that this response might even include the use of French tactical nuclear weapons.[44]

Mitterrand, on the other hand, emphasized the political rather than the military nature of the Franco-German security relationship. He preferred political or symbolic steps like summit meetings with Chancellor Kohl, the Joint Defense Council, and the Joint Brigade to promises of France taking part in the forward battle. As seen during the INF and SNF debates, Mitterrand's German strategy was more one of "giving the Germans what they want" than one of pursuing French interests as narrowly defined in Paris. Thus, in contrast to Chirac's suggestions of an "extended" French tactical nuclear deterrent, Mitterrand went out of his way to let the Germans know that France would *not* use its nuclear arms on German soil. "Nothing suggests," he declared while visiting the Federal Republic in October 1987, "that France's final warning to the aggressor would be delivered on German territory. France's nuclear strategy is directed to the aggressor, and only [to it.] Germany is a friendly country, she could not be an aggressor. Our deterrence strategy applies to the countries who could be."[45] Mitterrand understood that the Germans were more anxious to hear about peace than about war and that they still had more faith in the security relationship with the United States (and, increasingly, in Gorbachev) than they had in the force de frappe. The best way for France to cement the Franco-German relationship in Mitterrand's view was not by proposing nuclear guarantees or by emphasizing European defense but by being seen to promote arms control and détente.

In short, if Chirac's "Franco-German couple" was an attempt to build up the substantial and even nuclear European defense that would be necessary to compensate for an American withdrawal from Europe, Mitterrand's version was a political and symbolic alliance between the two most important actors in Europe. Chirac was seeking to secure Germany's defense, Mitterrand its trust.

The most significant difference between the security strategies of Right and Left during cohabitation concerned France's operational military doctrine. Chirac and the Right were apparently inclined toward a strategy of flexible response and a rapprochement with NATO whereas Mitterrand and the Left adhered strictly to the concept of pure deterrence.

The Right's interest in a more flexible military doctrine was evident not only in the types of weapons it favored—the S-4 mobile missile; the upgraded Hadès nuclear missile; the ASMP missile; and the neutron bomb—but also in the operational concepts it put forth. André Giraud was perhaps the administration's most outspoken advocate of flexible response, but the prime minister himself was also a frank and vocal proponent. In his 1986 speech to the IHEDN, Chirac suggested that France's "nuclear warning," which according to official doctrine was to be a single nuclear salvo meant to send a message to the aggressor, could take the form of a multiple tactical nuclear strike, a militarily useful part of the European battle. In language remarkably similar to that of Giscard and Méry (and Chirac himself) in 1975–1976, he argued that the objective of France's nuclear warning would be not only "to send an unequivocal signal to the aggressor but also *to check the momentum of the aggression.*" The French nuclear response could thus, the prime minister said, "be diversified and graduated in depth."[46] In his 1987 speech to the same audience, Chirac spoke of France's objection to flexible response in the past tense ("a doctrine whose premises we contested") and observed the "implicit rapprochement" between France's concept of deterrence and that of NATO.[47] He argued that new, more flexible, forces such as the ASMP and Hadès missiles "give our prestrategic component more versatility and thus more credibility in fulfilling its mission. . . . It is not a question of envisaging a nuclear battle from which Europe would emerge devastated, but of being in a position to restore deterrence in the case it would have failed at first."[48] Chirac had, thus, come full circle and was now espousing a nuclear doctrine that in its emphasis on "versatility," "greater credibility," and "range of means" was a direct descendant of that put forth during the mid-1970s, which the same Chirac had criticized after leaving the government in 1976.

Mitterrand, on the other hand, began to speak out against flexible response with an intensity that more than compensated for Chirac's enthusiasm. The president's argument was based on the now familiar concept of nonwar, the idea that the raison d'être of French nuclear weapons was to avoid war rather than to win it. As he put it in an important interview granted to Jean Daniel of the *Nouvel Observateur* in December 1987 less than one week after Chirac's speech to the IHEDN:

> I have many reservations about this strategy which offers a disturbing way out for our allies from across the ocean. I know that I am one of the few who think so. This opinion, most often, astonishes and shocks the Atlantic circles. . . . But I always come back to the same point. *Deterrence strategy is designed to prevent war, not to win it.* All that which moves away from this troubles me. Many people lose sight of this obvious point.[49]

Mitterrand reaffirmed that "there is no flexible response for France," that strategic nuclear deterrence remained France's "best guarantee," and that despite the suggestions of the prime minister, France's prestrategic "final warning" could not be "plural" but would have to be a single shot.[50]

Thus, as the May 1988 elections approached and defense questions began to assume a greater-than-usual role in the campaign, Mitterrand was using Gaullist language and logic to contrast his view with that of his opponents, the latter being identified with the American doctrine that France had long rejected. In his *Lettre à tous les Français* of April 1988, he repeated that the "objective of [the nuclear weapon] is to prevent war, not to win it" and just days before the presidential elections that a "graduated strategy" was not possible for France.[51]

Mitterrand's view was echoed by a number of his supporters on the Left, including Socialist party leader Lionel Jospin and future Defense Minister Jean-Pierre Chevènement. Although Chevènement, leader of the former CERES, differed from the president on other defense questions, in his critiques of NATO doctrine he was far more zealous than Mitterrand himself. He criticized what he saw as the Right's "Atlanticist drift toward battle" and argued that the French deterrent could, perhaps, be extended to Germany but only as an ultimate recourse, not as part of the battle.[52] In Chevènement's view, flexible response was no less than "a criminal aberration."[53]

COHABITATION IN RETROSPECT

As one looks back at the debates over the military program law, the INF and SNF negotiations, and France's European strategies during cohabitation, two conclusions seem appropriate. First, on all of these questions the positions of the Right were often militarily coherent and logically expressed, but in political terms they were unrealistic and likely to fail. Chirac's commitment to augment spending on military equipment was laudable in terms of building French military strength, but it was not necessarily in tune with a population tired of *rigueur* and interested in détente. His desire to keep the Euromissiles in place was impeccable from the point of view of deterrence, but because it contrasted with the wishes of France's neighbors, it was diplomatically out of step. And his emphasis on flexibility in French nuclear and conventional doctrine was rational as a means to defend Western Europe, but because it suggested fighting battles in Germany, it was politically and diplomatically troublesome.[54] To caricature somewhat, while Mitterrand was aligning himself with the Germans, disarmament, and the notion of nonwar, Chirac was supporting the United States, foreign missiles, and the doctrine of flexible response. Chirac apparently failed to recognize the extent to which military doctrine inevitably takes place in a political context, and in this sense Mitterrand was far more astute.

The second conclusion is that during cohabitation the Right and the Left tried their best to put forth a common front on questions of French strategy, but the combination of an upcoming election, a rapidly changing military environment, and genuinely different views about France's proper military role in Europe led to increasingly open divisions. One of the more ironic outcomes of these divisions was that by emphasizing the Atlantic Alliance, taking a hard line toward the Soviet Union, adopting a military strategy of flexible response and pushing for a reinforced military component to European defense, the "Gaullists" seemed to be reverting to the policies of the Fourth Republic. And at the same time, by emphasizing pure deterrence, independence, the Franco-German couple, and détente the Socialists were reverting to de Gaulle.

Seen from the outside, French defense policy from 1986 to 1988 was largely a policy of confusion and uncertainty. On one hand, both ends of France's political spectrum supported the Franco-German relationship, a more "European" defense, and the traditional nuclear and global pillars of French security policy; but with the country's two leaders in disagreement over precisely what these goals meant and how to achieve them, and with no one sure who would next be in power, it was unclear what to expect over the longer term. If the years of cohabitation came to an end without the explosion of any major crises and with France still able to talk about its "defense consensus," it was far from clear that the open questions about French defense had been resolved. The tensions long present in French security policy were magnified by a two-headed government that, despite its formidable efforts to mask those tensions, did not manage to do so.

PUTTING OFF THE CHOICES: MAY 1988–MAY 1989

A look at the year that followed cohabitation only reinforces the conclusions just reached. The victory of the Left in the presidential and parliamentary elections in 1988—Mitterrand won the second presidential round by an overwhelming 54 to 46 percent in May and the Socialists won a relative majority in June—did little to resolve the problems that had been building over the past several years. In fact, the year 1989 would be one during which the difficulties inherent in French defense policy from the start of the Fifth Republic—developing a military strategy to ensure national interests without conflicting with European ones; paying the increasing costs of maintaining nuclear, conventional, and global military roles; and finding an acceptable balance between defense and disarmament—would come to a head. By the summer of 1989, fundamental long-term choices clearly had to be made in France, but no one appeared willing or able to make them, and few agreed on which choices to make.

The main security debate of that year was over how to interpret the changes in the Soviet Union and, consequently, over the implications of those changes for French defense planning and programming. Within the government—no longer divided between Left and Right but now within the Left itself—two main "camps" emerged, each of which represented traditional strains of modern French socialism. On one side of the debate was the new defense minister, Chevènement, the main advocate of sustained military spending and representative of the Jacobin nationalist tradition. Chevènement warned against prematurely "lowering the guard" and against a lack of "vigilance" against the Soviet Union. He argued that "the Soviet Union has not slowed down its military effort since the arrival of Mr. Gorbachev" and that the Soviets maintained an "offensive military posture." Citing Napoleon, the defense minister based his argument on the logic that nations must "judge the capacities of the potential adversaries, not their intentions."[55] In these views Chevènement was joined by much of the French Right and center.

On the other side of the debate were Prime Minister Michel Rocard and Finance Minister Pierre Bérégovoy, representatives of pragmatic social democracy, both of whom believed the stability of the rest of the economy depended on savings made in the area of defense. Committed to increasing government spending on education, stimulating business investment, and maintaining the value of the franc, the prime minister argued for lower defense spending so that business taxes could be cut. For Rocard (in an obvious jibe at the "Gaullism" of Chevènement), "The respectability of a country [is] not measured simply in terms of the volume of its military budget."[56] But the Left-wing defense minister had his own comment about Rocard: "When I think that I am being asked to sacrifice defense in order to lower business taxes, it makes me ill."[57]

Choosing from hypotheses ranging from no defense cuts at all to the FFr70 bn proposed by his budget director, Michel Charasse, Mitterrand announced on May 24, 1989, that France would cut approximately FFr45 bn from its defense budgets over the next four years, but that no major programs would be sacrificed. Instead, procurement of some, the aircraft carrier Charles de Gaulle, the Orchidée radar, the Rafale fighter, and the advanced cruise missile, would be delayed, while orders for others, like the Mirage 2000 bomber and the Leclerc tank, would be reduced in numbers.[58] In other words, the president had decided to do what his own defense minister had warned could not be done—to cut severely French defense spending without sacrificing any of the major programs. He had decided that despite the pressures of a defense budget under strain and the opportunities of a changing European balance, the time was not yet ripe to reorient significantly French defense. Put another way, Mitterrand had decided "not to decide."[59]

This is not the place to explore fully why the president made such a choice. Perhaps he was seeking to entice the Right, which would seek to criticize whatever choice he might make, into taking a belligerent posture during a period of relaxed tensions in Europe.[60] Alternatively, Mitterrand may have believed that the changes taking place in Eastern Europe were still too uncertain to merit the cancellation of major equipment programs but already clear enough to warrant budgetary cuts. Both of these suggestions are plausible.

What is also true, however, is simply that Mitterrand felt compelled, like the other Fifth Republic leaders who preceded him, to uphold a certain set of commitments that had become sacrosanct in France. Mitterrand may well have agreed with his critics that "the status quo is impossible," that "choices are necessary," and that "France must sooner or later choose between her status of first-class nuclear power and her presence in the world."[61] But he was evidently unprepared to make those choices in a concrete manner. Any attempt to deal definitively with the pressures that had been building for years was being put off yet again.

Looking back at the final years of the 1980s, one cannot help but to conclude that by 1989 the end of a proverbial rope had been reached. The strategic inconsistencies that had always been mitigated by the American protectorate were surfacing as that protectorate receded; the financial demands of an ambitious defense program were becoming more acute as the need for France in Europe grew and military costs skyrocketed; and domestic political disputes always quieted by the desire for consensus were finally spilling into public view. As revisions in the new military program law were debated in May 1989—exactly thirty years after General de Gaulle came to power—it was arguable that the tensions always present in the Gaullist model had peaked and that pressures for change had come to a head. In other words, the year 1989 might have marked the end of an era even if the revolutions of that year had not taken place.

Part Three

FRANCE IN THE NEW EUROPE

CHAPTER SEVEN

The Gaullist Legacy Today

FRENCH SECURITY POLICY IN THE 1990S

A LOOK BACK: CONTINUITY SINCE DE GAULLE

The main conclusion that emerges from part 2 of this book is that French security policy during the 1970s and 1980s was profoundly influenced by Gaullist ideas and policies and that the Gaullist model was maintained by all of de Gaulle's successors. Whereas most analysts who have studied this period have emphasized change rather than continuity, I argue that despite the significant evolutions discussed in chapters 4 to 7, most Gaullist goals, practices, military doctrines, and political constraints remained largely in place. The case that during the 1970s and 1980s France abandoned the Gaullist model seems to assume either that de Gaulle wanted nothing to do with Europe or the Atlantic Alliance and/or that he intended the specific policies made during the 1960s to endure for decades to come. But neither of these arguments holds up very well to scrutiny.

The force and influence of the Gaullist national security legacy can be measured first by how much it appears against all odds to have guided and constrained de Gaulle's successors, particularly the latest two. Neither Valéry Giscard d'Estaing nor François Mitterrand came to office with any particular affinity for what was known as "Gaullism"; both were sharp critics of it. Moreover, neither Giscard nor Mitterrand was ever known for his admiration of Gaullist defense thinking; the former was at best diffident toward it while a young minister, and the latter was among its most vehement political critics. In spite of this, neither man, despite the enormous power of the French presidency in the domaine réservé of foreign and security policy, altered the basic orientation of de Gaulle's defense doctrine, which had been elaborated under very different circumstances with some very different requirements. Notwithstanding domestic political alternance, increased integration of France within the EC and a changing balance of military power in Europe, the last official update of France's defense doctrine as the 1980s ended remained the Gaullist-inspired white paper of 1972.

Nothing underscores this fundamental continuity more than a reminder of the basic guidelines by which French leaders felt compelled to abide. National leaders throughout the 1970s and 1980s had to (1) maintain the ideal of total autonomy of decision; (2) defend the theoretical independence of the nuclear force; (3) avoid any new explicit or automatic commitments to third country security; (4) refuse participation in any sort of integrated military command structure; (5) continue to claim for France an exceptional status and special global role; (6) deny the automatic use of or access to French territory in time of peace or crisis; (7) reject participation in "bloc-to-bloc" negotiations; (8) purchase the overwhelming majority (approximately 95 percent) of French armaments in France; and (9) claim the right and the need to produce (and export) the entire range of weapons that other military powers produced. Thus, it is important to distinguish—as de Gaulle surely would—between a break with specific policies and a break with the basic guidelines behind them; if some of the former evolved, the latter were well respected.

How were Gaullist ideas and policies able for so long to influence the policies of successive French leaders? and Why did they take such a hold upon the French? One can posit several plausible hypotheses. First, a doctrine so flattering to national sensibilities, one that readily proclaims national importance, is bound to appeal, especially in a country given toward national exceptionalism. Since the Great Revolution, the French have been more than ready to accept a role that distinguishes them from others and have assumed a universal interest in their own culture and ideas. Second, there are political necessities: a politician must be very cautious about appearing to break with a consensus that appears to be so widely held not only among national elites but to a large degree among public opinion—voters—as well. It has been in the interest of no political leader to open up the can of worms that a divisive defense debate can be; it has seemed better not to try to fix something that few consider broken. Third, a set of policies so closely identified with so powerful a figure as Charles de Gaulle has by itself a certain momentum and historical force; it would seem to take more than a certain amount of hubris on the part of a new French leader to proclaim publicly that he or she knows more about the military needs of France than the general who saved the country twice. French presidents since de Gaulle—if not lacking in self-esteem—have,nevertheless, appeared to be constrained by this concern. Finally, although some critics were very slow in accepting the particulars of Gaullist defense policy and were reluctant to accept their implications, subsequent developments—including the gradual erosion of the American nuclear guarantee, the growing need for a stronger European pillar, and the enduring differences in the perceptions of security among European states—arguably reinforced the fundamental validity of some key

Gaullist premises. It is, thus, not surprising that de Gaulle's legacy in this area was so lasting and influential.

Whatever the best explanation, the point here is simply that the security policies that France adopted during the 1960s were maintained to a very great extent during the two decades that followed. Although significant evolutions certainly took place *within* the Gaullist model, the most important elements of that model all remained in place as the 1980s came to an end. To paraphrase (and contradict) a quote from Jean-François Révél cited in chapter 5, French security policies might have been good and might have been bad, but one thing is for certain: they were fundamentally Gaullist.

It is against this backdrop of great continuity that the European revolutions of 1989 occurred. The purpose of this chapter is to ask how well that continuity—so clear in the 1980s—is holding up today and whether the French still accept the basic tenets of Gaullist defense. How has French policy adapted to a three-year period that has seen the collapse of Soviet military power, the establishment of democracy in Central and Eastern Europe, the unification of Germany, the Persian Gulf War, a civil war in Yugoslavia, and the dissolution of the Soviet Union itself? Have the very distinctive characteristics of French policy observed since the 1960s disappeared, or can French security policy still best be described as Gaullist? As one looks toward the future, what are the prospects for the "Gaullist model" in the post–Cold War world? It is probably too soon to answer these questions definitively, but with the first few years of the new era now past, some initial responses are starting to become clear.

FRANCE AND NATO IN THE 1990S

The period between the collapse of the Berlin Wall (November 1989) and the end of the Persian Gulf War (February 1991) offered a window of opportunity during which France might have greatly reduced its opposition to NATO integration and sought better military relations with the United States. French leaders could plausibly have argued that the European security situation had greatly changed since the 1960s, that Gaullist reticence toward a hegemonic United States was no longer necessary in the wake of the announced U.S. troop reductions, and that a new French attitude toward NATO had become both possible and necessary. With the dominant American role in Europe greatly reduced and as a means to balance the new German power, France could have cast its lot with the proponents of a "New Atlanticism" and sought to join its allies in a new transatlantic consensus.

A significant French rapprochement with the United States in NATO, however, has not taken place. Whether because NATO was unwilling to take sufficient account of French proposals for a genuine Europeanization of the alliance (as some French officials argue) or because the French, in fact, prefer a status quo in which they maintain a particular role (as many Americans believe), France decided not to take part in a number of aspects of NATO reform. Hopes that may once have been entertained that France would become a more cooperative Atlantic ally now seem to have been quite mistaken.

The French, of course, have continued to maintain that they seek the preservation of a strong and functional NATO, and French leaders from both the government and the opposition have all reaffirmed France's desire to work closely with both NATO and the United States. In response to American and some other complaints that France's promotion of a "European defense" would lead to competing security structures in Europe, the French have insisted that they seek arrangements that would complement NATO, not replace it. As President Mitterrand put it in an important speech in April 1991:

> The defense of Western Europe, for the present and for many years to come, can only be conceived of in a context of respect for the Atlantic Alliance. It is not a matter of creating a defense organization that will substitute for that of NATO. It is a matter of understanding the limits of the Atlantic Alliance and its military organization. . . . The Atlantic Alliance will continue fully to play its major role in the maintenance of peace.[1]

Other French officials have also underlined that France sees NATO and the United States as necessary to any new security arrangements for Europe: Defense Minister Pierre Joxe has called NATO "the defense system upon which our security is based"; Élysée spokesman Hubert Védrine has affirmed that "no one is trying to construct a system in competition with the one that exists"; and even Jean-Pierre Chevènement, a longtime critic of American imperialism and staunch defender of France's special national role, has stated that the American commitment to European security "remains indispensable."[2] French officials throughout the bureaucracy—in the Foreign Ministry, the Defense Ministry and the Élysée—all claim a solid commitment to the maintenance of NATO and U.S. troops in Europe and firmly deny suggestions that they want the Americans out. Rather than a debate about the existence of the alliance, the French debate is about NATO's organization, content, and scope.

Recent French critiques of NATO fall into three traditional categories: the principle of military integration; the political scope of the alliance; and the geographical scope of the alliance. It is not necessary here to review the history of these well-known French positions, but it is important to understand that the past few years have not caused them to disappear.

Military Integration

To the great disappointment of those hoping to see France take advantage of the new European context to rejoin NATO military commands, the French did not sign on to the July 1990 NATO summit decision to "rely increasingly on multinational corps."[3] Instead, both Defense Minister Chevènement and President Mitterrand declared (in the latter's words) that France had "no intention of changing [it's] particular position with regard to NATO's integrated command."[4] While expressing a continued desire to work closely with the alliance, French leaders have continued to make it clear that there could be "no question of rejoining covertly or more overtly NATO's military organizations" and that "France's relationship with NATO has not been modified."[5]

Military integration within NATO, of course, has long been a bête noire for the French: De Gaulle believed that NATO's integrated commands, perhaps necessary in 1951, by the 1960s served only to help sustain American political hegemony in Europe. There was always a certain element of cynicism in this position because France knew it could denounce integration, leave NATO commands, and expel SHAPE without threatening the integrated NATO forces that would continue to protect France. But de Gaulle argued that cooperating national forces—because responsible for their own defense—would be just as effective as integrated ones and much more responsive to the distinct interests of the nations involved.

The crux of the present French critique of integration is that with a greatly diminished Soviet threat, and given the implausibility of a large-scale battle in Europe, military integration has lost its only conceivable raison d'être. In the future, the logic runs, threats to security and stability will be much more diverse and unpredictable, requiring more flexible capabilities of response. As the French diplomat in charge of the issue put it in May 1991: "We are no longer in the perspective of the third world war, where we had to prepare for a massive response to a relatively clearly identified massive attack. . . . A permanent integrated structure could only be justified in this perspective."[6]

In place of "integration," which might limit national flexibility, French strategists have stressed "coordination" and "interoperability." They have argued that NATO forces should coordinate bilaterally through national defense staffs and that the NATO military committee (composed of national chiefs of staff) should "resume its preponderant place."[7] Not knowing where military crises might arise or which countries will be involved in meeting them, the French have sought European security structures built on independent elements capable of working together. "What will count," argues analyst Frédéric Bozo, "will not be integration of forces but on the contrary, for each country, the capacity to act together—or not—when the time comes."[8]

Not even the "lessons" of the allied experience in the Persian Gulf—where highly disparate allied units successfully performed complex air-land-sea operations under a unified command—seemed to convince the French that precrisis military integration on the NATO model is necessary. On the contrary, many French military and political leaders argue that the Gulf War demonstrated that France could fight alongside the Americans as well or better than many of its NATO-integrated allies, and that the war confirmed that ad hoc cooperation can be as effective as anything else.[9] Some French officials, including Defense Minister Joxe, have begun to acknowledge more explicitly than in the past that "in action itself . . . operational integration is the condition for success." But these leaders are quick to point out that such "operational integration," based on agreements between national armies and improved interoperability of equipment, must come only after independent political choices have been made. As Joxe put it to the National Assembly three months after the Gulf War, "What is important is to maintain overall control over our own forces, and thus to have them all under a single and national command. [This] is the case [today] and will continue to be the case."[10]

French leaders are not oblivious to arguments that NATO's integrated commands help ensure the U.S. presence in Germany and the German presence in NATO (both avowed French goals), and they are as concerned as anyone about the potential (in the absence of integrated commands) for the renationalization of European defenses. They are also interested in keeping Germany bound as closely to NATO as possible. But despite the diminishing American troop presence in Europe, the French still assume that any form of formal integration with the United States implies American domination or, at least, excessive U.S. constraints on French freedom of maneuver. Although some French officials now seem to believe that joining NATO's integrated commands would give France more influence over alliance policy (and would imply little risk because of NATO's declining role), most French leaders remain diffident about a military organization that they have long associated with subordination to the political decisions of Washington. If France's opposition to the *principle* of international military integration disappears, it is much more likely to happen in a European context than an Atlantic one.

The Political Scope of the Alliance

A second enduring French position in the transatlantic debate has been that NATO's role should remain limited to guarantees of mutual defense. Whereas some Americans have proposed to revalidate the alliance by extending its competencies into political, economic, and humanitarian domains, the French have insisted more than ever that NATO should remain primarily a security organization designed to preserve geopolitical balance in Europe. French leaders have seen proposals to politicize the alliance simply as American efforts to maintain leverage over a Europe no longer so dependent on the U.S. military umbrella.

In response to U.S. Secretary of State James Baker's December 1989 call for an institutional transatlantic partnership, for example, Foreign Minister Dumas expressed concern about "certain tendencies to see the alliance get involved with everything in all sorts of areas" and called on the Allies to "leave to each framework its specificity if we want it to keep its coherence and strength."[11] In June of the following year, Jean-Pierre Chevènement argued that it would be "neither desirable nor realistic to go down a path where the reinforcement of the political dimension of the alliance would mean the retraction of military questions" and that "[NATO] has no vocation [for] tasks such as cooperation in the areas of the environment, economics, or culture."[12] President Mitterrand himself, apparently concerned about the withering of NATO before anything else is in place, has been somewhat more ready than his ministers to accept new competencies of the alliance, and has admitted that "we cannot ask the U.S. to stay in Europe as a determining element of our security without keeping them informed on political issues." "But," Mitterrand is quick to add, "we must not think that the military alliance should occupy itself with everything and anything."[13] Holding to these principles, Mitterrand in November 1991 denounced NATO's "preaching" to the Soviet Union about economic reform, and France strongly opposed plans to have NATO coordinate and distribute aid there. French diplomats complained that these were not NATO's proper roles.[14]

The French have been adamant that questions of economics, reform in Eastern Europe, relations with the Middle East, and European politics (immigration, transportation, communication, etc.) are best left to European bodies such as the EC, the Conference on Security and Cooperation in Europe (CSCE), and Mitterrand's proposed "confederation," a new organization that would encompass all of Europe but would not include the United States.[15] For the French, NATO is useful, even indispensable, but it should not become the means for the United States to maintain its predominance in Europe or to prevent European institutions from maturing. American critics of the minimalist French view have argued that what France wants is a NATO in which the United States becomes a sort of "defender of last resort," with no say in any aspects of European policy but which risks being "dragged into another war." The French, however, have had their own perception, one that was made incessantly by de Gaulle: that the Americans want a NATO that allows the United States to control European affairs as if Europe were still an American protectorate.

The Geographical Scope of the Alliance

Just as France has opposed the broadening of NATO's scope, it has objected to NATO's geographical expansion. Ironically, during the first fifteen years of the alliance's existence it was France that sought a wider NATO, whereas the United States wanted to limit it to the North Atlantic area. France insisted on including its Algerian departments in the North Atlantic treaty's Article 6, saw its colonial wars of the 1950s as part of an anti-Communist contribution to NATO and the West, and repeatedly proposed that the Atlantic Alliance become a forum for the United States, France, and the United Kingdom to discuss and manage international political affairs.[16] By the mid-1960s, however, it was the United States, with responsibilities from Southeast Asia to Latin American to the Middle East, that wanted NATO's support in its activities and conflicts abroad, and France that wanted to limit it to Western Europe.

Recent French objections to extending the alliance's geographical scope have been as strong as ever, and French leaders still argue that NATO should not "extend its zone of competence and transform itself into a grand directory for world affairs."[17] Throughout 1991, Paris opposed increased links between NATO and the new democracies of Eastern Europe and only very reluctantly agreed to the formation of the North Atlantic Cooperation Council (NACC) that was set up between the alliance and the former Warsaw Pact states.[18] French officials argued that the NACC's missions were poorly defined, that its creation risked misleading the East Europeans into assuming security guarantees that NATO was not prepared to give, that the exclusion of "neutral" countries was illogical, and that the new institution's functions overlapped with those of the CSCE. French diplomats protested that the NACC would leave Europe with two pan-European security orgnizations but no fully functioning organization for mutual defense.[19]

France also continues to oppose the notion that NATO might develop capabilities and legal authority for interventions abroad such as the Persian Gulf War. Although they acknowledge that major European interventions abroad without the support of the United States are nearly inconceivable at present, French leaders argue that to allow NATO to take the lead in organizing security in Eastern Europe or the Third World is to short-circuit the growing potential for other, more appropriate bodies, such as the United Nations, the European Community, and the CSCE, to take on those roles. In short, a broadened geographical scope for NATO, like a broadened political scope, would only weaken the existing alliance security guarantees and serve as an excuse to maintain the U.S. leadership of Europe.

The vigorous French rejection of NATO's May 1991 decision to create a Rapid Reaction Corps (RRC) was illustrative of the tenacity of France's position on limiting NATO's scope.[20] This new NATO unit was not to be given an explicitly "out-of-area" role, and it could not be called a formal expansion of NATO's "zone." In the French view, however, the creation of a highly mobile fighting force in the immediate wake of the Persian Gulf War, with Yugoslavia breaking up, Eastern Europe calling for security guarantees, and a renewed focus on Turkey and the Mediterranean, was clearly a first step in this direction. In the Persian Gulf, after all, NATO technically was not involved, but it was clear to everyone that NATO's forces, equipment, commanders, and doctrines were being used.

From a French perspective, by creating the RRC, NATO was surreptitiously trying to appropriate new roles and missions by first creating the forces that would deal with them. By acting before the alliance strategy review was completed, NATO was, in Roland Dumas's words, "putting the cart before the horse."[21] France saw the creation of the RRC as a blatant attempt to preempt the creation of a more autonomous European security structure and instead to bring European forces under the aegis of the United Kingdom, United States, and NATO. French officials were apparently "livid" about what they saw as an "Anglo-Saxon" move to act within NATO before Europe had a chance to develop its own proposals.[22] According to one French observer, the objective of NATO's haste—the Defense Planning Committee meeting was moved forward from a previously set date—was "to reduce the European identity to a European pillar in an Atlantic Alliance under American control."[23]

The formal debate over NATO's out-of-area role was largely resolved at the alliance's November 1991 Rome summit, which not only reaffirmed that NATO's zone was limited to that defined in the Washington treaty but also formally recognized the possibility of an exclusively European force, which itself could, presumably, operate abroad. Still, a certain tension remains between the American view that the Atlantic Alliance should be adapted to the new era by including the broadest range of international security questions and the French insistence that NATO remain devoted exclusively to (West) European defense.

To describe these continuities in France's policy toward NATO is not to say that French thinking has not evolved since 1989, and there have been signs that some of the old NATO taboos are quietly being called into question in Paris. Some in France seem to believe that now that the European political union project has been launched (at the EC's Maastricht summit) and the United States has recognized the EC's security role (at NATO's Rome summit), France will be able to emerge from the relative immobilism of the early 1990s and proceed to develop closer, more fruitful, and more public ties with NATO. France, in fact, has already sought to improve its operational military cooperation with NATO (which was quite good in the first place), and Defense Minister Joxe has begun to speak of France "revising its accords with NATO to take account of the profound geostrategic changes that have taken place in Europe."[24] It is also clear, however, that there are limits to these evolutions, and other French leaders (such as Roland Dumas) still assert that there is no need for France to "modify [its] relationship with NATO and . . . enter straight into Atlanticism under American hegemony."[25] French vigilance against what is seen in Paris as American or NATO domination is no longer what is was in 1966 or even 1976, but it is apparently still acute.

FRANCE AND THE EUROPEAN SECURITY IDENTITY

As an alternative to a U.S.-dominated NATO, the French have been the most vocal supporters of a "European security identity" within the framework of the European Community. In the French view, this European identity would initially be formed around the Western European Union—presently nine of the twelve EC members—but would eventually "fuse" with the EC itself into a complete political union, perhaps in 1998 when the WEU's original fifty-year statute conveniently runs out. The new European Union would remain essentially intergovernmental where defense policy was concerned but would form a tightly knit and well-organized group of states capable of, and used to, cooperating closely in military affairs. It would cooperate closely on security matters with the United States but would not be subordinate to it.

During 1990 and 1991, France put forth—most often together with Germany—a series of broad proposals for creating such a new entity.[26] The proposals described a process by which Europe would develop a "true security policy that would ultimately lead to a common defense."[27] The French and the Germans have portrayed the WEU as a sort of "military arm" of the EC that would "enable the WEU, with a view to being part of Political Union in course, to progressively develop the European common security policy on behalf of the Union."[28] Whereas some of France's

European partners (in particular, Great Britain and the Netherlands) argued that the WEU should simply be a "bridge" between the European Community and NATO, France and Germany emphasized its direct links with the EC. In the months preceding the EC's December 1991 Maastricht summit, competing proposals on security policy were submitted by Britain and Italy on one hand and by France and Germany on the other, with the former emphasizing NATO's primacy and the latter, European autonomy.[29]

At Maastricht, summit leaders adopted important elements of the French-German design. They agreed that the Community's common foreign and security policy would include "the eventual framing of a common defense policy . . . which might in time lead to a common defense"; that the WEU would be "an integral part of the development of the European Union"; and that the Union would be able to call on the WEU "to elaborate and implement decisions and actions of the Union which have defense implications."[30] At the same time, however, France yielded to British sensitivities that plans for an EC-based defense should not imply a diminished European interest in NATO. In a separate declaration on December 10, leaders of WEU member-states also pledged that the WEU would act "in conformity with the positions adopted in the Atlantic Alliance" and that they would "intensify" their coordination on alliance issues, synchronize dates and venues of WEU and NATO meetings, and establish close cooperation between WEU and NATO Secretariats-General.[31]

Although the general themes of European political union and a stronger WEU were formally accepted at Maastricht, a number of important differences continue to separate France from some of its European partners. Great Britain, the Netherlands, and Portugal, for example, still believe European efforts should remain under the NATO umbrella, and they are unenthusiastic about the European Union's role in defense. These countries are concerned that European defense efforts will duplicate those of NATO and that European attempts to gain military autonomy will send a message to the United States that it is no longer needed in European affairs. They worry that new WEU command arrangements will confuse those already in place under NATO's integrated commands and argue that it will be excessively costly for Europe to attempt to do alone what it presently does together with the United States. For the smaller countries in particular, there is also a concern that an EC security structure would be dominated by a Franco-German "axis": these countries would prefer to entrust their security to the distant, powerful, and more disinterested United States than to the French and the Germans.[32] The debate between proponents of an "Atlantic Europe" and a "European Europe" is an old one and recalls the acrimonious struggles of the early 1960s between Paul-Henri Spaak, Joseph Luns, and Harold Macmillan, on the one hand,

and de Gaulle (and sometimes Konrad Adenauer) on the other. If the participants in the debate have changed, however, its basic arguments remain very much the same. The Maastricht agreement papered over these historic disputes, but it did not resolve them.

One of the most important of the Franco-German European defense initiatives in the period that preceded Maastricht was the October 14, 1991, proposal by President Mitterrand and Chancellor Kohl (reportedly without any substantial input from their respective foreign and defense ministries) to expand the Franco-German joint brigade into a fully fledged European corps.[33] Details about the new corps were initially sketchy (in fact, the idea was presented only as a footnote to a long letter on political union), but the first indications were that it would include thirty-five thousand troops under alternating French and German commands and with a headquarters in Strasbourg, France. France and Germany made it clear that invitations to participate in the corps were open to all WEU countries, and Spain, Belgium, and Italy immediately showed some interest. According to its architects, the corps' missions would include the defense of Western Europe in the context of the NATO or WEU treaties, peacekeeping or peacemaking interventions, and humanitarian tasks.[34]

Although no one could be sure that the proposed European corps would eventually develop into the "European army" supported by some of its proponents, the proposal itself was significant. It was the most concrete sign to date that France, Europe's most stalwart defender of national military sovereignty, was prepared to bring its national security policy into line with its pro-European rhetoric. The joint corps proposal reversed France's July 1990 decision to withdraw its forces from Germany; accepted for the first time since the late 1950s the "logic" of peacetime military integration; and provided for, through the joint headquarters to be established in Strasbourg, the first permanent peacetime stationing of foreign forces in France since 1966.

Another potentially important example of France's growing efforts to build a European defense has been the increasing willingness in Paris to discuss the possible Europeanization of the French nuclear force. After having insisted for more than thirty years on the total autonomy of their nuclear deterrent forces and doctrine, French leaders began in early 1992 to suggest that certain modifications of that autonomy might become possible. On January 10, 1992, for example, President Mitterrand asked rhetorically whether it was "possible to conceive of a European nuclear doctrine" and asserted that "this will very quickly be the major question of a common defense policy."[35] Nine days later, Defense Minister Joxe noted that there were "things that could be new in the future" where French "cooperation with [her] allies was concerned, including the nuclear domain" and alluded to possible discussions with Great Britain "on the conditions in which our nuclear weapons could be combined."[36] And on January 29, Secretary of State for Defense Jacques Mellick outlined several different ways in which the French deterrent force could theoretically be Europeanized, envisaging anything from "existential deterrence" (by which the French force would deter for all of Europe by its simple existence) to "concerted deterrence" (in which France would consult with its partners on nuclear questions) to a much more far-reaching (and for him implausible) European political authority responsible for nuclear weapons.[37]

"Europeanizing" French nuclear deterrence poses many difficult questions, and a number of French officials have pointed out that it will be "a long time" before a European nuclear deterrent can be developed.[38] Mitterrand was careful to speak only of elaborating a nuclear "doctrine," and no French official went as far as the French President of the EC Commission, Jacques Delors, who has envisaged "the transferring of nuclear weapons to a strong [European] political authority."[39] Mellick, in fact, stated that such a development was "very far away" and questioned whether it was even desirable. Nonetheless, the unprecedented allusions by French officials to a Europeanization of nuclear deterrence are significant. Together with the growing French acceptance of military integration in Europe and calls for political union, they may be a sign that France is prepared to abandon certain elements of national sovereignty in the name of creating the European defense identity that has become its priority.

What explains the strength of the French interest in the development of a European security identity? Why are the French unsatisfied with the notion of a NATO "second pillar" and so committed to European autonomy? And why do they now seem so much more willing to move down the path toward a genuine European defense than in the past?

The most important factor in explaining recent French positions on European defense has doubtless been the unification of Germany. In the past, France had always sought—and to a certain extent managed—to impose supranational constraints on Germany that would somehow not apply to France. But when the Federal Republic was transformed from a semisovereign, militarily dependent "equal" of France into a politically confident state of eighty million inhabitants, the old bilateral balance was thrown off. The French now seem to have concluded that they cannot expect Germany to accept the constraints of European integration, such as the devolution of control over the Deutsche mark to a European central bank, if France is unwilling to do the same in the military field. The only way to "contain" their powerful new neighbor, the French now seem to believe, is to embrace it; the new Germany must be joined as closely as possible with France under a European roof. (In this sense French strategy has come full circle: in 1950 France proposed a European army as an alternative to a German national army that might dominate Europe. France's motivations today are not altogether different.)

The second reason the French are so committed to the idea of a European security entity is simply as a matter of principle. If Europe is going to be a true, fully sovereign "political union," Frenchmen argue, it must be legally and actually capable of dealing with defense. This is a view, elevated to the European level, that echoes de Gaulle's often-made arguments that ensuring national defense was a sovereign government's very raison d'être. Just as de Gaulle argued in the 1960s that France could not maintain a state if it was not responsible for national security, French leaders today argue that a European Union without a common security policy and, eventually, a common defense "would be incomplete."[40] Nearly all French leaders accept (as de Gaulle accepted) that this defense entity could cooperate closely and formally with the United States. But it is simply unacceptable to them that a European Union not have the explicit right and capability to carry out its own policies in an area as important as defense. For the French, to borrow Pierre Lellouche's phrase, "*L'Europe sera stratégique ou ne sera pas*" (Europe will be strategic or it will not exist).[41]

A third, and more practical, reason the French seek a genuine European defense is as a matter of long-term insurance. Perhaps because they have been questioning American reliability in Europe for so long, many French leaders and analysts seem considerably less optimistic than their neighbors about the long-term American role there. As already seen, French leaders from across the political spectrum have come out clearly for an American presence on the continent, but these same leaders are far from convinced their appeals will be heard in Washington (or accepted in Bonn and Berlin). Many in France fear that the Americans—with enormous fiscal problems, pressing social difficulties at home, and deprived of a geopolitical "enemy"—will be tempted to turn inward in years to come. Moreover, they believe, Americans so used to unchallenged hegemony will prove incapable of playing a reduced role in the new alliance; they will insist on leading it, or they will leave. The careful Mitterrand will only go so far as to question whether "the United States will always be in the front row to defend Europe," but many French analysts and officials would concur with the more direct assessment of former prime minister Edith Cresson: "It is evident that the United States is disengaging from Europe. . . . It can't leave and ask us Europeans not to have a defense of our own."[42] Another former prime minister, Michel Rocard, pointed to U.S. inaction in Yugoslavia as an example of the sort of military crisis Europe might have to face without the United States.

Can Europeans be confronted with crises that do not concern the United States? To some, the very idea was seen as a blow to transatlantic solidarity. The conflict in Yugoslavia has changed all that. Rightly or wrongly, the United States decided that its interests and ideas of international stability were not at stake in this crisis, and it let the EC act independently. This is the type of crisis Europe is likely to face in the years to come, and it illustrates why Europe must have the military means to support its policies.[43]

The French thus seek to create an autonomous European defense as insurance for future contingencies in or around Europe—a conservative reaction in the former Soviet Union, instability or wars in Eastern Europe, or (perhaps most important) serious unrest in North Africa—that the United States would be unwilling or unable to deal with. The French clearly recognize that where useful and possible (as in the Persian Gulf) Europe and the United States must cooperate closely in international security affairs; but they are not convinced that in ten or twenty years the United States will be as capable and prepared to do so as it has been in the past.

The final attraction of a European security identity for French leaders seems to be as a tool for achieving French influence both within the alliance and throughout the world. As already argued, the French have never passively accepted exclusive American leadership of Western security affairs and believe a capable and credible independent European military capacity would ensure that Europe would not be ignored by either Washington or some global adversary. The French have clearly not abandoned their interest in a respected voice and global role and increasingly believe these can be exercised only through Europe. As President Mitterrand has argued, "France will be all the more influential, prosperous, and radiant in the world if she plays her role in Europe, and this role will be consistent with her history, a determining role."[44] Nicole Gnesotto, the French deputy director of the WEU's Institute for Security Studies, also sees a European security entity as a necessary means to global influence.

> Does the European Community see itself in the future as a purely civilian and economic entity with a strictly European vocation . . . ? Or does it see itself as a world power with global responsibilities and influence? . . . The French clearly choose the second option. This is neither a militaristic vision of international relations nor a willingness to build Europe as a third bloc, but a matter of principle. . . . Europe . . . cannot be an effective diplomatic actor . . . if its authority is not backed by serious military power.[45]

And Roland Dumas's comment on Europe's role in the Middle East peace process is also indicative of the French view of Europe's proper role. "Europe doesn't want to be a mere observer in the peace process in the

Mideast. . . . Europe is seeking to participate in the same capacity as the United States and the Soviet Union with which it can rightly be compared given its 340 million inhabitants. . . . it wants a major role as participant and co-sponsor."[46] Although few in France would object to these perspectives, it is instructive to ask whether the above statements could have been made anywhere in Europe but in France.

Despite the ambitious rhetoric, the French view of the European security identity should not be seen as more dogmatic or zealous than it really is. Whereas French leaders certainly seem to believe in a more autonomous and more robust European security policy, they are not optimistic about creating it anytime soon and do not want to abandon any Atlantic guarantees in the meantime. Indeed, even the most fervent French proponents of a European security entity recognize that any concrete manifestation of such an entity will take many years to build. President Mitterrand, for example, has admitted that although "inevitable" in the long run, the creation of an autonomous European military capacity "does not seem imminent," and Foreign Minister Dumas has distinguished between the "real" (NATO) and the "eventual" (EC defense).[47] As Defense Minister Joxe explained: "The constitution of a true European defense identity will take some time. In order to command, a single authority is necessary, and that does not yet exist at the European level. Even before that, a political agreement about the goals to be pursued is also necessary, especially in time of crisis."[48] Thus, French leaders are not naive about the short-term prospects for an integrated European security identity, and they do not expect one to be in place and fully functioning anytime soon. But they are clearly committed to setting in motion a process that they believe would help bind the Germans closely to Europe, lay the foundations for European political union, ensure against an American withdrawal, and (ideally) enhance French international influence—all traditional French goals.

THE LESSONS OF THE PERSIAN GULF WAR: THE VIEW FROM PARIS

Perversely, nothing demonstrates the existence of continuities in recent French security policy better than the one event that was supposed to mark the end of continuity—the Persian Gulf War. To be sure, some saw France's participation in the U.S.-led coalition as a watershed that would signal France's return to the Atlantic fold and lead it to abandon some of its loftier aspirations to independence and power. Although the French were reluctant to follow the U.S. lead at the onset of the crisis, once the war began, French support was unambiguous: French troops served effectively under U.S. commands; French public opinion strongly supported American policy; French leaders officially backed U.S. diplomacy; and the French military seemed to begin drawing lessons about its supposed "independence." By the end of the conflict, senior French officials were referring to the "synergy" between the French and American positions, a nationalist and somewhat anti-American defense minister had resigned, and President Mitterrand had initiated a far-reaching review of French military policies and force structures.[49] When in March 1991 Mitterrand confirmed French support for U.S. policies at an affable summit with George Bush, and France reversed an earlier decision not to participate in NATO's strategy review, it seemed as if the Gulf War might prove a major turning point in French foreign and security policy.[50]

A closer look at French conclusions about the Gulf War, however, shows that France's reconsideration of its global military role may not be as fundamental as some initially thought. Although the war certainly reminded the French of the need for transatlantic cooperation and of their own military deficiencies (discussed later), it by no means convinced them to abandon their traditional political aims. On the contrary, French participation in the war and cooperation with the United States can be explained as much by a French desire to avoid "marginalization" as by any resignation to a minor or subordinate alliance role. Even under de Gaulle, after all, the French always took the position that when conditions warranted it, France should cooperate with the United States. That this was the case for the duration of the Gulf War by no means implies that it will be so in future cases. As Elysée spokesman Hubert Védrine put it just after the war: "One does not express [political] differences just for fun. One does so when it is necessary, which is not the case today."[51]

For the French government, if the Gulf War exposed (in Roland Dumas's words) Gaullist "illusions" about France's special relations with the Arab world, it also confirmed some long-standing Gaullist views about American leadership, international statecraft, and the relationship between military and political power.[52] It was not lost on French leaders that the decision to go to war was taken primarily in Washington—because the Americans had the vast majority of the forces present in the region—and that Europe was faced with a fait accompli when President Bush decided to augment the U.S. troop presence in November 1990. The French, moreover, saw it as an "affront to Europe" when Saddam Hussein allowed his foreign minister to meet with the American secretary of state but refused to receive a European Community delegation.[53] Some French officials were reminded of Stalin's condescending question about how many divisions the pope had in World War II and were insulted by the comparison; without military force, France and Europe's political roles were negligible.

Along similar lines, with the Americans and British leading the efforts to organize the peace after the war, Mitterrand's adviser Michel Vauzelle expressed fears of another "Yalta," from which France would again be excluded, and Defense Minister Chevènement worried that Europe was being "relegated to a secondary role."[54] President Mitterrand elected in his first speech after the war to emphasize not the liberation of Kuwait but that France had "upheld its role and its rank"; the president did not even mention Europe in his speech.[55] Even French public opinion, thought to be less interested in "grandeur" than the political elites, appeared to resent France's inferior political and military position: 60 percent of French people surveyed thought France was "too subordinate to the United States," and only 37 percent thought they were not.[56] In other words, as clearly as the Gulf War revealed French military inadequacies, it would be a mistake to assume that France will conclude from the Gulf War that military power and political influence are futile or beyond its reach. Much like the Suez crisis of 1956, the Persian Gulf War may lead the French to pursue more aggressively their objectives of international status and influence—perhaps this time, in a more European context—rather than to give them up.

In addition to confirming French anxieties about diplomatic subordination, the Gulf War taught the French a number of lessons about the weaknesses of their conventional military forces and their capacity for intervention abroad. First, French means of force projection were clearly inadequate to the task at hand, despite the 1983 creation of the FAR and the traditional emphasis on France's "global" role. To get even its limited and relatively light equipment to the Gulf, France—with only three modern landing platform docks (LPDs)—had to execute more than 100 military DC-8 missions, more than 200 Transall and Hercules missions, 37 trips of 747 cargo planes, and 50 missions of civilian ships. All of this took more than three weeks, and underlined the gap between France's global rhetoric and the country's lift, logistics, and force projection capabilities.[57] Second, most of France's tactical aircraft in the Gulf (Jaguars built in the late 1960s and early 1970s) had never been adequately modernized over the years, and their outdated equipment and lack of avionics made it impossible for them to fly in bad weather or at night. Although France did send an aircraft carrier (the *Clemenceau*) to the Gulf, its aging Crusaders were so inadequate for modern air warfare that they were not deployed, and the carrier transported only helicopters and trucks.[58] France's more advanced planes, the Mirage 2000Ns, were not configured for conventional missions and remained inactive in France.[59] Third, President Mitterrand's decision not to send conscripts to fight in a foreign war meant that the number of soldiers available for duty in the Gulf was severely limited. Not only was the overall percentage of conscripts in the

French armed forces high (55 percent for the army; 26 percent for the navy; and 37 percent for the air force), but several key units, including the FAR and the *Clemenceau* crew, were made up largely of nonprofessional soldiers who could not be sent abroad. This was the primary reason that France—with an army of 280,000 and a rapid action force of 47,000— was only able to put together 12,000 troops for its land-based Daguet division. In an often made comparison, Great Britain—with a professional army of only 160,000—was able to send 35,000 troops to the Gulf.[60] Finally and perhaps most important (as will be discussed below), France's military intelligence capability was severely limited in the Gulf, requiring French forces to rely heavily on the Americans for vital information.

As a result of these military lessons, France has already begun to make a number of changes in its force structure and organization. The military command structure is being redesigned to facilitate force projection and interventions abroad, and most of France's rapid deployment forces will be made up of professional soldiers or conscripts who have agreed to fight overseas.[61] The French nuclear priority, now seen to be largely responsible for the underfunding of critical conventional military programs, is being deemphasized (in fact, if not yet in rhetoric) and nuclear spending is scheduled to decline as a share of French military budgets. Decisions taken in 1991–1992 to cancel the S-45 mobile missile, freeze production of the Hadès, disband without replacing two Pluton regiments, delay production of the new generation nuclear submarine, and declare a one-year moratorium on French nuclear testing in the Pacific all belied new Prime Minister Bérégovoy's contention that the force de frappe remained "the cornerstone of French defense."[62] To compensate for logistical shortcomings, French military planners are also seeking to purchase additional heavy transport aircraft and are reviewing France's civilian air transport mechanisms and in-flight refueling systems.

Nowhere, however, are French military changes greater—and the desire in Paris for greater military and political autonomy more evident— than in the domain of military intelligence and communications. An independent capability for the collection and processing of battlefield information—primarily through the use of advanced reconnaissance and communications satellites—has, in fact, become the new symbol of France's aspiration to political "rank," much in the way nuclear weapons were in the 1960s. Pierre Joxe has asserted that "space means will bring about changes as important as those caused by nuclear strategy and deterrence," and that "the same reasons that led France to equip itself with an autonomous capacity for nuclear deterrence, must now lead us to develop an autonomous capacity for space observation.[63] As another government official put it, reflecting a widespread French view: "Intelligence should be an absolute priority. If we played a real military role in the Gulf, we [nonetheless] remained permanently dependent on the Americans for intelligence from space. This is no longer acceptable."[64] According to *Le Point*, "One of the principal lessons of [the Gulf War] is that France can only hope to uphold the rank to which it aspires if it has effective intelligence systems at its disposal."[65]

Such an emphasis on satellite observation and communication seems not only to have the support of President Mitterrand, who was reportedly incensed when American officials would not allow the French to keep the satellite photos they showed them, but has become the top priority of Joxe and the Ministry of Defense. Joxe now speaks of "the absolute necessity for Europe to endow itself with its own means of space observation" and argues that "there will come a time when simply having high-resolution observation systems will give such power that those who do not have them will be disarmed, whatever their other weapons."[66] He has proposed to give military intelligence—to which he devoted his entire first address as defense minister to the IHEDN—the status of an official "branch" of the armed services, and (within the context of a declining overall 1992 defense budget) to increase the 1992 budget for military space programs by nearly 18 percent.[67] Such ambitions in space, moreover, are scarcely limited to the Defense Ministry or the present government. Even Edouard Balladur, a supposedly Atlanticist leader of the RPR, has argued that Europe must have its own observation satellites "in order to avoid [a situation in which] European countries are blind if they do not benefit from information supplied by the Americans."[68]

As evident from the Joxe and Balladur statements, French leaders have now begun to speak of "autonomy" and "independence" largely in a European context (rather than a national one), and the French are making great efforts to rally the other Europeans to their cause. Their success has been limited so far but includes Italian and Spanish agreements to fund partially the Hélios intelligence satellite (with 14.1 and 7 percent shares respectively), an agreement with Great Britain to study the development of a network of European military telecommunication satellites, and a June 1991 decision by the WEU to set up a satellite data interpretation center in Torrejon, Spain.[69] France has also sought more ambitious European and WEU space cooperation from Germany, but Bonn does not seem as ready to pay for such capabilities as Paris would like.

Thus, renovation of France's armed forces in the wake of the Gulf War is considerable, and Joxe is not exaggerating when he speaks of "a new era for [France's] defense . . . a cycle that will probably be on the order of a generation, like the one that began at the beginning of the 1960s."[70] As important as these military lessons are, however, they should not obscure—indeed, they go far to confirm—the political lessons previously discussed. France did not conclude from the Gulf War that its only future military option is to ally itself more closely to the United States. On the contrary, France's determination to develop its force projection and military intelligence capabilities are evidence of a renewed French desire to liberate Europe from its military dependence on Washington. One might say that the French reaction to their experience in the Gulf was not so much "How wonderful to cooperate so well with the Americans!" but "How can we avoid being so dependent next time around?"

CONCLUSIONS: CONTINUITIES AMID CHANGE

Has French security policy, then, remained "Gaullist" or not? Have the revolutions of 1989 brought about the end of the Gaullist influences observed over the past thirty years, or do vestiges of those influences remain? Two contradictory tendencies seem to be present.

On one hand, it is manifest that France has begun to rethink some of the most basic pillars of what has been called the "Gaullist model." French leaders are not nearly as reticent toward NATO as they were during the 1960s (or even the 1970s or 1980s); they seem willing to accept much greater military integration within the European Community than ever before; their emphasis on national independence has faded significantly; and strategic nuclear weapons are no longer the *nec plus ultra* of French defense strategy that they once were. Gaullist policies were implemented and maintained at a time when the United States dominated the Atlantic Alliance, the Soviet threat hung heavily over a bipolar Europe, Europe's role in the world was in the shadows of the superpowers, and the Europeans had serious disagreements among themselves about how best to ensure their defense. All of these factors are in the process of changing or have already changed, and French policy is changing as a result.

On the other hand, some important Gaullist policies and perspectives have clearly endured. In the 1990s as in the 1960s, France has opposed American leadership on a number of levels; criticized the concept of Atlantic military integration; refused to take part in NATO's integrated commands; sought to construct a European defense that could act autonomously within or outside Europe; maintained the notion of a presidential domaine réservé; and continued to assert France's global role and "rank." As Alexis de Tocqueville once observed (and as French history demonstrates), national policies and practices tend to be passed on from one epoch to another, and even revolutions are sometimes not enough to wash them away. No one should have expected that the main elements of the Gaullist model would be jettisoned within the space of a few years.

What, then, are the prospects for continuity in the future? Are Gaullist influences likely to endure, or has France started down a slippery slope that will soon lead to the definitive abandonment of the Gaullist model?

Will the Gaullist period become that "brilliant parenthesis" referred to at the beginning of this book, one that was neatly closed one hundred years after the General's birth, fifty years after he founded the Free French, and twenty years after his death? Or will Gaullist ideas and perspectives continue to influence French thinking about security in France and abroad?

Certainly, a strong argument can be made that the continuities of the past few years are largely the result of inertia and that within a few more years the Gaullist legacy will be a thing of the past. The changes that have taken place in Europe have left French policy wanting in a number of areas: The pursuit of independence has left French armed forces less closely involved with the Americans than they would like to be; the end of the Cold War renders the Gaullist association between military power and national prestige less valid than before; the French defense budget is significantly overstretched; and, perhaps most of all, the deepening of European integration means the national character of French military doctrine and procurement will be more difficult to maintain. With the Cold War over, Germany united, military power devalued, the Americans withdrawing from Europe and French defense spending out of hand, the policies of the Gaullist years are clearly coming under strain.

In the past, moreover, French leaders all had an interest in upholding the "consensus," and none was ever willing to risk fundamental change when continuity served them just fine. On the rare occasions when major change was attempted, such as in 1976 under Giscard d'Estaing, the innovators were quickly beaten back within the safe parameters of conservatively interpreted Gaullist "rules." Today, however, the arguments for change seem stronger than before, the arguments against it are weaker, and in any case, those in France who have always vigilantly defended Gaullist orthodoxy—often in a manner "more Gaullist than de Gaulle"— are no longer in a position to block a new course. In short, it cannot be excluded that some of the main elements of the Gaullist model will be fundamentally revised in the years ahead. The present generation of political leaders in France (most of whom have been around for decades) will soon give way to a new generation, and a new leader may decide that Gaullist means and goals are no longer appropriate for a greatly changed world. François Mitterrand, after all, is probably the last French president who will have been an adult (and even a prisoner of war) during World War II, and few of his potential successors possess the strong sense of the nation and sense of history that Mitterrand shared with de Gaulle. The current French president may well prove to be the last one whose foreign and security policies could be described as "fundamentally Gaullist."

At the same time, however, it would not be surprising if some basic Gaullist perspectives were to continue in many ways to influence French policy. The French still seem more concerned with their national image and prestige than most of their neighbors—a recent poll showed that 72 percent of the French still believe France is a "great power" (and that just as many believe this is so because of the force de frappe)—and French elites have not abandoned their vigilant watch over their national political rights in the international arena.[71] French military leaders have no qualms about cooperating closely with the United States (they never have), but they, and their political mentors, are still jealous of their own national prerogatives and are still clearly interested in playing a prominent global role. Unlike Germany, France does not have a past that prohibits it from playing a high-profile international military role, and unlike Great Britain, France does not have the linguistic and cultural links with the United States that might enable it to exercise international influence through Washington. A national strategic culture with deep roots in history and geography is not easily abandoned.

Given these contradictory influences—the compelling need for change and the enduring influence of the past—the future evolution of French policy is likely to depend greatly on the international environment in which French policy is made. If, for example, the United States comes to treat the European Community as a political and economic equal, EC integration proceeds harmoniously in the direction of a federal entity, and the recent trends toward peaceful resolution of international conflicts are confirmed, the French may come to conclude that Gaullist arguments about the centrality of the nation-state, the importance of nuclear deterrence, and the need for a strong national defense are no longer relevant in a greatly changed world. The Gaullist period would become a fascinating historical chapter in French history whose final pages would have been turned in 1989 (or shortly thereafter). But if, on the other hand, the United States gives the impression that it seeks global political hegemony at the expense of France and Europe, European integration is sidetracked by divergent national interests, the new Germany begins to throw its weight around, or armed conflicts break out to Europe's east or south, France may find itself more Gaullist than ever. In this case, de Gaulle's arguments about enduring national interests and the need to protect them, even with military means, would become relevant once again. Recent trends suggest the former scenario may be more likely than the latter, but if the early 1990s have taught analysts anything, it is to remain skeptical about recent trends.

Epilogue

THE GAULLIST LEGACY AND THE
POST–COLD WAR WORLD

ARE GAULLIST IDEAS about France and national security still relevant more than twenty years after the General's death? One might be tempted to answer in the negative if it were not for some striking similarities between the Europe of de Gaulle's vision and the Europe that seems to be evolving today. The reestablishment of the nation-states of Eastern Europe, the collapse of ideology and resurgence of nationalism, the disintegration of the Soviet Union (and reemergence of Russia), the continuing development of a European Community still based on national interests and mutual consent, and the erosion of the dominant American role in Europe are just some of the present realities that remind observers of de Gaulle's goals and predictions. Comparing de Gaulle's arguments about the desirable and natural state of European affairs with the "post–Cold War world" suggests that reflections on the Gaullist legacy may be more than a simple historical or intellectual exercise.

This is not to say that the new situation in Europe is in every way like the one de Gaulle foresaw, that he was right about when or how Europe's changes would take place, or even that he helped bring the new situation about. In fact, de Gaulle probably believed the Cold War would end sooner than it did, that East European leaders would play a greater role in that process than they did, and that his own policies would be more instrumental than they were. Still, the potential emergence in the 1990s of a "Europe from the Atlantic to the Urals" makes a critical look back at de Gaulle's vision of Europe seem worthwhile. Given the General's emphasis on the long term and given the enduring influence of his ideas on French policy, it seems useful to conclude this book by reconsidering the relevance of Gaullist perspectives in a very new context.

DE GAULLE'S POST–COLD WAR WORLD

It can be argued, if perversely, that de Gaulle did not really want to see a Gaullist world come about and that he was only cynically taking advantage of a status quo that gave France uncommon room for maneuver. In this view, de Gaulle, whose primary goals were national power and influence, knew that France would have more of both in a divided world than it would in a multipolar one. De Gaulle's France, for example, could never have flattered itself as the privileged interlocutor of the Soviet Union or as mediator between East and West had the decried "two-bloc" system not been in place. Without the Cold War, which ensured stability in Europe, American protection and the division of Germany, France would be a weak and small fish in a big pond, and it could never have pretended to play the leading global and European roles of de Gaulle's dreams.

De Gaulle, this argument continues, knew full well that in a Europe "from the Atlantic to the Urals," in which Germany would be reunited and the Americans would largely go home, Germany and Russia (not France) would be the continent's dominant powers. France would no longer be the relatively large and militarily superior state in the heart of *l'Europe des Six* but a relatively weak and militarily inconsequential state on the periphery of Europe as a whole. A calculating (and diplomatically astute) de Gaulle, then, was improving his own position by disingenuously professing to seek a revision of the status quo while hoping and, indeed, believing that things would never really change.

Although this interpretation has its grain of truth, it overlooks a very fundamental point made in chapter 1: De Gaulle was far too well aware of the inevitability of change and the power of nationalism to accept that the divided Europe of the Cold War would go on forever. In his mind, history and geography were, in the long run, much more permanent and influential factors in world affairs than individuals, governments, or ideologies. "No regime," de Gaulle wrote in 1958, "can hold up against the wills of nations."[1] His clamoring for an end of superpower hegemony may have hidden a certain fondness for a status quo that artificially inflated France's importance. He certainly used this temporary situation to enhance France's status and to build a nuclear force behind the American shield. But in the longer term—the term in which de Gaulle placed his aspirations for *la France éternelle*—it is difficult to believe that Gaullist revisionism was a mere diplomatic game.

De Gaulle's conviction that the Cold War could not endure was the foundation for his policies of détente, which began in earnest in 1965, peaked with his spectacular visit to Moscow in June 1966, and included visits to Warsaw and Bucharest in 1967 and 1968. The Moscow visit (not unintentionally) reminded observers of the Franco-Russian alliance of the 1890s and the de Gaulle-Georges Bidault policies of 1944–1946, and the Eastern Europe tour conjured up thoughts of France's interwar "little entente." In Moscow, de Gaulle declared that "comprehension and collaboration were eminently natural" between the French and the Russians and spoke of a "deliberate rapprochement between the Soviet Union and

France."[2] To everyone's surprise (and consternation—France had just left the NATO commands), he even proclaimed Russia to be "powerful, prosperous, and full of pacific ardor."[3] While the United States and West Germany were still maintaining a political "quarantine" on the Communist superpower, de Gaulle began to deal with it.

Several different arguments seem plausible in explaining de Gaulle's pursuit of détente with the East. First, one can make the case already mentioned that de Gaulle was resigned to a Europe that would remain divided for the foreseeable future and that his efforts in the East were only crafted to increase French bargaining power within the Western Alliance. He was well aware, this argument ran, that the Russians had not changed, but he wanted to augment French leverage and avoid American hegemony all the same. Second, one can argue that the General knew it would still be some time before the Cold War would end and that his détente was only a temporary expedient designed to urge the process along. In this view, de Gaulle (rightly or wrongly, probably the latter) believed cooperation with the Soviets and his own example of independence within the West would promote fissures in the bipolar system and progressively bring about the crumbling of the two blocs. This was particularly true of his visits to Wladislaw Gomulka's Poland and Nicolae Ceaucescu's Romania, both of which he mistakenly hoped would soon seek to leave the Soviet bloc. Third, it is possible that de Gaulle's policies toward the East were meant neither to take advantage of the status quo (the first argument) nor to break it apart (the second) but were merely a way to leave a door open for Russia when that country did change, to avoid, as Stanley Hoffmann has put it, "insulting the future."[4] In this view de Gaulle was trying to show that whatever the "present nature of the regime," the eternal Russians, with whom Europeans were fated to share a continent, would eventually have to be dealt with.

There is some truth in all of these points, which are not as contradictory as they might appear. One can take advantage of a particular situation even while trying to promote both short- and long-term change. Indeed, even if a reversal of the status quo is one's goal, one can scarcely be blamed for taking advantage of that status quo in the meantime. If de Gaulle's attempts to draw the Soviet Union into the world's community of nations at the same time increased French stature and importance within that community, all the better for de Gaulle.

If each of the preceding explanations have some validity, however, they nonetheless leave out a fourth and much simpler argument that is too often overlooked: de Gaulle was not only calculating and manipulating but really did believe the Cold War was coming to an end. In this view, de Gaulle, as was his wont, looked attentively at the situation around him and became convinced that the time was ripe for change. Not only was

France free from its Algerian burden and endowed with the beginnings of a force de frappe, but the world around France had also evolved in such a way that détente seemed possible. Given de Gaulle's dynamic geopolitical vision as described, this would have been a highly reasonable interpretation of the circumstances for him to make and would have been perfectly compatible with his long-term view of Europe and the world.

During his first years in power after 1958 (to say nothing of his tenure as leader of the anti-Communist RPF), there was of course no question that de Gaulle knew the Cold War was still on. He saw the Soviet Union as "the most terribly imperialist and colonialist power that has ever been known" and denounced its "totalitarian and threatening ideology."[5] His greatest fear during these years was not so much American Cold War belligerence but "superpower condominium" and Anglo-Saxon "sellouts." As is often pointed out, de Gaulle took the firmest possible stands against Moscow during the crises of the early 1960s in Berlin, at the 1960 Paris summit, and during the Cuban missile crisis. From 1958 to 1964, de Gaulle's policies toward the Soviet Union showed little nostalgia for any historic "special relationships."

But de Gaulle, unlike many of his contemporaries, had not "given up" on the Russians, even during the coldest of the Cold War years.[6] As the East-West tensions of the Cuban crisis abated and the superpowers each moved back from the brink, de Gaulle began to see what he thought were signs that a new era was about to emerge. And no one can deny that such signs were not at least to be taken seriously. On the eastern side of the Cold War, the Communist world was now manifestly divided, with the Chinese and Russians shooting at each other across their endless border. The reckless and dangerous Khrushchev, who had served the good purpose of revealing Stalinist crimes and introducing domestic reforms, was now gone in favor of a Soviet leadership that promised to be more conservative and less adventuristic. Third World States, once feared to be lining up in some sort of Marxist International, were proving far more nationalist than internationalist or Marxist. And there were signs, particularly in Romania but also in Poland and Czechoslovakia, that East European states (beginning to recover from the shock of the 1956 invasion of Budapest) were seeking some independence from the Warsaw Pact. This all led de Gaulle to conclude by 1964 that "the monolithic character of totalitarianism [was] in the process of falling apart."[7]

On the Western side there were also powerful signs of change: the United States was becoming increasingly bogged down and distracted by Vietnam, had a new president (Lyndon Johnson) who was much more interested in domestic politics than in European affairs, and had even begun to show signs of willingness to cooperate with the Soviets in arms control, signing a limited nuclear test-ban treaty in 1963. The tensions

that had peaked in October 1962—and the factors that produced them—
had apparently begun to fade.

Given his views of human nature and political ideology, de Gaulle
probably believed that in Russia he would find interlocutors interested in
improving the Soviet standard of living, aware that they could not sup-
press East European nationalism forever, and willing to deal with the
manifestly more prosperous West. He went to see not the Communist
leader of a Soviet empire but the "Russian" (in fact, Ukrainian) leader
that he believed to be hiding underneath, a European like himself. The
problem, however—and what de Gaulle apparently failed to see—was
that Brezhnev's nationalism (unlike de Gaulle's) was not enlightened
enough to accept that maintaining an empire against the will of the colonies could be more of a national burden than a source of security or
strength. As the crushing of the Prague Spring and implementation of the
"Brezhnev Doctrine" brutally made clear two years later, the Soviets of
the 1960s were not quite ready for de Gaulle's post–Cold War world of
free nation-states. The Cold War was not over but would last for decades
to come.

If de Gaulle, then, was right to perceive that certain factors were working against the maintenance of the two blocs and leading to a more plural
world, he seems to have misjudged the speed and extent of the process. In
1965, a domestic evolution in Moscow may, indeed, have been "already
underway," but it was premature to conclude from this that "the Cold
War that [had] lasted for twenty years [was] in the process of disappearing."[8] At age seventy-six and with a burning desire to see his grand design
come to fruition—to see the division of Europe come to an end—de
Gaulle was apparently too quick to believe that the conditions necessary
for pan-European cooperation had come about.[9]

The implication of this for de Gaulle's Eastern policies, and, thereby,
his security policies, was all too clear: as long as the Soviet Union maintained its Cold War ideology, its exceptional military force, and its hold
on Eastern Europe, de Gaulle's ideas about "détente, entente, and cooperation" would never fully correspond to the realities on the ground. It is at
least arguable that the Europe of 1958–1989—the Europe de Gaulle and
to some extent his successors tried to pry away from the tutelage of the
United States—was unable to deter and defend without American military force and leadership. As de Gaulle's opponents at the time argued,
the Soviets really *were* threatening, there really *was* a conventional military imbalance in Europe, and only the United States seemed able, for the
time being at least, to right it. What is certain, in any case, is that most
Europeans believed this to be true and that even de Gaulle's arguments
about a more independent French and European defense were based on
the premise that the United States guarantee was for the time being firmly

in place. De Gaulle's vision of an independent Europe could not fail to attract the sympathy of many on the continent, but as long as the Soviet military threat remained real, most Europeans preferred the insurance that only the other superpower could provide.

Was Gaullist détente thus a failure, based on a misunderstanding of the European situation and an ill-conceived plan to bring about change? Such a reading would be too harsh. Although it is true that de Gaulle's revisionist European policies failed, it is also true that in the longer run his fundamental assumptions proved powerful and his skepticism about the status quo proved correct. Would not Soviet ideology, empire, and force all erode with time? Would not communism, like all other ideologies, eventually "pass"?[10] And was dealing with Russia not both necessary and inevitable, as de Gaulle's Western allies would soon come to accept? An enlightened Soviet leader (Mikhail Gorbachev), aware of the failure of the Soviet system and the need for better relations with the West, happened to come to power on Mitterrand's watch and not on de Gaulle's. But was it really unreasonable to expect that Khrushchev or Brezhnev would come to realize what Gorbachev eventually realized all too late?

For Charles de Gaulle, a Europe "from the Atlantic to the Urals" made up of nation-states but inevitably interdependent, would be a more natural, lasting, and satisfactory state of affairs than a continent divided into two opposing blocs. He may have prematurely judged conditions ready for this Europe to come about, but he also understood that in the longer run the continent's bipolar division could not be a permanent arrangement. His "Europe beyond the blocs" was not a cynical adage that hid a secret preference for the status quo but a genuine goal that he sought, albeit in vain, to bring about.

GAULLIST MILITARY LOGIC AND THE NEW EUROPE

If de Gaulle's vision of the future was fairly prescient, how well did he prepare France for the European situation that he thought would inevitably come about? Did de Gaulle, as is often said, take advantage of the short-term protection provided by the United States as he created the military and political structures necessary for the longer term, or were his policies simply more appropriate to a nostalgic past than to the present or to the future? How well is Gaullist military logic, as examined in earlier chapters, holding up in the Europe that appears to be evolving today?

Somewhat perversely, as relatively accurate as de Gaulle's geopolitical intuitions were, the security policies with which he left France do not seem particularly appropriate for the very world he in many ways envisaged and desired. However grand the Gaullist adventure was, however useful in giving the downhearted French something in which to believe, and however fundamentally right de Gaulle's argument about the injustices of the bipolar world, it seems increasingly clear in the 1990s that the model on which French security policy has been based since the early 1960s is no longer well-suited for the present European context. In a number of ways, the end of the Cold War has condemned some of de Gaulle's most important hopes and expectations for France and has called into question some of the fundamental assumptions of the Gaullist national security model.

The first apparent failure of the Gaullist vision of Europe's future has to do with the relative power and stature of France itself. In the mid-1960s, it was quite plausible to believe that France was on its way to becoming the leading power in Western Europe and that its economic and political fortunes were increasing rather than in continued long-term decline. De Gaulle had replaced the weak and unstable Fourth Republic with a new one designed to facilitate strong leadership, had extracted the country from its debilitating Algerian war, and through his own heroism had restored the faith and hopes of his compatriots. Moreover, and more importantly, French economic growth rates during the Gaullist years were among the highest in Western Europe; from 1960 to 1968, for example, France's GDP grew at an annual rate of 5.4 percent to Germany's 4.1 percent.[11] With France's birthrate also significantly higher than that of its neighbors, it was not impossible to believe that France would come to surpass West Germany (unification seeming unlikely anytime soon) as not only the richest but also the most populous West European state. For the greater part of his presidency, de Gaulle's belief in the possibility of a French-led Europe was not simply a function of nationalistic conceit.

In the 1990s, however, such aspirations for France seem nostalgic at best. The French economy, first thrown off track by the economic crisis of 1968 and unable to respond as well as West Germany to the oil shocks of 1973 and 1979, has not kept up its impressive past growth, and French GDP in 1989 was still 24 percent less than the Federal Republic's. With German unification in 1990, Germany's GDP is now close to 40 percent greater than France's, and if recovery in eastern Germany proves a success, this gap will only increase. Unification has also prevented France from "catching up" demographically, and Germany now has nearly 80 million inhabitants to France's 56 million.[12] De Gaulle's reasonable hope that France would be the strongest European economic as well as nuclear power is no longer realistic.

A second and related element of the Gaullist vision that may now be out of date is the General's belief that France could compensate for German economic superiority—to the extent that Germany maintained the larger economy—with French military and political power. De Gaulle came from an era in which national power was measured more by military prowess than by economic performance, and he was confident that France's military power and political prestige were at least as important as German economic success. What the General apparently failed to see, however, was that French military superiority was only an advantage so long as Germany was concerned about its security in the east and its legitimacy in the west. Now that de Gaulle's own aspiration for a united Europe has largely come about, the security relationship he so carefully cultivated with the Federal Republic has lost much of its importance. Germany, united and fully sovereign, no longer needs what France had most to offer—political legitimacy in Europe and (to a lesser extent) military support. Indeed, it could now be argued that France in the 1990s is today endowed with a great nuclear arsenal and global military role about which most Germans could not care less, while Germany, in turn, is concentrating on producing goods, building trade surpluses, and accumulating wealth, the true sources of power in the decades to come. France may have the Inflexible, the Hadès and a garrison in Djibouti, but Germany has Siemens, the Bundesbank, and Daimler-Benz.

A third and very specific area in which the Gaullist model seems out of step with post–Cold War security requirements in Europe is nuclear deterrence. The force de frappe was primarily an effort to augment French status, prestige, and ultimately security in de Gaulle's own time, but the General—with his pessimistic, Hobbesian assumptions about enduring struggle among states—probably believed that France would need an autonomous nuclear force even once Europe's bipolar division had been overcome. His arguments about the need for an autonomous nuclear force in Europe were usually based on the argument that no one could predict what the world would look like twenty or thirty years hence (when the American interest in European security might not be so acute), and he assumed that when such a time came the French nuclear force would be more relevant than ever.

A look at the present European situation challenges these assumptions. As the past forty years have demonstrated, nuclear weapons may be useful deterrents against other nuclear weapons and against direct invasions, but they are not very useful against anything else. With the Warsaw Pact disbanded and Russia apparently on the path toward some sort of pro-Western democracy, it is difficult to imagine just what country's army might directly invade French territory or even plausibly threaten to do so. And although the breakup of the Soviet Union has produced at least three new nuclear powers in Eurasia, it is also difficult to see what sort of military conflicts could arise between France and the new nuclear states. Finally, even if nuclear proliferation continues in the Third World, a French threat of massive retaliation may not be the most effective or appropriate means of deterring an irrational rogue or terrorist state. As will be suggested, some sort of French nuclear force, ideally "Europeanized" in one way or another, is probably worth maintaining, but it nonetheless seems clear that France's absolute priority on the force de frappe—and the military spending choices that priority implied—must be rethought in a world where limited conventional battles, peacekeeping roles, and humanitarian interventions seem much more likely than any sort of nuclear war. As the Persian Gulf War so starkly showed, thirty years of emphasis on the strategic nuclear deterrent has left French conventional forces relatively poorly prepared for the sorts of missions for which they are now most likely to be employed.

De Gaulle's emphasis on national independence, the cornerstone of his defense policy, is a fourth element of the Gaullist model that no longer seems so appropriate in the post–Cold War world. As I have argued in this book, France's "isolation" from its Atlantic and European partners has often been exaggerated, and the Gulf War also showed that France's insistence on "independence of decision" does not mean that French decisions will be different from those of its allies. This would be all the more true in a European crisis. Still, it is uncontestable that the will to be independent has prevented France from taking full advantage of the potential benefits of Atlantic and European integration, and it seems increasingly absurd that a country like France procures 95 percent of its military forces domestically. When one considers the sorts of diplomatic and military crises that are likely in the post–Cold War era, it is difficult to imagine the areas in which France will want to—or be able to—act alone.

Finally, the end of the Cold War has also challenged the value of the Gaullist legacy in the one area in which it was most unquestionably successful, the psychological one. As military power becomes increasingly less useful as a means of influence in international affairs, the French, who have long associated their national stature with the possession of military power, have come to question the legitimacy and utility of such an association. They have begun to wonder whether the "grandeur" they have heard so much about since de Gaulle's time may not have been an illusion and whether it should still be an important goal in an economically oriented world. Indeed, the malaise that overcame France in the early 1990s—demonstrated by the unpopularity of all the major political parties, the periodic student and working class protests, the growing anxiety about a potential Fifth Republic constitutional crisis, and the rise in support for the extremist National Front—was in part the result of a fear that France entered the 1990s unprepared on the economic terrain that counts. Could it be that de Gaulle, a product of the nineteenth century with a reputed disdain for economics, placed all of France's eggs in the nuclear, diplomatic, and military baskets but failed to see that those baskets would bring little in the marketplaces of the twenty-first century? The French, nearly united in their support for Gaullist defense policies since the late 1970s, began in the early 1990s to wonder whether those very policies did not leave them seriously unprepared to play a major role in the very world that de Gaulle held forth as France's salvation.

The military legacy left by General de Gaulle, then, is scarcely flawless, and the French would be well advised to ask themselves if the Gaullist model should continue to serve as the basis for their defense and security policy. De Gaulle's alleged "anachronism," however, should not be exaggerated, and several important points should be brought to mind before any definitive conclusions are reached.

First, one should not forget that de Gaulle left power in 1969, and that analysts today study him from the perspective of the 1990s. As much as the General talked about preparing France for the future, he cannot be held responsible for the way his ideas have been implemented by his successors, no matter how much they have referred to his name and example. Charles de Gaulle the national leader should be judged first by his accomplishments and failures in his own time, and when one asks how appropriate his ideas are thirty years after he held them one should be aware of the difficult criteria one is applying.

Second, and more specifically, it would be wrong to argue that de Gaulle's France was excessively profligate in the military domain and that it squandered its resources to the detriment of the economy. To be sure, de Gaulle and his successors poured significant amounts of money into the creation and maintenance of a national nuclear force. But as discussed in chapter 2, the French nuclear force was paid for through cutbacks in conventional forces rather than with new spending, and overall military budgets declined regularly from the early Gaullist years on. French military spending as a share of GDP in the Gaullist and post-Gaullist period was consistently less than Great Britain's, only slightly more than Germany's, and often less than half of those of the United States. De Gaulle—who after all staked his life in 1940 on the conviction that Western economic power would prove more decisive than German military prowess—was very sensitive to the role of the economy as a factor in international power. If, in the 1990s, his views about national industrial policy seem out of fashion, his views about the importance of industry are not so at all.

Third, as suggested earlier, Gaullist views on the need for nuclear deterrence in Europe may not yet be irrelevant. As long as nuclear weapons exist in the world (which will probably be for a long time) and as long as they proliferate (which may be longer than most people would like), France and its allies in Western Europe will probably want some sort of autonomous nuclear capability as an ultimate recourse, and without such a capability they could find themselves in a position of not only military but potential political vulnerability. With the long-term U.S. role in European security still uncertain, the existence within Western Europe of an autonomous nuclear capability is probably an insurance policy worth keeping intact, and de Gaulle may one day be appreciated for having endowed Europe with its own means of nuclear deterrence.

Finally, although the post–Cold War world will certainly be marked by growing international integration and interdependence, the role of the nation and of national military forces cannot yet be done away with. If one lesson of the Persian Gulf War was that even great nations can no longer act alone in an interdependent world, another was that multinational military forces are only as good as the sum of their parts. It was, after all, not the United Nations that defeated the Iraqi army, but the United States along with the allies that fought under its command. Both the Gulf War and the civil war in Yugoslavia, moreover, have also demonstrated that Europeans—for all their progress toward unity—still do not have completely common international interests and views. Not even the most profoundly "European" Frenchman can be sure that an Islamic insurrection in North Africa or a civil war in Eastern Europe would be perceived in the same fashion in Paris as it would in Berlin. The creation of a powerful United Nations Security Council, a functioning CSCE, and a truly integrated European defense are all worthy goals that one hopes will continue to reduce the need for uniquely national military organizations. None of these goals, however, have yet been fully achieved, and it would be naive and premature to dismiss the need for decisive and independent national political and military decisions.

In sum, the most reasonable conclusion about de Gaulle's military legacy and the post–Cold War world is not that de Gaulle failed to foresee the security requirements of the sort of world he envisaged but that the "Gaullist model," implemented flexibly but without fundamental modifications for more than thirty years, must be brought up to date in the wake of revolutionary geopolitical change. As I have argued throughout this book, after all, one of the most important lessons of the Gaullist model itself is that policies and doctrines should be based on a sober and realistic assessment of circumstances and that if changing events should ever prove one's past assumptions wrong, the policies should be changed. It would be absurd to think—and de Gaulle himself would never have so thought—that the force structures, military doctrines, and alliance relationships that de Gaulle designed for France in the 1960s should be maintained in the same form today. Thus, to say that some fundamental Gaullist insights still seem valid is not to say that Gaullist policies need not be fundamentally revised, and it would be unfortunate (although not unprecedented) if a narrow reading of the General's legacy were to prevent France from adapting to changing conditions. It would be no small irony if the man who made his name in the 1930s by criticizing France's out-moded military doctrines should come to leave such doctrines as a legacy of his own.

RECONCILING DE GAULLE WITH EUROPE

The question of adapting Gaullist security policies to a very new environment raises once again some of the fundamental questions with which this book began: Is a Gaullist defense policy compatible with the need for France to contribute to the common security of Western Europe? Can France now begin to pursue more far-reaching European cooperation without betraying the national heritage of Charles de Gaulle? Is there anything about the new situation in Europe that makes it more likely that France can now finally accept more extensive European defense coopera-tion than in the past? The difficulty French leaders have had in reconciling the national requirements of their Gaullist legacy with their growing de-sire to cooperate in Europe and the growing need for them to do so has been apparent throughout this book. But when the Gaullist view of Euro-pean defense is reassessed in light of recent events, it is by no means clear that the Gaullist model and European defense are irreconcilable concepts.

It is true, of course, that Charles de Gaulle always put *French* independ-ence first and European second and that he was in no circumstances willing to let his country play a subordinate role. Throughout World War II and then into the 1950s and 1960s, de Gaulle was much more con-cerned with augmenting French status within the Western Alliance than in ensuring the most efficient functioning of that alliance. Convinced by the mid-1950s that war was unlikely anyway, de Gaulle took advantage of propitious circumstances to concentrate on elevating French rank while he left the duties of defending Western Europe to others.

De Gaulle always believed, moreover, that questions of domestic poli-cies and economics should be decided in a national context, not under the influence of supranational institutions. He would doubtless continue to believe that where agricultural subsidies or national investment policy was concerned, European states had sometimes competing interests and that those interests should be traded off at the bargaining table, not de-cided by unelected European Community bureaucrats. The idea that a British commissioner in Brussels might tell the French government whether or not it could subsidize Renault would surely have gone against the grain of the man who nationalized that firm in 1945; one will never know if de Gaulle would ever have been able to accept the sharing of French economic sovereignty that the European Community of the 1990s entails.

Yet for all this, the concept of a much closer European Union—one that would deal even with the primordial questions of security and defense—is not alien to the Gaullist view of Europe and the world. On the contrary, de Gaulle never failed to argue that although European states had to maintain ultimate control over their own fates and the ability to decide for themselves, they also had an abiding interest in getting together to form a stronger force in the world. De Gaulle did argue for and try to create a European entity, and if his design for that entity was very different from the one proposed by his opponents, it was not thereby insincere or merely a diversionary ploy. De Gaulle's vision of European unity was also, it should be remembered, a dynamic one: "[If] we go down this path," he argued about his plan for a European confederation, ". . . links will multiply, habits will form, and then, with time doing its work, little by little, it is possible that new steps will be taken toward European unity."[13] The European states would begin by developing "the habit of living and acting together," and over time, step by step, they would develop common practices and common views.[14]

There is, of course, no way of knowing how de Gaulle's thoughts and actions on European unification would have evolved into the 1970s, 1980s, and 1990s. And surely, his specific ambitions for France often got in the way of progress toward his own European goals. But it is clear that de Gaulle was interested in a European security arrangement, and it requires no great leap of faith to imagine the General supporting some such arrangement today. Indeed, looking at how the world has changed over the past two decades—and, particularly, over the past two or three years—the notion of closer European defense cooperation seems much more compatible with Gaullist perspectives than it ever was in the past. Many of the justifications that de Gaulle had for insisting so strongly upon French *national* defense during the 1960s have been attenuated, and some have even disappeared.

First, as explained in the preceding chapters, de Gaulle objected not so much to NATO itself but primarily to the fact that is was so heavily dominated by the United States. Because France's role in this massive, American-led organization would be no more that a highly subordinate one subject to the leadership of others, de Gaulle refused to play much of a role at all. France was barely more than a defeated nation of World War II, and de Gaulle refused to let it sink into a subordinate position that would only breed irresponsibility and resentment. (Neither the General's predecessors nor his successors, it might be added, were much more willing to do so.) De Gaulle's nationalism and pride, useful or not, precluded

France's accepting the only sort of European defense that was available at the time—one led and dominated by the United States.

In the 1990s, however, it is far less likely that European defense—even if NATO itself continues to exist—will be so dominated by Washington. Although nobody knows which of the old security structures in Western Europe will survive, it is safe to assume that there will be some such structures and that they will be more European- and less American-led than in the past. The United States, financially strapped, already in the process of reducing its troops in Europe, and no longer driven by a Communist threat, seems unlikely to maintain its hegemonic postwar role. A united Germany, for all its economic and financial power, is probably neither well disposed nor well suited to lead a military coalition or play the role of Europe's face on the world. Great Britain, with France Europe's other nuclear and "global" power, is probably neither committed enough to Europe nor rich enough to play such roles. In such a context, France— with its history of global activity and influence, its relatively large armed forces, its defense technology base, and its political and military ambitions—seems indispensable to any new European security arrangements.

To be sure, France's role in a European defense system would not be the primordial one that de Gaulle had always assumed to be natural, and France's allies in such an arrangement would not, in the 1990s, look to Paris to "trace out the plan and appoint the leader," as de Gaulle had once hoped.[15] A brooding General, were he still around, might shoot down European defense as he threatened to shoot down the European Community in the mid-1960s, using a version of what Alfred Grosser has called the language of Samson: "If I cannot have it my way, than I'll bring the whole structure down, and you value its existence more than I do!"[16] But it is more likely that de Gaulle, whose expectations for France were probably never as great as the rhetoric he used to exhort the French, would have recognized that if France's role would not be the dominant one he had always imagined, it would probably be important enough to be worth playing. France would be a major actor with maximum influence over its fate; that is what its leaders have always wanted it to be.

A second reason de Gaulle objected to NATO and U.S. hegemony was that he feared that in such an organization France and the Europeans would be subject to American decisions, whims, and mistakes that could easily run counter to their interests. Examples of these included American "adventurism" in Vietnam and U.S. commitments in the Middle East or Asia that risked setting off an East-West war in Europe that the Europeans would not want. At the same time, the Americans would control the military strategy with which that war would be fought: they would decide whether or not it would be a nuclear war and could even choose to limit the battle fighting to European soil. De Gaulle wanted no part of a bind-ing organization that might drag Europeans into a war they did not want to fight and make them fight it on terms they could not choose.

Again, such concerns seem far less important today. The American global battle with the Soviet Union is finally over, and, in any case, even very hypothetical U.S.-Russian conflicts in the Third World are unlikely to spill over onto the European continent as was feared in the past. Even if the Persian Gulf crisis raised again the specter of Washington deciding alone whether to start a war and how to fight it (which the French still strongly resist), European security is not put directly at risk as it might have been when the Soviets would have automatically been on the other side. The Americans are in the process of reducing their deployment in Europe by at least one-half in the coming several years, may be required (for budgetary or political reasons) to reduce it by much more than that, and are already committed to extensive devolution of responsibilities within the Western Alliance. They have also abandoned the military doctrine of flexible response, which, after all, was so critical (rhetorically, at least) in de Gaulle's decision to leave NATO commands in the first place. The Gaullist concern that Washington would control the fate, action, or inaction of a future European defense organization has largely been removed.

A third reason de Gaulle and his successors were reluctant to accept a more far-reaching European defense is that "Europe," as a concept, institution, and political reality, was at the time still relatively embryonic. As seen in chapter 1, de Gaulle's argument was that it had taken European states one thousand years to grow into distinct entities and that it would, thus, take a lot longer than a couple of decades for them to fuse into a single entity or anything even close to one. De Gaulle believed—and his successors have all explicitly agreed—that a common European defense could not precede the creation of a common European polity and that the latter was still some years away. Europe, of course, remains a long way from the single, homogeneous political community a Charles de Gaulle would have believed necessary to the creation of a completely common defense. But even the General would have to admit that the last forty years have seen a spectacular harmonization of interests in Europe and the development of the sort of interstate cooperation he always claimed to support. The old colonial empires that once divided European interests are gone, cultural and political histories have been harmonized by the Cold War and through the European Community, European economies have converged in both policy and production terms, and most important of all, the habit of doing things together—the *reflexe communautaire*— has become a very real part of European thinking. The West European grouping of the 1990s is surely a more propitious terrain on which to try to organize a common defense than was the collection of former enemy nations that were just beginning to cooperate during the 1950s and into the 1960s.

A fourth obstacle to a European defense along Gaullist lines has always been that such a defense required, or at least seemed to require, the sort of massive, integrated organization that de Gaulle believed violated national needs. Because postwar Russia was so abnormally powerful and the old European powers were so relatively weak, European security could only be ensured by building up an ungainly alliance that arranged multinational forces all along a vulnerable central front. If de Gaulle already believed in the 1960s that such a mechanism was unnecessary, his neighbors all disagreed, and their desire for security was incompatible with the Gaullist aversion to integration. Today, multinational military integration seems both more possible and less necessary. It is more possible for all the reasons just given about European defense in general, but it is less necessary because the military threat has been so greatly reduced. If the French continue for whatever reason to find military integration anathema or incompatible with their national principles, this should not be the obstacle to European defense it always was in the past. With the Soviet threat gone and nothing similar likely to take its place, a true common European defense need no longer be built around multinational units and permanently integrated commands.

Finally, and perhaps most importantly, in the 1990s, a Gaullist France should be better disposed to enter into an arrangement for European defense because France itself is much better prepared for it than in the past. The country de Gaulle inherited was ideologically divided, militarily weak, nonnuclear, inflationary, and insecure, and it would remain so for some time. Progressively, the Fifth Republic has become a rather stable democratic regime (recent French apprehensions notwithstanding), France's economy has become more than respectable, and the French can be proud of their political, technological, and social accomplishments. De Gaulle proclaimed so frequently the *redressement* of France after 1945 and 1958 because he knew deep down that it had yet to be fully realized. And as has arguably become apparent with the breakup of the Soviet Union and Yugoslavia, a country must establish (or reestablish) its sovereignty before it can willingly share it. Because de Gaulle so emphatically accomplished the first of these tasks, the second now seems much more realizable.

This set of arguments that a major French role in European defense is more conceivable now that France would be among its leaders should obviously not be taken to suggest that France can somehow replace the United States as the protector of Western Europe and the gendarme for its interests abroad. As has been seen, even in the context of the *Pax Americana*, France was already unable to afford all of its self-appointed roles.

Credible strategic and tactical nuclear forces, flexible and well-armed conventional forces, a navy capable of projecting French force abroad, and a prominent French role in space and military technology were difficult if not incompatible goals for a country of France's size and resources, and they led to predicaments and disputes over military budgets and strategies that may have become insurmountable by the late 1980s. Moreover, it is unlikely that other West European countries would be willing to accept France as an outright leader of their military alliance; they were never willing to in the past, and there is no reason they would be willing to today. French means are certainly not equal to American ones, and French military "hegemony" is no more attractive or tolerable than American.

Yet, if France clearly cannot play all the security roles formerly assumed by the United States, Europe may not be able to afford to neglect them. And surely, a united Europe of 340 million or more people and a greater combined gross product than any other region in the world can afford the means necessary to ensure its security and interests in the world in the decades to come. This does not mean that Europe is now ready to rush into the adoption of a new version of the federalist European Defense Community that failed in 1954. The political prerequisites for such an organization are probably closer to existing today than they were then, but they are probably still not in place. Instead, the great challenge of the early 1990s is to find a way to implement the sort of far-reaching, cooperative European security organization that de Gaulle always claimed as a goal but was ultimately never willing or able to bring about. Whether the French will fulfill their indispensable role in this European defense only the future will reveal. But if the arguments here have any merit, they will not be able to use their Gaullist legacy as an excuse not to do so.

Notes

Preface

1. Nearly two thousand books, in forty-five countries, have been written about de Gaulle. According to the Institut Charles de Gaulle, in France alone more than six hundred works on the General had been published by 1989 before the proliferation during the 1990 anniversary of his birth. See André Passeron, "Près de deux mille ouvrages, déjà," *Le Monde*, March 19, 1990; and *Le Point*, September 5–11, 1988.

2. For specific references, see the bibliography and chapter 1.

3. These authors are all cited in chapters 4 to 6.

4. See Patrick McCarthy, "France Faces Reality: *Rigueur* and the Germans," in David P. Calleo and Claudia Morgenstern, eds., *Recasting Europe's Economies: National Strategies in the 1980s* (Lanham, Md.: University Press of America, 1990), p. 68.

Chapter One
Perspectives on de Gaulle

1. The best examples of this view are those of Stanley Hoffmann, in particular the essays found in *Decline or Renewal? France since the 1930s* (New York: Viking Press, 1974); and Jean Lacouture, *De Gaulle*, vol. 1, *Le rebelle* (Paris: Editions du Seuil, 1984); *De Gaulle*, vol. 2, *Le politique* (Paris: Editions du Seuil, 1985); and *De Gaulle*, vol. 3, *Le souverain* (Paris: Editions du Seuil, 1986).

2. See the works of Alfred Grosser, notably *La IVe République et sa politique extérieure* (Paris: Librairie Armand Colin, 1961; 3d ed. 1972); idem, *La politique extérieure de la Ve République* (Paris: Editions du Seuil, 1965); and idem, *Affaires extérieures: La politique de la France 1944–1984* (Paris: Flammarion, 1984). See also Jean Touchard, *Le gaullisme: 1940–1969* (Paris: Editions du Seuil, 1978).

3. See, for example, John Newhouse, *De Gaulle and the Anglo-Saxons* (New York: Viking Press, 1970); Alexander Werth, *De Gaulle*, new ed., (Baltimore, Md.: Penguin Books, 1967); and Robert Aron, *An Explanation of de Gaulle* (New York: Harper and Row, 1966).

4. See Lacouture, *De Gaulle* 3:7.

5. See, for example, Michael M. Harrison, *The Reluctant Ally: France and Atlantic Security* (Baltimore, Md.: Johns Hopkins University Press, 1981); Edgar S. Furniss, Jr., *De Gaulle and the French Army: A Crisis in Civil-Military Relations* (New York: Twentieth Century Fund, 1964); and Grosser, *La Ve République*.

6. Paul Kennedy, *The Rise and Fall of the Great Powers: Economic Change and Military Conflict from 1500 to 2000* (New York: Random House, 1987), p. 402.

7. Charles de Gaulle, *Mémoires d'espoir*, vol. 1, *Le renouveau, 1958–1962* (Paris: Plon, 1970), p. 7.

8. On the true Russian nature of the Soviet Union, for example, de Gaulle once explained: "You scratch a little bit, and you think you find Marx and Lenin. But no! You discover Gogol and Tarass Boulba." Perhaps even more prescient was this comment: "I do not know if Khruschchev's successor will be Marxist, Leninist, Maoist, Titoist *or, who knows, capitalist.* All I can affirm is that he will be Russian." Cited in Pierre Viansson-Ponté, *Histoire de la République gaullienne: Mai 1958–avril 1969* (Paris: Robert Laffont, 1984), p. 177 [emphasis added].

9. See de Gaulle, *Mémoires de guerre*, vol. 1, *L'appel, 1940–1942* (Paris: Plon, 1954), p. 232.

10. See Charles de Gaulle, *La discorde chez l'ennemi* (Paris: Librairie Berger-Levrault, 1924); idem, *Le fil de l'épée* (Paris: Librairie Berger-Levrault, 1932), published in English as *The Edge of the Sword* (New York: Criterion Books, 1960); and idem, *Vers l'armée de métier* (Paris: Librairie Berger-Levrault), published in English as *The Army of the Future* (Philadelphia: Lippincott, 1941).

11. De Gaulle claims in his war memoirs that he announced future colonial independence to President Truman as early as August, 1945. But as Jean Touchard points out, this revelation comes fourteen years after the fact and is published just after de Gaulle's September 1959 declaration on Algerian self-determination. A careful examination of de Gaulle's positions on Indochina in the 1940s and Africa in the 1950s gives little indication that the General was prepared to accept the dissolution of the French empire. For de Gaulle's claim, see his *Mémoires de guerre*, vol. 3, *Le salut, 1944–1946*, paperback ed., (Paris: Plon, 1959), p. 249. For Touchard see *Le gaullisme*, p. 85. On de Gaulle's early positions on "the Empire," see Touchard, *Le gaullisme*, pp. 117–19; Lacouture, *De Gaulle* 3:154–83; Werth, *De Gaulle*, pp. 255–82; and Jean-Pierre Rioux, *La France de la Quatrième République*, vol. 1, *I. L'ardeur et la nécessité, 1944–1952* (Paris: Editions du Seuil, 1980), pp. 127–28.

12. De Gaulle, *Mémoires de guerre* 3:45–47. For de Gaulle's early postwar views on "the German Problem," see Pierre Maillard, *De Gaulle et l'Allemagne: Le rêve inachevé* (Paris: Plon, 1990), pp. 83–118; Alfred Grosser, *La IVe République*, pp. 136–41, 210–12; and F. Roy Willis, *France, Germany and the New Europe: 1945–1967*, rev. ed. (London: Oxford University Press, 1968), pp. 15–16.

13. De Gaulle's comments on German unification and the conditions under which it should take place actually seem quite prescient in retrospect: "The reunification of the two fractions into a single Germany, which would be completely free, seems to us to be the normal destiny of the German people, provided that [Germany] does not question her present borders . . . and that she inclines toward integrating herself into a contractual organization of all Europe for cooperation, liberty and peace" (de Gaulle's March 25, 1959, press conference in *Discours et messages* 3:84–85).

14. See Raymond Aron, *Mémoires: 50 ans de réflexion politique* (Paris: Julliard, 1983), p. 254.

15. From a February 1960 speech to the general assembly of the Conseil d'Etat. Cited in Edmond Pognon, *De Gaulle et l'histoire de France* (Paris: Albin Michel, 1970), p. 252.

16. Press Conference of September 5, 1960, see de Gaulle, *Discours et messages* 3:244–45.

17. See de Gaulle's November 3, 1959, speech to the Ecole Militaire, ibid., 3:126.

18. Press Conference of September 5, 1960, ibid., 3:245.

19. Cited in Touchard, *Le gaullisme*, p. 309.

20. As Renan put it in his *Qu'est-ce qu'une nation?*, "The existence of a nation is a daily plebiscite." See the texts and commentary in Raoul Girardet, *Le nationalisme français* (Paris: Editions du Seuil, 1983), pp. 62–69.

21. Press conference of September 5, 1960, see de Gaulle, *Discours et messages* 3:245.

22. Grosser, *La IVe République*, p. 231.

23. For Drieu La Rochelle, see Raoul Girardet, ed., *La Defense de l'Europe* (Brussels: Editions Complexe, 1988), p. 164. For Toynbee, see Arnold J. Toynbee, *A Study of History* (London: Oxford University Press, 1940). For Carr, see Edward Hallet Carr, *Nationalism and After* (London: Macmillan, 1965), p. 51. For Herz, see John H. Herz, "The Rise and Demise of the Territorial State," *World Politics* 9 (July 1957): 474. On the decline of the nation-state in general, see Ernst B. Haas, *Beyond the Nation State* (Stanford, Calif.: Stanford University Press, 1964).

24. The was an argument made frequently by the early "Europeans." See, for example, Robert Schuman, *Pour l'Europe* (Paris: Editions Nagel, 1964), esp. pp. 28–29.

25. De Gaulle, *Mémoires de guerre* 1:1.

26. See, in particular, Hoffmann, *Decline or Renewal?*; and Lacouture, *De Gaulle*, vol. 3.

27. De Gaulle, *Mémoires de guerre* 1:1.

28. From a speech in Bordeaux on April 15, 1961, as cited by Jean-Baptiste Duroselle, "Changes in French Foreign Policy since 1945," in Stanley Hoffmann, et al., *In Search of France: The Economy, Society, and Political System in the Twentieth Century* (New York: Harper and Row, 1963), p. 352.

29. From General de Gaulle's New Year's speech to the French people of December 31, 1963, see de Gaulle, *Discours et messages* 4:155 (emphasis added).

30. From a radio-TV speech from the Elysée on December 31, 1967. See ibid., 5:252.

31. Speech given at the Hôtel de Ville in Paris on June 18, 1959. See ibid., 3:98.

32. Televised speech from the Elysée, March 26, 1962, ibid., 3:396–97.

33. Lacouture, *De Gaulle* 3:315.

34. See Hoffmann, "De Gaulle's Memoirs: The Hero of History," in *Decline or Renewal?*, p. 196.

35. Odile Rudelle, *Mai 1958: La République* (Paris: Institut Charles de Gaulle, 1988).

36. The study of French and other authors' influence on de Gaulle has been a cottage industry in the literature of Gaullism. Two interesting general discussions can be found in Touchard, *Le gaullisme*, pp. 291–343; and Lacouture, *De Gaulle* 1:34–56 (esp). On de Gaulle's place in the French Right in general, see René Rémond, *Les droites en France* (Paris: Aubier, 1982), pp. 313–49.

37. De Gaulle, *Mémoires de guerre* 1:2.

38. See Harrison, *Reluctant Ally*, p. 49. Along the same lines, Stanley Hoffmann has written that "Independence is the condition of grandeur." See Stanley Hoffmann, "De Gaulle, Europe, and the Atlantic Alliance," *International Organization* 18 (Winter 1964): 2.

39. See, for example, Newhouse, *De Gaulle and the Anglo-Saxons*; Edward L. Morse, *Foreign Policy and Interdependence in Gaullist France* (Princeton, N.J.: Princeton University Press, 1972); Werth, *De Gaulle*; Jean François Révél, *Le style du général: Précédé de la légende vivante au mythe posthume* (Paris: Editions Complexe, 1988); and Robert Aron, *Explanation of de Gaulle*.

40. See Newhouse, *De Gaulle and the Anglo-Saxons*, p. 52.

41. Robert Aron, *Explanation of De Gaulle*, p. 188; and Révél, "De Gaulle: Le droit à l'erreur," *Le Point*, Septembre 5–11, 1988, pp. 52–53.

42. From an Elysée press conference of October 28, 1966. See de Gaulle, *Discours et messages* 4:97–98.

43. De Gaulle, *Mémoires d'espoir* 1:177.

44. De Gaulle, *Mémoires de guerre* 1:70. Translation taken from Charles de Gaulle, *War Memoirs*, vol. 1, *The Call to Honor*, trans. Jonathan Griffin (New York: Viking Press, 1955), pp. 88–89.

45. De Gaulle, *Mémoires de guerre* 1:209.

46. For the classic statement of this argument, see de Gaulle's November 3, 1959, Ecole Militaire speech, *Discours et messages* 3:126. The statement on defense as "the first duty of the state" is from de Gaulle's press conference of June 30, 1955, ibid., 2:645.

47. Ibid., 3:127.

48. The episode that comes to mind in particular here is the American willingness to evacuate Strasbourg for strategic reasons toward the end of World War II, leaving it open to a Nazi reoccupation. De Gaulle recognized the American logic from a global or from an American point of view but protested that such logic intolerably negated the interests of France and, especially, of the Strasbourgeois. He was not convinced that similar circumstances would not arise if another European war were to break out. See de Gaulle's perspective of the Strasbourg incident in his *Mémoires de guerre* 3:168–77.

Chapter Two
The Missing Pillar

1. See Harrison, *Reluctant Ally*, p. 153.

2. See General André Beaufre, *NATO and Europe*, trans. Joseph Green (New York: Alfred A. Knopf, 1966), pp. 37–38.

3. Indicative of this feeling was Gaston Monnerville's argument to the Constit-

uent Assembly in May 1945: "Without the Empire, France today would be no more than a liberated country. Thanks to her Empire, France is a victorious country." Cited in Grosser, *Affaires extérieures*, p. 39.

4. See Allan B. Cole, *Conflict in Indochina and International Repercussions* (Ithaca, N.Y.: Cornell University Press, 1956), p. 259.

5. Total Marshall Plan grants and loans to France were about four billion dollars. See Jean Godard, "L'Aide américaine à la France," *Revue de science financière* 17, no. 3 (July–September 1956): 446.

6. See Jean Planchais, "Le tournant de 1958," *Pouvoirs*, no. 38 (1986): 6.

7. North Atlantic Council, "Resolution to Implement Section IV of the Final Act of the London Conference" (para. 4), in North Atlantic Treaty Organization, *NATO: Facts and Figures* (Brussels: NATO Information Service, 1971), p. 330.

8. See Planchais, "Le tournant de 1958," p. 8.

9. The remaining one-third division was Canadian. See International Institute for Strategic Studies, *The Military Balance* (London: International Institute for Strategic Studies, 1959), p. 8 [hereafter cited as IISS].

10. See Lothar Ruehl, *La politique militaire de la Ve République* (Paris: Presses de la Fondation Nationale des Sciences Politiques, 1976), pp. 328–30.

11. Herriot was cited by Socialist René Mayer during the 1949 NATO debates in Washington. See Grosser, *La IVe République*, p. 228.

12. See Raymond Aron, "French Public Opinion and the Atlantic Treaty," *International Affairs*, no. 1 (January 1952): 1–8; J. B. Duroselle, "The Crisis in French Foreign Policy," *The Review of Politics* 16, no. 4 (October 1954): 412–37; and John T. Marcus, *Neutralism and Nationalism in France: A Case Study* (New York: Bookman Associates, 1958).

13. See General Paul Ely's "Pourquoi l'Indochine," in his *L'armée dans la nation* (Paris: Arthème Fayard, 1961) p. 159 (essay originally published in *Défense nationale* in 1954); and Deputy André Mutter in Assemblée Nationale *Journal officiel de la République française*, [hereafter cited as *Journal officiel*], June 10, 1949, p. 3,298.

14. See Vincent Auriol, *Mon septennat: 1947–1954*, journal entries selected by Pierre Nora and Jacques Ozouf (Paris: Gallimard, 1970), p. 44.

15. See Brigadier Kenneth Hunt, *NATO without France: The Military Implications*, Adelphi Paper no. 32 (London: IISS, 1966), p. 10.

16. For arguments that the difference between the Fourth and Fifth Republic's security policies was essentially one of style and tone, see Grosser, *La Ve République* p. 25; and David P. Calleo, *The Atlantic Fantasy: The U.S., NATO, and Europe* (Baltimore, Md.: Johns Hopkins Press, 1970), p. 60.

17. For good, comprehensive narratives of Gaullist security policy, see Harrison, *Reluctant Ally*; Ruehl, *Politique militaire*; and Wilfred L. Kohl, *French Nuclear Diplomacy* (Princeton, N.J.: Princeton University Press, 1971).

18. Lacouture, *De Gaulle* 3:474.

19. From a speech at Nîmes on January 7, 1951, de Gaulle, *Discours et messages* 2:405.

20. See de Gaulle's speech to a meeting of the RPF in Nancy on November 25, 1951, *Discours et messages* 2:478.

21. See Grosser, *La IVe République*, p. 393.

22. See de Gaulle's May 15, 1962, press conference in *Discours et messages* 3:413.

23. For some earlier attempts to assess the costs of the force de frappe, see Kohl, *French Nuclear Diplomacy*, pp. 192–200; and Morse, *Foreign Policy and Interdependence*, pp. 147–203.

24. See Assemblée Nationale, *Projet de loi de programme relative à certains équipements militaires*, no. 784 (Paris: Imprimerie nationale, 1960).

25. On the second program law, see Assemblée Nationale, *Rapport du gouvernement sur le programme d'équipement militaire* (Paris: Imprimerie nationale, 1964); and the detailed analysis in Ruehl, *Politique militaire*, pp. 287–97.

26. See Kohl, *French Nuclear Diplomacy*, p. 198.

27. Several outside observers, by including indirect costs, have estimated the nuclear share to be as high as 35 percent, whereas the government has tended to put the figure closer to 20–25 percent. See the Ministère de la Défense Nationale, *Livre blanc sur la défense nationale* (Paris: Ministère de la Défense Nationale, 1972), 1:63; and Kohl, *French Nuclear Diplomacy*, p. 198.

28. Pierre Messmer, "L'armée de demain," *Revue des deux mondes* (February 15, 1962): 487.

29. See Pierre Messmer, "Notre politique militaire," *Revue de défense nationale* (May 1963): 748–49.

30. See IISS *Strategic Survey 1970–71* (London: IISS, 1971), p. 23; and David S. Yost, "French Defense Budgeting: Executive Dominance and Resource Constraints," *Orbis* 23, no. 3 (Fall 1979): 582.

31. See Guy de Carmoy, *The Foreign Policies of France: 1944–1968* (Chicago: University of Chicago Press, 1970), p. 345.

32. See Wolf Mendl, *Deterrence and Persuasion: French Nuclear Armament in the Context of National Policy, 1945–1969* (London: Faber and Faber, 1970), p. 18.

33. For the Mitterrand citation, (from his 1965 presidential election campaign), see Harrison, *Reluctant Ally*, p. 214.

34. Raymond Aron, *The Great Debate* (New York: Doubleday, 1965), p. 109.

35. See Aron, *Great Debate*, pp. 100–43.

36. Jacques Isnard, *Le Monde*, July 11, 1968. Cited in de Carmoy, *Foreign Policies of France*, p. 345.

37. See Robbin F. Laird, *France, the Soviet Union, and the Nuclear Weapons Issue* (Boulder, Colo.: Westview Press, 1985), p. 93.

38. For an examination of the various "political" rationales for the force de frappe, see Philip H. Gordon, "Charles De Gaulle and the Nuclear Revolution," paper presented at the Nuclear History Program conference "Cold War Statesman and the Nuclear Revolution," Athens, Ohio, September 19, 1991 (forthcoming).

39. De Rose cited in Kohl, *French Nuclear Diplomacy*, p. 78.

40. The first quote is cited in Alexander Werth, *De Gaulle* (Baltimore, Md.: Penguin Books, 1967), p. 343. The second is cited in André Passeron, *De Gaulle parle*, vol. 1, *Des institutions, de l'Algérie, de l'armée, des affaires étrangères, de*

la Communauté, de l'économie et des questions sociales (Paris: Plon, 1962), 1:361.

41. See de Gaulle's speech in Strasbourg in November 1961, *Discours et messages* 3:369.

42. For the first quote, see Lacouture, *De Gaulle*, vol. 3, *Le souverain* p. 298; and for the second, Michel Debré, *Au service de la nation: Essai d'un programme politique* (Paris: Editions Stock, 1963), p. 158.

43. See Pierre Messmer, "Notre politique militaire," p. 760. One can only imagine the French reaction if a German defense minister had written the same words in 1963!

44. See Alexandre Sanguinetti, *La France et l'arme atomique* (Paris: René Julliard, 1964), p. 32.

45. For Furniss, see Edgar S. Furniss, Jr., *De Gaulle and the French Army: A Crisis in Civil-Military Relations* (New York: Twentieth Century Fund, 1964), p. 246 (emphasis added). The notion that France developed certain weapons systems simply to keep the army in line has long been rejected by French officials: "One does not build weapons to keep soldiers happy," Pierre Messmer told me in an October 1988 interview.

46. See Kohl, *French Nuclear Diplomacy*, pp. 3, 6.

47. Edward Kolodziej, *French International Policy under de Gaulle and Pompidou* (Ithaca, N.Y.: Cornell University Press, 1974), p. 102.

48. See Messmer, "Notre politique militaire," p. 761.

49. *Le Monde*, December 4, 1964.

50. Cited by Kolodziej, *French International Policy*, p. 100.

51. Cited in Hubert Beuve-Méry, *Onze ans de règne: 1958–1969* (Paris: Flammarion, 1974), p. 360.

52. See Harrison, *Reluctant Ally*, p. 108.

53. Aron, *Great Debate*, p. 120.

54. See Ambassade de France, *The First Five Years of the Fifth Republic of France, January 1959–January 1964* (New York: Service de Presse et d'Information, 1964), p. 19.

55. From a speech to the American Club of Paris on February 24, 1964. See ibid., p. 193.

56. See Raymond Aron, "Défense européenne," *L'Express*, November 19, 1982, p. 43.

57. See John Lewis Gaddis, *Strategies of Containment: A Critical Appraisal of Postwar American Security Policy* (New York: Oxford University Press, 1982), p. 183.

58. See IISS *Military Balance* (1975–1980); and Edward Luttwak, *The Strategic Balance: 1972*, Washington Papers no. 3 (New York: Library Press, 1972), pp. 18–21.

59. See IISS *Military Balance*, (1969).

60. See Gaddis, *Strategies of Containment*, p. 207.

61. See Robert S. McNamara, "Statement," in United States Department of Defense, *The Fiscal Year 1969–73 Defense Program and the 1969 Defense Budget* (Washington, D.C.: U.S. Government Printing Office, 1968), pp. 27–32, 80–82.

62. From De Gaulle's January 14, 1963, press conference, See *Discours et Messages* 4:73.

63. The notion of America as an "ordinary country" comes from Richard Rosecrance, ed., *America as an Ordinary Country* (Ithaca, N.Y.: Cornell University Press, 1976).

64. From 1938 to 1945, Germany's GNP declined by two-thirds, Italy's by about 40 percent (reverting to the 1911 level), and France's by one-half. Excluding the Soviet Union, Europe's GNP as a whole fell by about 25 percent. See Paul Bairoch, "Europe's Gross National Product: 1800–1975," *Journal of European Economic History* 5 (1976): 291–92; and Paul Kennedy, *Rise and Fall of the Great Powers*, pp. 357–72, 368 (for figures).

65. These costs are what David P. Calleo refers to as the American "imperial deficit." Even with current account surpluses, the U.S. "basic account" (which omits short-term capital flows to consider only the "real" economy—goods, services, and long-term investments) was in deficit, owing largely to "overseas military expenditures, foreign aid, [and] direct capital investments abroad by American corporations." See David P. Calleo, *The Imperious Economy* (Cambridge, Mass.: Harvard University Press, 1982), esp. pp. 9–24.

66. From 1959–1964, consumer inflation in the United States averaged only 1.2 percent annually. See United States, *Economic Report of the President: 1981* (Washington, D.C.: U.S. Government Printing Office, January 1981), p. 293.

67. See Andrea Boltho, *The European Economy: Growth and Crisis* (London: Oxford University Press, 1982).

68. In 1980, U.S. GNP was around $2.6 bn and that of the EEC was $2.9 bn. See Kennedy, *Great Powers*, p. 436.

69. French economic growth during the 1950s was 4.6 percent, and from 1959 to 1970 it was 5.8 percent. See Jean Fourastié, *Les trente glorieuses ou la révolution invisible de 1946 à 1975* (Paris: Fayard, 1979); and Jacques Guyard, *Le miracle français* (Paris: Editions du Seuil, 1965).

Chapter Three
Manipulating Ambiguity

1. For a good analysis of the background and logic of flexible response, see David N. Schwartz, *NATO's Nuclear Dilemmas* (Washington, D.C.: Brookings Institution, 1983), chap. 6.

2. See, for example, the speeches and press conferences of November 3, 1959; September 5, 1960; and May 15, 1962, in de Gaulle, *Discours et messages* 3:127; 249; 413.

3. Examples of such noncooperation with NATO include a 1963 incident in which French army forces on a war-game maneuver remained on the western side of the Rhine and "bombed" West Germany and another in 1965 in which France failed to deploy her forward troops consistent with NATO's forward defense. Their very weak pretense was that adequate installations were not available, even though American facilities there had just been vacated. In 1965 also, all French tactical air forces, including those assigned to NATO, were consolidated into a new national tactical air command, the force aérienne tactique (FATAC). Most impor-

tant, though, was the 1966 French decision not to participate in the long-planned Fallex 1966 NATO military exercises, which planned a nonnuclear response to a hypothetical Soviet aggression. On the incidents and Fallex, see Harrison, *Reluctant Ally*, pp. 130, 139. On the FATAC, see Diego Ruiz-Palmer, "Between the Rhine and the Elbe: France and the Conventional Defense of Central Europe," *Comparative Strategy* 6, no. 4 (1987): 475.

4. See de Gaulle's February 15, 1963, speech to the Ecole Militaire in *Discours et messages* 4:86–87.

5. Ibid., pp. 86–87.

6. See General Charles Ailleret, "Opinion sur la théorie stratégique de la 'flexible response,'" *Revue de défense nationale* 20 (August 1964): 1323–40; and idem, "Evolution nécessaire de nos structures militaires," *Revue de défense nationale* 21 (June 1965): 947–55.

7. See Ailleret, "Opinion sur la théorie stratégique," p. 1,336.

8. Ibid., p. 1337.

9. See Ailleret, "Evolution nécessaire," p. 949.

10. Gallois's major work on nuclear strategy in the 1960s was *Stratégie de l'âge nucléaire* (Paris: Calmann-Lévy, 1960), published in English as *The Balance of Terror: Strategy for the Nuclear Age*, trans. Richard Howard (Boston: Houghton Mifflin, 1961).

11. See Aron, *Great Debate*, p. 141.

12. See Gallois, *Balance of Terror*, pp. 110–42.

13. Ibid., pp. 139–40.

14. This was because "thermonuclear weapons neutralize the armed masses, equalize the factors of demography, contract distance, level the heights, limit the advantages which until yesterday the Big Powers derived from the sheer dimensions of their territory." Cited in Aron, *Great Debate*, p. 102.

15. See Gallois, "U.S. Strategy and the Defense of Europe," *Orbis* 8 (Summer 1963): 247.

16. To be fair, Gallois does not seem to be advocating the use of doomsday machines or the deployment of the proverbial "mad colonel" at the nuclear button. By "automatic" deterrence he seems to mean providing for autonomous presidential control, something with which de Gaulle would have doubtless agreed. See Gallois, *Balance of Terror*, pp. 122–29.

17. See de Gaulle's January 14, 1963, press conference in *Discours et messages* 4:74.

18. See the press conference of July 23, 1964, in de Gaulle *Discours et messages* 4:223.

19. Ibid.

20. Ibid., p. 231.

21. Even Raymond Aron, so skeptical about the utility of an independent force de frappe, accepted that multilateral deterrence could have a positive effect by adding "yet another factor to those the Soviet high command . . . must take into account." See Aron, *Great Debate*, p. 142; and idem, *Penser la guerre: Clausewitz*, vol. 2, *L'âge planétaire* (Paris: Gallimard, 1976), p. 179.

22. See Beaufre's major works, *Introduction à la stratégie* (Paris: Armand Colin, 1963) and *Dissuasion et stratégie* (Paris: Armand Colin, 1964). The trans-

lations I have used for quotes are André Beaufre, *An Introduction to Strategy* (New York: Frederick A. Praeger, 1965); and idem, *Deterrence and Strategy*, trans. Major General R. H. Bary (New York: Frederick A. Praeger, 1965).

23. Beaufre, *Introduction to Strategy*, p. 83.

24. See Beaufre, *Deterrence and Strategy*, p. 79.

25. Ibid., p. 84.

26. Many American observers, of course, objected that it was preposterous that the United States would ever start a strategic nuclear war simply because France had attacked the Soviet Union with nuclear weapons. (The French, after all, claimed the U.S. nuclear guarantee was not even credible if the *Soviets* attacked *France*!) For a discussion of some ways in which "nuclear triggering" might work, see Glenn Snyder, *Deterrence and Defense* (Princeton, N.J.: Princeton University Press, 1961), pp. 162–64.

27. See Beaufre, *Deterrence and Strategy*, p. 88.

28. See Hoffmann, "De Gaulle," p. 9 (first emphasis added; second is Hoffmann's).

29. See the radio-TV speech of August 10, 1967, de Gaulle, *Discours et messages*, 5:203.

30. See General Charles Ailleret, " 'Défense dirigée' ou défense tous 'azimuts,' " *Revue de défense nationale* 23 (December 1967): 1,926–27. This translation taken from the article reprinted as General Charles Ailleret, "Defense in All Directions," *Atlantic Community Quarterly* (Spring 1968): 24.

31. See Ailleret, " 'Défense dirigée,' " P. 1,926.

32. See Lacouture, *De Gaulle* 3:477–80.

33. See de Gaulle's speech at the Ecole Militaire of November 3, 1959 in *Discours et messages* 3:27.

34. See the article and "authorized" summary of the talk in *Le Monde*, January 30, 1968, and the version reconstructed by Lacouture in *De Gaulle* 3:480.

35. At the NATO foreign minister's meeting of November 16, 1968, the French supported a final communiqué stating that "[the] North Atlantic Alliance will continue to stand as the indispensable guarantor of security" and that "recent events [had] demonstrated that its continued existence is more than ever necessary" (communiqué in NATO, *NATO: Facts and Figures* [1971], pp. 369–71).

36. See General Michel Fourquet, "Emploi des différents systèmes de forces dans le cadre de la stratégie de dissuasion," *Revue de défense nationale* 25 (May 1969): 757–67. The speech was reprinted in English as "The Role of the Forces" in *Survival* 11, no. 7 (July 1969): 206–11. I have taken the next citations from this translation.

37. Fourquet, "Role of the Forces," p. 208.

38. Ibid., p. 208.

39. Ibid., p. 207.

40. Author's interview with General Fourquet, May 1991. See also Lacouture, *De Gaulle* 3:481–82.

41. Ibid., p. 481.

42. See Fourquet, "Role of the Forces," p. 208.

43. Ibid., p. 209.

44. See Alfred Grosser, *The Western Alliance: European-American Relations since 1945* (London: Macmillan, 1980), p. 290.

45. The ministers from the Action Committee were Valéry Giscard d'Estaing (Finance), René Pleven (Justice), Jacques Duhamel (Agriculture), and Joseph Fontanet (Employment). See Grosser, *Affaires extérieures*, pp. 237–38.

46. Just after the new government was formed in the summer of 1969, Prime Minister Chaban-Delmas called French nuclear policy "irreversible." See Kohl, *French Nuclear Diplomacy*, P. 374.

47. Cited in ibid., p. 374.

48. See the "Loi de Programme 1971–1975," in Dominique David, ed., *La politique de défense de la France: Textes et documents* (Paris: Fondation Pour les Etudes de Défense Nationale, 1989), p. 187.

49. Ibid., p. 188.

50. In 1969, when Pompidou was elected, the United States still led the Soviets in ICBMs (1,054:1,028), SLBMs (656:196), and bombers (560:145). By 1974, the Soviets had moved ahead in both ICBMs (1,575:1,054) and SLBMs (720:656). (Bombers declined on both sides with the United States still ahead at 437:140.) This was also the period in which the Soviets developed MIRVs, which would further subtract from American advantage. All numbers refer to launchers. See IISS, *Military Balance (1977–1978)*, p. 80.

51. See Ministère de la Défense Nationale, *Livre blanc sur la défense nationale* vol. 1 (June 1972).

52. Ibid., p. 6. All translations in text are the author's.

53. Ibid., pp. 1–2, 22.

54. Ibid., p. 8.

55. Already discarded de facto by financial considerations, *"tous azimuts"* was now explicitly repudiated even as a hypothetical goal. The white paper stated that "to claim that [France's] defense objectives cover the whole world would be so absurd an exaggeration as to put in doubt the very notion of defense" (ibid., p. 6).

56. Ibid., p. 9.

57. Ibid., p. 9.

58. Ibid., p. 8.

59. Ibid., pp. 20, 9.

60. Ibid., p. 22.

61. The Ailleret-Lemnitzer and Fourquet-Goodpaster accords of 1967 and 1970 established liaisons between French and NATO commands, foresaw the deployment of French forces in the central sector of the alliance, established coordination between French and NATO air defenses, and made specific which French divisions would be initially available. On the various agreements linking France to NATO after 1966, see General François Maurin, "L'originalité française et le commandement," *Défense nationale* 45 (July 1989): 45–57.

62. Ibid., p. 21.

63. Michel Debré, "France's Global Strategy," *Foreign Affairs* 49, no. 3, (April 1971): 395–406.

64. Jean Guitton from *La pensée et la guerre* (Paris: Desclée de Brouwer, 1969), cited by Fourquet, "Role of the Forces," p. 207.

65. Debré, "France's Global Strategy," p. 401.

66. See François de Rose, *Contre la stratégie des curiaces* (Paris: Julliard, 1983). The call to avoid a Western "strategy of the Curiatii" was actually first issued by François Mitterrand in his 1980 book *Ici et maintenant* (Paris: Fayard, 1980), p. 232.

67. See the "Aide-mémoire du gouvernement français aux représentants des gouvernements de l'Alliance Atlantique, 8 et 10 mars, 1966," in David, *Politique de défense*, p. 135.

68. See Lucien Poirier, "Dissuasion et puissance moyenne," *Revue de défense nationale* 28 (March 1972): 369.

69. See, for example, Frédéric Bozo, *La France et l'OTAN: De la guerre froide au nouvel ordre européen* (Paris: Masson, 1991), esp. pp. 150–60.

Chapter Four
Giscard's Balancing Act, 1974–1981

1. See Réne Rémond, *Notre siècle: 1918–1988* (Paris: Fayard, 1988), p. 764.

2. See Rémond, *Les droites en France*.

3. Cited by Rémond, *Notre siècle*, p. 772.

4. Giscard caused quite a stir among the Gaullists in his coalition when he somewhat casually noted that France would soon represent less than 1 percent of the world's population. On the president's remark and the RPR's reaction, see Rémond, *Notre siècle*, p. 816.

5. Cited in Grosser, *Affaires extérieures*, p. 280.

6. For the text of the program law, see Assemblée Nationale, "Loi No. 76-531 du 19 juin 1976 portant approbation de la programmation militaire pour les années 1977–1982," *Journal officiel de la République française* (June 20, 1976): 3,700 (henceforth cited as "Loi de programmation 1977–1982").

7. See "Loi de programmation 1977–1982," p. 3,700.

8. See Valéry Giscard d'Estaing, "Allocution de M. Valéry Giscard d'Estaing, Président de la République, à l'occasion de sa visite à l'Institut des Hautes Etudes de Défense Nationale," *Défense nationale* 32 (July 1976): 15.

9. Ibid., p. 17.

10. For Chirac, see his February 10, 1975, speech at Mailly, "Au sujet des armes nucléaires tactiques françaises," *Défense nationale* 31 (May 1975): p. 12; and for Méry, see his September 1975 speech, "Réflexions sur le concept d'emploi des forces," *Défense nationale* 31 (November 1975): 21.

11. See Général d'Armée G. Méry, "Une armée pour quoi faire et comment?" *Défense nationale* 32 (June 1976): 11–24. Where indicated, translations of the Méry speech used are taken from the excerpts printed as "Comments by General Guy Méry, March 15, 1976," *Survival* 18, no. 5 (September–October 1976), pp. 226–28.

12. Méry, "Comments," p. 227.

13. Ibid., pp. 226–27.

14. Ibid., p. 227.

15. See Giscard d'Estaing, "Allocution," pp. 5–20.

16. Ibid., p. 15.

17. Those circumstances were (1) if the front crumbled too quickly; (2) if the French decision to intervene came too late; or (3) if French movements were hindered by enemy action. See Méry, "Une armée pour quoi faire," p. 16.

18. See Giscard d'Estaing, "Allocution," p. 17 [emphasis Giscard's].

19. See Chirac, "Des armes nucléaires tactiques," pp. 11–15; and Méry, "Une armée pour quoi faire," pp. 17–18.

20. See "Loi de programmation 1977–1982," p. 3,701.

21. See Giscard d'Estaing, "Allocution," p. 15 [emphasis added]. According to Jacques Isnard of *Le Monde*, Giscard had even planned originally to describe TNWs as "an artillery" in the speech, but this reference was removed before the official text was presented. See Jacques Isnard in *Le Monde*, June 11, 1976.

22. Two of the best analyses of the reorganization of the armed forces under Giscard are Ruiz-Palmer, "Between the Rhine," 480–86; and David S. Yost, *France's Deterrent Posture and Security in Europe*, Pt. 1, *Capabilities and Doctrine*, Adelphi Paper no. 194 (London: IISS, 1984–1985), pp. 55–60.

23. See Yost, *France's Deterrent Posture*, p. 56.

24. Before the reorganization, the "planned" size of the army was 360,000 and its "actual" size was 331,000. The new planned size was to be 310,000. The reduction was, thus, 14 percent in terms of plans and 6 percent in real terms. See Yvon Bourges, *Notre politique de défense* (Paris: Ministère de la Défense, 1976), p. 17; and Harrison, *Reluctant Ally*, p. 200.

25. See "Loi de programmation 1977–1982," pp. 3,702–3 and 3,705–6; and also Méry, "Comments," p. 226.

26. See "Loi de programmation 1977–1982," p. 3,705.

27. See Messmer, "Notre politique militaire," pp. 751–52.

28. See the interview with General Claude Vanbremeerch (then commander of the First Army) in André Bloch, "Si la France s'estime directement menacée, elle utilisera l'arme nucléaire quelle que soit la décision de l'OTAN," *L'Aurore*, February 4, 1980, p. 2. In 1983, the Third Corps would be transferred to Lille where it would take on an even more "forward" role.

29. See Jacques Isnard, "La 1ère armée française en 1979," *Le Monde*, April 4, 1979.

30. See "Loi de programmation 1977–1982," p. 3,702.

31. See "Loi de programmation 1977–1982," pp. 3,705, 3,707; and the analysis in *Le Monde*, May 7, 1976.

32. For Bourges, see Assemblée Nationale, *Journal officiel*, November 9, 1977, p. 7,239. For Méry, "Comments," p. 20.

33. See "Loi de programmation 1977–1982," p. 3,705; and the *Rapport sur la programmation des dépenses militaires et des équipements des forces armées pour la période 1977–1982* (Paris: Service d'Information et de Diffusion du Premier Ministre, 1976), pp. 12, 19–20; and Gérard Vaillant, "Défense en France," *Défense nationale*, 32 (July 1976): 146–48.

34. See the revelations in the article by Princeton University Professor Richard H. Ullman, "The Covert French Connection," *Foreign Policy*, no. 75 (Summer 1989): 22.

35. Ibid., p. 8.

36. It might, thus, be argued that by refusing U.S. nuclear assistance to the

French, it was the Americans who were responsible for the "independent" force de frappe, not de Gaulle. For examples of French efforts to elicit nuclear assistance from the Americans, see Kohl, *French Nuclear Diplomacy*, pp. 64–67, 222–23.

37. Ullman's 1989 article was highly controversial on both sides of the Atlantic, in the United States because it suggested U.S. laws on the export of nuclear technology (the amended Atomic Energy Act) had been broken and in France because political taboos were definitely broken. Some security analysts in France criticized the article for appearing to suggest that strategic (as well as tactical) nuclear targeting coordination also took place, for failing to emphasize that military cooperation between the two countries was nothing new, and for what they saw as its sensational tone. No one, however, has contested the existence of the nuclear cooperation, and high-level sources in both France and the United States (interviewed since) have confirmed that it took place. One former French military leader of the highest authority confirmed to me that French-American technical cooperation was "very important" to France and that it had saved the French considerable time and money. I was also told, however, by a former top Defense Ministry official that although French and American scientists did work together, France "never collaborated with anyone at all" on tactical nuclear targeting, contradicting what has been affirmed by an equally high-level source in the United States. The most authoritative public testimony so far on this issue is that of Valéry Giscard d'Estaing, who discusses the origins and motivations of the nuclear cooperation in the second volume of his memoirs, *Le pouvoir et la vie: L'affrontement* (Paris: Compagnie 12, 1991), pp. 183–92. See also the French Defense Ministry's brief communiqué of May 28, 1989, confirming technical cooperation on questions of nuclear "safety" and "security" but insisting that this in no way compromised France's nuclear independence. For a critical French assessment of Ullman's revelations, see Frédéric Bozo, *La France et l'Otan: de la guerre froide au nouvel ordre européen* (Paris: Masson, 1991), pp. 119–22.

38. See, for example, the very progressive UDF security platform prepared for the 1981 elections, *Une doctrine de défense pour la France* (Paris: UDF, 1980), presented by Jean-Marie Daillet.

39. See, for example, Pierre Gallois, "French Defense Planning—The Future in the Past, *International Security* 1; no. 2 (Fall 1976): 15–31; and idem, *Le renoncement: De la France défendue à l'Europe protégée* (Paris: Plon, 1977). See also Général Lucien Poirier, "Quelques problèmes actuels de la stratégie nucléaire française," *Défense nationale* 35 (December 1979): 43–61; and Jean Klein and Jacques Vernant, "Indépendance nationale et défense," *Paradoxes*, no. 39 (April–May 1980). Chevènement's position—that Giscard was realigning with NATO and possibly trying to prevent the Left from coming to power in France—is discussed in Pascal Krop, *Les socialistes et l'armée* (Paris: Presses Universitaires de France, 1983), pp. 63–83.

40. Pierre Messmer cited by David S. Yost, "The French Defense Debate," *Survival* 23, no. 1 (January–February, 1981): p. 20. If Messmer really said this, one wonders about his point of reference: a "leap backward of ten years" from 1976 is to 1966, during Messmer's tenure as minister of the Armed Forces.

41. See Yost, *France's Deterrent Posture*, pt. 1, p. 65 nn. 20, 21.

42. The speech was reprinted as Raymond Barre, "Discours au Camp de Mailly," in David, *Politique de défense* (1989), pp. 245–59.

43. See Barre, "Discours au Camp de Mailly," p. 253.

44. General Poirier, for example, argued that Barre's suggestion that France's deterrent might apply to "neighboring territories" was "to ruin, with a single phrase, the coherence of a strategic discourse that is otherwise of exemplary rigor" (cited in Yost, "French Defense Debate," p. 23).

45. See Barre, "Discours au camp de Mailly," pp. 245–46.

46. Ibid., pp. 246–47, 250.

47. Giscard d'Estaing, "Allocution," p. 17.

48. See the parliamentary report cited by François de Rose, "La politique de défense du Président Giscard d'Estaing," in Samy Cohen and Marie-Claude Smouts, eds., *La politique extérieure de Valéry Giscard d'Estaing* (Paris: Presses de la Fondation Nationale des Sciences Politiques, 1985), p. 193.

49. See Giscard d'Estaing, "Allocution," p. 16. See also Bourges' statement that "our conventional forces must be prepared to fight battles and, if necessary, to completely engage in battle" (Bourges, *Notre politique de défense*, p. 16).

50. See Giscard d'Estaing, "Allocution," pp. 15–16.

51. For the critique of Jobert, see the interview with Giscard in *Le Figaro*, May 21, 1975, cited by Pierre Hassner, "Les mots et les choses," in Cohen and Smouts, *La politique extérieure*, p. 234.

52. See Harrison, *Reluctant Ally*, p. 189.

53. See Méry, "Comments," p. 227.

54. Giscard elaborated on his view that a political Europe would have to precede a strategic Europe in a November 12, 1975, interview on *Antenne 2* cited in Hassner, "Les mots et les choses," in Cohen and Smouts, *La politique extérieure*, p. 234. For Méry's view that "there cannot be a European defence without political union of Europe," see Méry, "Comments," p. 228.

55. See the discussion entitled "Témoignages et interventions sur la France et la défense de l'Europe," in Cohen and Smouts, *La politique extérieure*, p. 242.

56. See Jean Klein, "France, NATO and European Security," *International Security* (Winter 1977): 33.

57. See United States Arms Control and Disarmament Agency, *World Military Expenditures and Arms Transfers: 1986* (Washington, D.C.: United States Arms Control and Disarmament Agency, 1987), p. 74 [hereafter cited as ACDA]. Using a deflator based on consumer (and not defense sector) price indices, the real increase in military expenditure for 1977–1980 was 12 percent. See IISS, *Military Balance* (1981–1982), p. 110.

58. Figure for 1960 from Assemblée Nationale, Raymond Tourrain, *Rapport d'Information*, no. 1730, May 22, 1980; Figures for 1970s and 1980s from Ministère de la Défense, *Regards sur la défense: 1981–1986* (Paris, 1986), p. 18. For French defense budgets as a share of GDP during the 1970s and 1980s, see table 5.2.

59. See Christian Sautter, "France," in Andrea Boltho, ed., *The European Economy: Growth and Crisis* (London: Oxford University Press, 1982), pp. 449–71.

60. Reported by Charles Hernu in "Une défense moderne et crédible," *Le Monde*, July 12, 1985.

61. See Yost, "French Defense Budgeting," p. 590.

62. See Jacques Chirac, "Jacques Chirac s'exprime sur la défense nationale," *Le Nouveau Journal*, March 7, 1981.

63. See Chirac in *Le Monde*, February 14, 1980, and the RPR report on defense presented by Michel Aurillac, RPR, *Réflexions sur la défense* (Paris: RPR, 1980), pp. 38–40. The RPR platform should be compared with the very Atlanticist UDF defense platform, *Une doctrine de défense pour la France*, presented by Jean-Marie Daillet in May 1980.

64. See François de Rose, "La politique de défense du Président Giscard d'Estaing," in Cohen and Smouts, *La politique extérieure*, p. 183.

Chapter Five
Mitterrand's Adaptations, 1981–1986

1. See Parti Socialiste, *Changer la vie: Programme de gouvernement du parti socialiste*, présentation de François Mitterrand (Paris: Flammarion, 1972), pp. 198–206.

2. See Mitterrand's views in Convention des Institutions Républicaines (CIR), *Un socialisme du possible* (Paris: Editions du Seuil, 1970), p. 96.

3. See Parti Socialiste, *Pour la France des années 80* (Paris: Club Socialiste du Livre, 1980), p. 340.

4. See Krop, *Les socialistes et l'armée*, p. 87; and Harrison, *Reluctant Ally*, p. 216.

5. During the internal party debates, Mitterrand (who still had his reservations about nuclear weapons) apparently told Hernu, "Go ahead, convince the party and I will support you" (cited in Julius W. Friend, *Seven Years in France: François Mitterrand and the Unintended Revolution, 1981–1988* [Boulder, Colo.: Westview Press, 1989], p. 196).

6. Cited in Jean Guisnel, *Les généraux: Enquête sur le pouvoir militaire en France* (Paris: Editions la Découverte, 1990.), p. 57. In fact, Mitterrand had foreseen this outcome as early as 1969: "I said during my presidential campaign of 1965 that I would abolish the force de frappe. I will soon no longer be able to say so. The military policy of General de Gaulle has been approved by the French who reelected him before reelecting the successor to his line of thought. Soon our atomic armament will be an irreversible reality" (*François Mitterrand, l'homme, les idées* [Paris: Flammarion, 1974]as cited in Krop, *Les socialistes et l'armée*, p. 62). For a similar argument by Hernu, see Charles Hernu, *Soldat citoyen: Essai sur la défense et la sécurité* (Paris: Flammarion, 1975), p. 54.

7. See Dominique Moïsi, "French Foreign Policy: The Challenge of Adaptation," *Foreign Affairs* 67, no. 1 (Fall 1988): 164.

8. This is the title given to Hoffmann's assessment of Mitterrand's foreign policy in a 1987 book. See Stanley Hoffmann, "Mitterrand's Foreign Policy, or Gaullism by Any Other Name," in George Ross, Stanley Hoffmann, and Sylvia Malzacher, eds., *The Mitterrand Experiment: Continuity and Change in Modern France* (New York: Oxford University Press, 1987), p. 294.

9. See A. W. DePorte, "France's New Realism," *Foreign Affairs* 63, no. 1 (Fall 1984): 147, 145.

10. See Robert S. Rudney, "Mitterrand's New Atlanticism: Evolving French Attitudes toward NATO," *Orbis* 28, no. 1 (Spring 1984): 83.

11. See Jolyon Howorth, "Consensus of Silence: The French Socialist Party and Defence Policy under François Mitterrand," *International Affairs* 60, no. 4 (Autumn 1984): 579–600.

12. See Révél, *Le style du général*, pp. 42–45.

13. François Mitterrand, *Le coup d'état permanent* (Paris: Plon, 1965).

14. On the presidential dominance of foreign and security policies under Mitterrand and all of his predecessors, see Samy Cohen, *La monarchie nucléaire* (Paris: Fayard, 1986).

15. François Mitterrand at the National Assembly, April 24, 1964, cited in Cohen, *La monarchie nucléaire*, p. 21.

16. Mitterrand's words were "La pièce maîtresse de la stratégie de dissuasion en France, c'est le chef de l'Etat, c'est moi; tout dépend de sa détermination" (text of the president's televised interview on November 16, 1983, cited in *Le Monde*, November 18, 1983).

17. From speeches on January 20, 1983, and June 9, 1983, printed in François Mitterrand, *Réflexions sur la politique extérieure: Introduction à vingt-cinq discours (1981–1985)*, (Paris: Fayard, 1986), pp. 195, 211.

18. The plans for the seventh submarine were later canceled but were indicative of the new president's enthusiasm for nuclear weapons. Giscard, after all, had only approved the sixth nuclear submarine under pressure from the Gaullists. For the decision, see *Le Monde*, July 26–27, 1981, p. 6.

19. See the summary and analysis of the program law in Ministère de la Défense, *La programmation militaire: 1984–1988* (Paris: SIRPA, 1983). For the program law itself, see Assemblée Nationale, "Loi No. 83-606 du 8 juillet 1983 portant approbation de la programmation militaire pour les années 1984–1988" (Paris: Imprimerie de l'Assemblée Nationale, 1983).

20. See Robbin F. Laird, "French Nuclear Forces in the 1980s and 1990s," *Comparative Strategy* 4, no. 4 (1984): 406.

21. See Hernu quoted in *L'Express*, October 15, 1982, p. 100. Even de Gaulle's foreign minister, Maurice Couve de Murville, one of the more vigilant guardians of the Gaullist legacy, admitted that the Socialists had "done a good job" in the nuclear domain. Author's interview with Couve de Murville in February 1989.

22. See the Mitterrand speech to the United Nations on September 28, 1983, reprinted in Mitterrand, *Réflexions*, pp. 225–26.

23. See Jeannou Lacaze, "La politique militaire: Exposé du chef d'état-major des armées au Centre des Hautes Etudes de l'Armament, le mardi 29 septembre 1981," *Défense nationale* 37, (November 1981): 10.

24. See the February 7, 1984, speech at The Hague, printed as "Le réveil de l'espérence européenne," in Mitterrand, *Réflexions*, pp. 276–77.

25. See François Heisbourg, "French Security Policy Under Mitterrand," in Robbin F. Laird, ed., *French Security Policy: From Independence to Interdependence* Boulder, Colo.: Westview Press, 1986, p. 43.

26. See Lacaze, "La politique militaire," pp. 9–10. This translation is taken from David S. Yost, "Franco-German Defense Cooperation," *Washington Community Quarterly* 11, no. 2 (Spring 1988): 178.

27. See Hernu's interview in *Le Monde*, July 11, 1981.

28. See Lacaze, "La politique militaire," p. 9.

29. See Pierre Mauroy, "Vers un nouveau modèle d'armée," *Défense nationale* 38 (November 1982): 17.

30. See Assemblée Nationale, "Projet de loi portant approbation de la programmation militaire pour les années 1984–1988," (Paris: Imprimerie Nationale, 1983), no. 1452. It is interesting to note that de Gaulle's defense minister, Pierre Messmer, had also declared that "it is a mistake to consider [the tactical nuclear weapon] as super-artillery" (from a press conference on October 21 1966, cited in *Air et cosmos*, October 29, 1966).

31. See Jacques Isnard, "Un arsenal pré-stratégique," *Le Monde*, October 31, 1984.

32. See Catherine Nay, *Les sept Mitterrand ou les métamorphoses d'un septennat* (Paris: Grasset, 1988).

33. See Michael M. Harrison, "Mitterrand's France in the Atlantic System," *Political Science Quarterly* 99, no. 2 (Summer 1984): 234.

34. Quoted in *Le Monde*, June 10, 1983.

35. See Mitterrand's press conference of June 9, 1982, reprinted in *Le Monde*, June 11, 1982.

36. Rogers cited in Ian Davidson, "France rejoins its allies," *Financial Times*, May 3, 1983.

37. France also permitted the United States to stockpile medical supplies (as long as the containers they were stored in were French!). See Ullman, "Covert French Connection," p. 22.

38. Ibid., p. 22.

39. See the January 20, 1983, Bundestag speech printed as "Il faut que la guerre demeure impossible," in Mitterrand, *Réflexions*, pp. 192–93.

40. See Claude Cheysson, "French Defense Policy and the U.S.," *Wall Street Journal*, February 25, 1983.

41. See Assemblée Nationale, "Loi no. 83–606" p. 2,115.

42. Statement by Cheysson at the Madrid meeting of the CSCE, cited in Grosser, *Affaires extérieures*, p. 303.

43. For the former quote, see François Mitterrand, *Ici et maintenant* (Paris: Fayard, 1980), pp. 241–42. The latter is from the Bundestag speech, printed in Mitterrand, *Réflexions*, p. 193.

44. Mitterrand in the introduction to *Réflexions*, p. 9.

45. Cited in the 1985 Socialist Party security platform *La sécurité et l'Europe* (Paris: Parti Socialiste, June 1985), p. 2.

46. The quote from the February 1982 meeting is from Yost, "Franco-German Defense Cooperation," p. 173.

47. See the *International Herald Tribune*, October 23–24, 1982; and the "Déclaration du Président de la République à l'issue des consultations franco-allemandes des 21 et 22 octobre 1982 à Bonn," in Ministère des Relations

Extérieures, *La politique étrangère de la France: Textes et documents. Octobre-novembre-décembre 1982* (Paris: Documentation Française, 1983).

48. See the text of the Elysée treaty reprinted in the annex of Karl Kaiser and Pierre Lellouche, eds., *Le couple franco-allemand et la défense de l'Europe* (Paris: Institut Français des Relations Internationales, 1986), pp. 329–33.

49. For details on the Franco-German Commission, see André Adrets (pseudonym of a former Defense Ministry official), "Les relations franco-allemandes et le fait nucléaire dans une Europe divisée," *Politique étrangère*, no. 3 (Fall 1984): 649–64.

50. See Jacques Isnard, "Relance spectaculaire de la coopération militaire franco-allemande," *Le Monde*, May 30, 1984, p. 1.

51. The terms of Germany's entry into the WEU in 1954 (after the failure of the European Defense Community) included limits on German conventional armaments production and military logistics. The removal of these limits took away the stigma of discrimination that had always marked the WEU in German eyes. On the 1954 Paris Accords providing for German accession to the WEU, see Alfred Grosser, *La IVᵉ République*, pp. 320–26. On the agreement to "relaunch" the WEU, see *Le Monde*, February 25, 1984.

52. These are Hernu's words cited in Yost, "Franco-German Defense Cooperation," p. 2.

53. Cited in *Le Monde*, November 5, 1983, p. 9.

54. See the statement in testimony before the National Assembly's Defense Commission in *Le Monde*, June 24, 1983.

55. See the statement by General Etienne Doussau in *Le Monde*, June 9, 1983. For Hernu, see *Le Monde*, December 7, 1982.

56. See Hernu's "Intervention devant des diplomats français: 6 mars, 1984" in David, *Politique de défense*, pp. 273–74.

57. See Lucien Poirier, "La greffe," *Défense nationale* 39 (April 1983): 22.

58. General Jeannou Lacaze, "Politique de défense et stratégie militaire de la France," *Défense nationale* 39 (June 1983): 21.

59. The words of Defense Minister Paul Quilès from a speech at Pforzheim, FRG. Cited in Yost, "Franco-German Defense Cooperation," p. 179.

60. Arthur Paecht's arguments on behalf of the UDF in the debate over the 1987–1991 program law. See Ministère de la Défense, *Débats parlementaires*, "1987–1991 loi de programmation militaire," (Paris: SIRPA, 1987), p. 64.

61. See the February 28, 1986, declaration in *Le Monde*, March 2–3, 1986, p. 4.

62. See Hernu in *Le Monde*, June 22, 1985, p. 1.

63. Cited in *Le Monde*, June 1, 1983.

64. See Mitterrand's speech at a royal dinner in Brussels on October 12, 1983, in Ministère des Relations Extérieures, *La politique étrangère*, (October 1983): 84–85.

65. For an analysis of French economic developments during these critical years, see Peter Hall, *Governing the Economy: the Politics of State Intervention in Britain and France* (New York: Oxford University Press, 1986), pp. 192–226.

66. The "help" the French needed and got was the German willingness to

accept a 5.5 percent EMS revaluation while the French only devalued by 2.5 percent. This not only saved the French government from additional political embarrassment but it allowed them to avoid an even greater domestic deflation to make the devaluation work. On the reasons for the French decision against protectionism, see Hall, *Governing the Economy*, p. 202.

67. See Patrick McCarthy, "France Faces Reality: *Rigueur* and the Germans," in David P. Calleo and Claudia Morgenstern eds., *Recasting Europe's Economies: National Strategies in the 1980s* (Lanham, Md.: University Press of America, 1990), p. 67.

68. Critics of defense spending under the Socialists were numerous, particularly in the preliminaries to the 1986 legislative elections. For examples of the opposition's case, see the UDF's *Redresser la défense de la France* (Paris: UDF, 1985); and the RPR's *La Défense de la France: 4 ans de gestion socialiste. Propositions pour le renouveau* (Paris: RPR, 1985). See also "Le RPR critique sévèrement les insuffisances de la politique militaire du gouvernement," *Le Monde*, June 26, 1985.

69. See, for example, Georges Mesmin, "1986: L'année des choix décisifs pour la défense," *Défense nationale* 42 (April 1986): 54; and Pierre Lellouche, *L'avenir de la guerre* (Paris: Mazarin, 1985), p. 55.

70. See IISS *Military Balance* (1987–1988), p. 236.

71. Ministère de la Défense, *Regards sur la défense*, p. 18.

72. This is the well-founded thesis of Jolyon Howorth in "Of Budgets and Strategic Choices: Defense Policy under François Mitterrand," in Ross, Hoffmann, and Malzacher, *Mitterrand Experiment*, pp. 306–23.

73. The first public incident of army discontent was a letter, eventually leaked to the press, from Army Chief of Staff General Jean Delaunay that criticized the "sacrifices demanded of the army" and argued that those cuts weakened French defense. See Jean-Michel Helvig, "Armée: une fuite inopportune pour le gouvernement," *Libération*, December 7, 1982.

74. See "Le Général Arnold dénonce le 'retard' de l'armée blindée française," *Le Monde*, November 2, 1985; and Jacques Isnard, "La grogne de certains officiers," *Le Monde*, November 28, 1985.

75. See Joseph Macé-Scaron, "Le général Méry dénonce les dérives de la politique de défense," *Le Figaro*, November 19, 1985. Other public criticism of the defense spending cuts by military officers—this time from the navy and air force—can be found in Admiral Yves Leenhart, "Réflexions pour une stratégie navale d'avenir," *Défense nationale* 41 (August–September, 1985): 11–34; Bernard Capillon, "L'Armée de l'air d'hier à aujourd'hui: Le fait aérien, une nouvelle dimension de la défense," *Défense nationale* 41 (June 1985): 23–30; and Michel Forget, "Le changement dans la troisième dimension," *Défense nationale* 41 (June 1985): 31–40.

76. See General Jeannou Lacaze, "The Future of French Defense," in Laird, *French Security Policy*, p. 52. See also "Le Général Lacaze sonne l'alerte," *Le Point*, July 1, 1985, p. 49.

77. See the interview with Lacaze in *L'Express*, March 26, 1981. This quote was reported again in "Défense: Le non des généraux," *L'Express*, December 10, 1982, p. 90.

Chapter Six
Tensions in the "Consensus," 1986–1989

1. See McGeorge Bundy, et al. "Nuclear Weapons and the Atlantic Alliance," *Foreign Affairs* 60, no. 4 (Spring 1982): 753–68

2. See, for example, the critical German response to the "no first use" article, in Karl Kaiser, et al. "Nuclear Weapons and the Preservation of Peace," *Foreign Affairs* 60, no. 5 (Summer 1982): 1,157–70.

3. See Valéry Giscard d'Estaing, "Pour une expression de solidarité européenne," *Le Monde*, November 8, 1986, p. 4.

4. See Moïsi, "French Foreign Policy," p. 155.

5. See Edward Luttwak, "Why the INF Pact Means the Nuclear Era is Over," *Washington Post*, Outlook, November 29, 1987.

6. See Lionel Barber, "Curbs on Defence Herald Major Restructuring," *Financial Times*, February 19, 1988.

7. For the estimates of the costs of defending Western Europe, see the Defense Department's *Report on Allied Contributions to the Common Defense* (Washington, D.C.: Department of Defense, 1985); and Richard Halloran, "Europe Called Main U.S. Arms Cost," *New York Times*, July 20, 1984, p. A2.

8. The quote is from Secretary of Defense Frank Carlucci in Molly Moore, "Carlucci Reminds NATO of Budget Restraints," *Washington Post*, December 3, 1987. For some of the official and nonofficial calls for burden sharing and troop withdrawals, see George C. Wilson, "NATO Payments 'Imbalance' Assailed," *Washington Post*, March 2, 1988; Richard Halloran, "Navy Chief Suggests Forces in Europe Be Cut," *New York Times*, January 14, 1988; Pat Schroeder, "Our Allies Must Pay More for Defense," *Washington Post*, October 13, 1987; Irving Kristol, "Reconstructing NATO: A New Role for Europe," *Wall Street Journal*, August 12, 1982, p. 18; and Melvyn Krauss, *How NATO Weakens the West* (New York: Simon and Schuster, 1986).

9. See "L'offensive Giraud," *L'Express*, July 10–16, 1987, p. 40. See also President Mitterrand's warning that American disengagement was "a real danger" (interview with Mitterrand by Jean Daniel entitled "La Stratégie, par François Mitterrand," *Le Nouvel Observateur*, December 18–24, 1987, p. 25 [hereafter cited as Mitterrand, "La Stratégie"]).

10. See Andrew J. Pierre, "Enhancing Conventional Defenses: A Question of Priorities," in Andrew J. Pierre, ed., *The Conventional Defense of Western Europe: New Technologies and New Strategies* (New York: Council on Foreign Relations, 1986), p. 12.

11. David P. Calleo, *Beyond American Hegemony: The Future of the Western Alliance* (New York: Basic Books, 1987), p. 160.

12. On the 1977 commitment by NATO member states to increase defense spending by 3 percent annually, see David Greenwood, "NATO's 3% Solution," *Survival* 23, no. 1 (November–December 1981): 252–60. For General Rogers's call for "only one percent more," see his "The Atlantic Alliance: Prescriptions for a Difficult Decade," *Foreign Affairs* 60, no. 5 (Summer 1982): 1,155.

13. For a good expression of skepticism about NATO's new strategies and new weapons, see Pierre, "Enhancing Conventional Defense," pp. 9–39.

14. See NATO, *NATO and the Warsaw Pact: Force Comparisons* (Brussels: NATO Information Service, 1984), p. 45.

15. See Robert W. Komer, "Is Conventional Defense of Europe Feasible?" *Naval War College Review* 35 (September–October, 1982): 3.

16. For a discussion of some of the institutional dilemmas of cohabitation where defense is concerned, see Raphaël Hadas-Lebel, "La défense, pierre d'achoppement pour la cohabitation?" *Le Monde*, October 29, 1986.

17. See "M. Chirac veut exercer pleinement son rôle de premier ministre en matière de défense," *Le Monde*, July 12, 1986, p. 8.

18. Chirac cited in Jacques Isnard, "La fin du domaine réservé," *Le Monde*, July 12, 1986, p. 8.

19. See, for example, Pierre Hassner, "Un chez d'oeuvre en péril: le consensus français sur la défense," *Esprit* (March–April, 1988): 71–82; Jacques Amalric, "Menaces sur le consensus entre l'Elysée et la majorité en matière de défense," *Le Monde*, March 1, 1988; and Jacques Jublin, "Défense: Le consensus s'effrite," *La Tribune de l'Expansion*, May 5, 1988.

20. See Chirac's July 10, 1986, speech to the Suippes military camp, "Pour une nouvelle loi de programmation militaire," *Lettre de Matignon* (Paris: Service d'Information et de Diffusion), no. 196, August 4, 1986, p. 3.

21. For a concise official assessment of the 1987–1991 program law, see the special issue of *Armées d'aujourd'hui* entitled "1987–1991: la loi de programmation militaire," no. 120, 1987.

22. For the Defense Ministry's estimates, see Assemblée Nationale, *Rapport fait au nom de la Commission de la Défense Nationale et des Forces Armées sur le projet de loi de programme (No. 432) relatif à l'équipement militaire pour les années 1987–1991*, François Fillon, rapporteur, no. 622 (Paris: Imprimerie Nationale April 7, 1987) p. 45.

23. See "Le projet de loi de programme militaire," *Le Monde*, November 7, 1986.

24. See Ministère de la Défense, *Débats parlementaires*, "1987–1991 loi de programmation," p. 38.

25. See "Le projet de loi de programmation 1987–1991," *Le Monde*, November 7, 1986.

26. See Isnard, "Le stratège et l'ordonnateur," *Le Monde*, November 7, 1986, p. 2.

27. See Jacques Amalric, "L'affaire des euromissiles divise la majorité," *Le Monde*, March 6, 1987.

28. See "Désarmement et déséquilibre nucléaire," *Armées d'aujourd'hui*, no. 120 (1987): 24. For the widespread opposition in France to the proposed INF Treaty, see, for example, "La dénucléarisation de l'Europe ne fait pas recette auprès des militaires Français" *Le Monde*, April 18, 1987; "Paris urges U.S. to keep missiles in Europe," *Financial Times*, October 22, 1987; and "M. Chirac et le désarmement: 'Prenons garde aux mesures symboliques,'" *Le Monde*, October 6, 1987.

29. According to Gallois, "Ronald Reagan [was] . . . the most spectacular victim of Moscow's propaganda" (General Pierre M. Gallois, "Un marché de dupes," *Le Figaro*, December 9, 1987).

30. See Mitterrand, "La Stratégie," p. 24.

31. François Mitterrand, *Lettre à tous les Français*, document distributed as supplement to many French newspapers on April 7, 1988, p. 12.

32. See Mitterrand, "La Stratégie," p. 25.

33. For Chirac, see the *Financial Times*, March 4, 1988, p. 3; and "M. Chirac prône la vigilance à l'égard de l'Union soviétique," *Le Monde*, March 2, 1988, p. 2. For Mitterrand, see Claire Tréan, "M. Mitterrand se déclare hostile à la modernisation des armes nucléaires de l'OTAN," *Le Monde*, February 27, 1988.

34. See Jublin, "Défense: Le consensus s'effrite, "*La Tribune de l'Expansion*, May 5, 1988.

35. See Barre's call for vigilance in the face of a continued Soviet military buildup in Professor Raymond Barre, the Alastair Buchan Memorial Lecture: "Foundations for European Security and Co-operation," *Survival* (July–August, 1987): 291–301.

36. After Giscard's fateful visit with Brezhnev in Warsaw following the Soviet invasion of Afghanistan (after which the French president wrongly assured his allies that Russian divisions would soon be withdrawn), Mitterrand had called him Brezhnev's "little messenger boy." For the Mestre quote, see "Cohabitation: l'Otan de la différence," *Liberation*, March 2, 1988, p. 7.

37. See "L'effet Gorbatchev' menacerait le consensus des Français en matière de défense nationale," *Le Monde*, February 25, 1988.

38. Ibid.

39. By late 1988, for example, 57 percent of the French believed that France's defense budget should be diminished "in order to contribute to general disarmament," up from only 39 percent in 1983. See, for the first figure, Conseils-Sondages-Analyses (CSA), "Les Français et les dépenses militaires," sondage des 22 et 23 novembre 1988, (Paris: CSA, November 1988), pp. 3–5; and for the second figure, Société Française d'Enquêtes et de Sondages (SOFRES), "Les Français et les problèmes de la politique extérieure," (Paris: SOFRES, April 1987), p. 6.

40. The term *Solzhenitsyn effect* (or *Gulag effect*) comes from the reaction of the formerly pro-Soviet French intelligencia to the 1974 release in Paris of Alexander Solzhenitsyn's *The Gulag Archipelago* (New York: Harper and Row, 1974). For an analysis of the impact of the Solzhenitsyn effect on French politics, and especially on the French Left, see Friend, *Seven Years*, pp. 74–80.

41. See, for example, Jacques Chirac, "Construction de l'Europe et défense commune," *Le Monde*, February 28, 1986, pp. 1, 9; and André Giraud, "La défense de la France et la sécurité européenne," *Défense nationale* 44 (May 1988): 11–19.

42. See Jacques Chirac, "La France et les enjeux de la sécurité européenne," allocution du premier ministre le 12 décembre 1987, devant les auditeurs de l'Institut des Hautes Etudes de Défense Nationale, *Défense nationale* 44 (February 1988): 17.

43. See Chirac, "La politique de défense de la France," Allocution du premier ministre le 12 septembre 1986, lors de la séance d'ouverture de la 39ᵉ session de l'Institut des Hautes Etudes de Défense Nationale," *Défense nationale* 42 (November 1986): 11.

44. See Chirac, "La France et les enjeux," p. 16.

45. Mitterrand's remarks in Germany can be found in "La stratégie nucléaire de la France s'adresse à l'agresseur et à lui seul," *Le Monde*, October 21, 1987; and "Le chef de l'Etat confirme son intention de réviser la doctrine sur l'emploi des armes préstratégiques françaises," *Le Monde*, October 22, 1987.

46. See Jacques Chirac, "La politique de défense," p. 12 (emphasis added).

47. See Chirac, "La France et les enjeux," p. 15.

48. Cited in Jublin, "Défense: Le consensus s'effrite *La Tribune de l'Expansion*, May 5, 1988."

49. See Mitterrand, "La Stratégie," p. 25 (emphasis added).

50. Ibid., pp. 25–26.

51. See François Mitterrand, *Lettre à tous les Français*, April 7, 1988; and Jublin, "Défense: Le consensus s'effrite *La Tribune de l'Expansion*, May 5, 1988."

52. For Jospin, see Lionel Jospin, "L'option dissuasion," *Le Monde*, December 5, 1987, pp. 1–2. For Chevènement, see SIRPA, *Débats parlementaires*, "1987–1991 Loi de programmation militaire," p. 47; and Chevènement's speech to the IHEDN on November 22, 1988, cited in Ministère de la Défense, *Propos sur la défense*, (November–December 1988): 72.

53. See Jean-Pierre Chevènement, "Vers la rupture du 'consensus nucléaire,'" *La lettre de République moderne* (November 1986): 1, 8.

54. The observation that the positions of Chirac and his supporters were "critically coherent . . . but politically maladroit" has been made by French analyst Pierre Hassner, to whom I am indebted for having helped me develop this theme. Hassner's own analysis of this period can be found in "Un chef-d'oeuvre en péril," pp. 72–74.

55. See, for example, "M. Chevènement: l'Union soviétique n'a pas ralenti son effort militaire depuis l'arrivée de M. Gorbachev," *Le Monde*, November 23, 1988, p. 12; and "M. Chevènement accuse les Soviétiques de maintenir une 'posture offensive' de leurs forces armées," *Le Monde*, September 8, 1988.

56. Rocard had always been concerned that excessive defense spending would ruin an otherwise effective fiscal policy. Rocard cited in Assemblée Nationale, 1re séance du 24 mai 1989, *Journal officiel de la République française, Débats parlementaires*. Première et Seconde Sessions Ordinaires de 1988–1989, compte rendu intégral, 25 mai 1989, p. 1,165.

57. See "Budget: Valse-hésitation à quatre temps," *Le Point*, October 16, 1989, p. 46.

58. See Jacques Isnard, "Des programmes militaires seront réduits ou retardés," *Le Monde*, May 25, 1989, pp. 1, 14.

59. See Erik Jones, *French Defense since Cohabitation: Consensus and Military Planning for 1990–1993*, Topical Papers no. 2, Université Libre de Bruxelles (July 1989): 11–14.

60. If this was, indeed, Mitterrand's strategy, it largely succeeded: Jacques Chirac called the president's decision no less than "an insidious calling into question of French defense." See Jacques Chirac, "Une remise en cause insidieuse de notre défense," *Le Monde*, June 10, 1989, pp. 1, 18.

61. The quotes on making choices are from François Heisbourg, "Défense française: L'impossible status quo," *Politique internationale* 36 (Summer 1987): 137–53; Jacques Isnard, "Désaccord entre M. Rocard et M. Chevènement sur la programmation militaire," *Le Monde*, April 25, 1989; and François Fillon, "Défense européenne: La coopération politique," *Défense nationale* 45 (May 1989): 20.

Chapter Seven
The Gaullist Legacy Today

1. See the text of Mitterrand's April 11, 1991, closing speech at the Forum de l'Ecole Supérieure de Guerre, in Ministère de la Défense, *Propos sur la défense*, no. 20 (March–April, 1991): pp. 82–90.

2. For Joxe, see his November 13, 1991, speech to the National Assembly during the presentation of the 1992 defense budget, "Compte-rendu des débats parlementaires sur les crédits 1992 du Ministère de la Défense," text provided by SIRPA. For Védrine, see "Paris tente de rassurer Washington sur la pérennité de l'alliance atlantique," *Le Monde*, May 29, 1991, p. 4. For Chevènement, see his June 1990 speech (as French defense minister) to the Royal Institute for Defense Studies in London, in Ministère de la Défense, *Propos sur la défense*, no. 15 (May–June 1990): 112.

3. See "London Declaration North Atlantic Council, July 5–6, 1990," U.S. Department of State, Bureau of Public Affairs. Excerpts from the NATO declaration can be found as "This Alliance Must and Will Adapt," *Washington Post*, July 7, 1990, p. A18.

4. For Chevènement, see David White, "French minister rejects idea of multinational forces," *Financial Times*, June 8, 1990, p. 5. For Mitterrand, see the text of the postsummit press conference in Ministère de la Défense, *Propos sur la défense*, no. 16 (July–August 1990): 14.

5. Roland Dumas cited in Claire Tréan, "La relation de la France à l'OTAN n'est pas modifiée," *Le Monde*, March 23, 1991.

6. Cited in Claire Tréan, "France-OTAN: Le chat et la souris," in *Le Monde*, May 4, 1991, p. 3.

7. An unnamed French official cited in Edward Mortimer, "Europe's teetering pillar," *Financial Times*, May 1, 1991, p. 15.

8. See Frédéric Bozo, "La France et l'Otan, vers une nouvelle alliance," *Défense nationale* 47 (January 1991): 30.

9. Interviews conducted with French officials in May and June 1991 revealed this to be a widespread view in France.

10. See Joxe's speech to the National Assembly on June 6, 1991, text provided by SIRPA, pp. 33–34. Joxe's discussion of the notion of "independence" for French forces was remarkably similar to past French doctrine. "Our independence may also be expressed in our disengagement from an affair in which we would [otherwise] be implicated, if we were to judge that the combat in which we would find ourselves would no longer be our own, in its form, in its objective, or in both" (p. 33).

11. Dumas at December 14, 1990, meeting in Brussels. See Joseph Fitchett, "Mitterrand Mutes Objections to U.S. Proposals on Europe," *International Herald Tribune*, December 19, 1989.

12. See Chevènement's June 1990 speech in London cited in Ministère de la Défense, *Propos sur la défense*, no. 15 (May–June 1990): 112.

13. The statement came one week after Mitterrand had been urged by President Bush at the Martinique French-American summit to accept that NATO begin to deal with economic and political issues as well as military ones. See Ian Davidson, "France and Germany align defence positions," *Financial Times*, April 27, 1990. For an interesting discussion of the (ultimately unsuccessful) French and American efforts to agree on NATO during the spring of 1990, see Frank Costigliola, *France and the United States: The Cold Alliance since World War II* (New York: Twayne Publishers, 1992), pp. 228–30.

14. See Claire Tréan, "M. Mitterrand a dénoncé le 'prêchi-prêcha' de l'OTAN," *Le Monde*, November 10–11, 1991; and Pierre Haski, "L'OTAN vole au secours de l'ennemi d'hier," *Libération*, December 20, 1991, p. 18.

15. For Mitterrand's original proposal for a European "confederation," see Claire Tréan, "M. Mitterrand souhaite une 'confederation' européene avec les pays de l'Est," *Le Monde*, January 2, 1990, pp. 1, 5.

16. See Harrison, *Reluctant Ally*, chap. 1.

17. The words of Roland Dumas cited in "M. Dumas prône la cohésion des Douze face à la crise yougoslave," *Le Monde*, October 6–7, 1991, p. 5.

18. When proposals were first made to develop regular diplomatic links between NATO and Eastern Europe, French officials reacted by calling such logic "bizarre," and Foreign Minister Dumas argued that NATO should not take advantage of political changes to "extend its military role." See Claire Tréan, "Paris et Washington réduisent leur divergences sur la défense," *Le Monde*, June 8, 1991, p. 8; and Jean de la Guérvière, "Le renforcement des compétences de l'OTAN et le rôle des Européens restent controversés," *Le Monde*, December 20, 1990, p. 28. On France's reluctant acceptance of the NACC, see Jean de la Guérvière, "La France accueille avec scepticisme le projet de 'Conseil de coopération de l'Atlantique nord,'" *Le Monde*, October 30, 1991.

19. Interviews in Paris, April 1992. See also Dumas's speech to the March 1992 meeting of the North Atlantic Cooperation Council, "Réunion du Conseil de Cooperation Nord-Atlantique: Intervention du Ministre d'Etat," *Bulletin d'Information*, March 11, 1992, no. 6 (1992), French Foreign Ministry.

20. The Rapid Reaction Corps was formally decided at the NATO Defense Planning Committee's May 28–29, 1991 meeting in Brussels. The RRC will consist of seventy thousand to one hundred thousand troops (two British divisions and two multinational ones), with a headquarters in Germany and under British command. It will also include a much smaller (approximately five-thousand-man) ACE mobile "immediate reaction force." See *Le Monde*, May 29, 1991, p. 4; and David White, "Smaller, Faster, Cheaper," *Financial Times*, June 1–2, 1991, p. 7.

21. Cited in William Drozdiak, "U.S. Shows Arrogance to Allies, French Say," *Washington Post*, June 12, 1991. See also Pierre Joxe's critical declaration to the WEU parliamentary assembly on June 4–5, 1991 in "MM. Dumas et Joxe critiquent la réforme de l'OTAN," *Le Monde*, June 6, 1991.

22. See Joseph Fitchett, "France Is Miffed at NATO Plan for Rapid Force," *International Herald Tribune*, June 5, 1991. See also Dumas's comment that Americans "should not dictate to Europeans what they should do for their own security" in William Drozdiak, "U.S. Shows Arrogance to Allies, French Say," *Washington Post*, June 12, 1991.

23. See André Dumoulin, "Les forces multinationales," *Défense nationale* 47 (August–September 1991): 69.

24. See Joxe's November 29, 1991 speech to the Cours Supérieur Interarmées, "Allocution de M. Pierre Joxe, Ministre de la Défense, à la cérémonie de clôture de la session plénière du Cours Supérieure des Armées," text provided by French Ministry of Defense, p. 8.

25. See the interview Dumas gave just one day after Joxe's speech to the Cours Supérieure Interarmées: "Roland Dumas contre une Europe des technocrates," *Libération*, December 6, 1991, p. 18.

26. The four most important Franco-German proposals were the Kohl-Mitterrand statement on political union of April 19, 1990; the Kohl-Mitterrand letter to the Rome intergovernmental conference of December 6, 1990; the Dumas-Genscher letter on security policy cooperation of February 4, 1991; and the Kohl-Mitterrand letter to the Dutch EC presidency calling for a European corps of October 14, 1991. See "Text of Statement by Mitterrand and Kohl on EC Union," Reuter Press Agency, transcript, April 19, 1990; "Letter sent by German Chancellor Kohl and French President Mitterrand to the EC Chairman," *FBIS-WEU-90-238*, December 1, 1990, p. 1; "Security Policy Cooperation within the Framework of the Common Foreign and Security Policy of the Political Union," February 4, 1991," in Agence Internationale d'Information pour la Presse, *Europe Documents*, February 21, 1991, p. 2; and the text of the October 1991 initiative in *Le Monde*, October 17, 1991, p. 4.

27. See the text of the December 6, 1990, Kohl-Mitterrand letter to the acting Italian presidency of the European Community printed as "La lettre commune de MM. Kohl et Mitterrand," *Le Monde*, December 9–10, 1990.

28. See the February 4, 1991 letter, "Security Policy Cooperation within the Framework of the common Foreign and Security Policy of the Political Union," *Europe Documents*, February 21, 1991, p. 1.

29. See the British-Italian initiative of October 4, 1991; text furnished by the British Embassy, Washington, D.C. The British view was clearly expressed by Foreign Secretary Douglas Hurd: "An approach which emphasized the separateness of Europe would seriously weaken our real security. . . . The common foreign and security policy should include some broad security issues . . . but it should not compete with the military tasks in Nato." See Douglas Hurd, "No European Defence Identity without Nato," *Financial Times*, April 15, 1991, p. 13.

30. See the "Treaty on Political Union, Final draft by the Dutch Presidency as modified by the Maastricht Summit," *Europe Documents*, no. 1750/1751, December 13, 1991, p. 19.

31. See the "Declaration of the Member States of Western European Union which are also members of the European Union on the role of WEU and its relations with the European Union and with the Atlantic Alliance," December 10, 1991; text furnished by WEU Secretariat General.

32. See, for example, the concerns expressed by Dutch Foreign Minister Hans van den Broek in "Europe ne doit pas être soumise au consensus franco-allemand," *Le Monde*, October 18, 1991; and "Les Pays-Bas se disent 'outrés' par les méthodes de MM. Dumas et Genscher," *Le Monde*, October 9, 1991.

33. See the text of the Kohl-Mitterrand proposal in "MM. Mitterrand et Kohl proposent de renforcer les responsabilités européennes en matière de défense," *Le Monde*, October 17, 1991, pp. 1, 4–5. See also Quentin Peel and Ian Davidson, "Political Changes First, Says Bonn," *Financial Times*, October 17, 1991, p. 2.

34. See Henri de Bresson, "Paris et Bonn définissent les missions du corps franco-allemand," *Le Monde*, May 13, 1992, p. 4. For more on the Franco-German corps and its implications, also see Philip H. Gordon, *French Security Policy after the Cold War: Continuity, Change and Implications for the United States*, R-4229-A (Santa Monica, Calif.: RAND, 1992).

35. See Jacques Amalric, "La France suggère à ses partenaires d'étudier une 'doctrine' nucléaire pour l'Europe," *Le Monde*,, January 12–13, 1992, p. 1; and the (somewhat overstated) article by Ian Davidson, "France Signals Reversal of National Defense Doctrine," *Financial Times*, January 11–12, 1992.

36. See "M. Pierre Joxe insiste sur la nécessité d'une réflexion concernant l'avenir de la force de dissuasion française," *Le Monde*, January 21, 1992.

37. See "M. Mellick recense les différentes formules d'une doctrine nucléaire européenne," *Le Monde*, February 4, 1992, p. 18. Note also the March 19, 1992, *Libération* article (coauthored by a French Defense Ministry official) that questioned France's long-term ability to pursue European political union but maintain purely national nuclear deterrence. See Serge Grouard and Patrice van Ackere, "Pour une dissuasion européenne," *Libération*, March 19, 1992, p. 25.

38. See Joxe and Mellick in the articles cited previously and also Armed Forces Chief of Staff Jacques Lanxade's comments in "L'amiral Lanxade: La défense nucléaire européenne 'n'est pas pour demain'," *Le Monde*, January 17, 1992.

39. Delors's words were "I cannot help but think that if, one day, the European Community has a very strong political union, then why not [envisage] the transfer of nuclear weapons to that political authority?" See Jacques Amalric, "La France suggère à ses partenaires d'étudier une 'doctrine' nucléaire pour l'Europe," *Le Monde*, January 12–13, 1992, p. 1.

40. From the Franco-German proposal of February 4, 1991. See "European Security Policy: The Franco-German Proposals at the Intergovernmental Conference of the Twelve on Political Union," *Europe Documents*, no. 1690, February 15, 1991.

41. See Pierre Lellouche, "L'Europe sera stratégique ou ne sera pas," *Le Monde*, December 21, 1988, p. 2.

42. See the interview with Mitterrand in *Le Monde*, October 23, 1991, p. 10. Cresson is cited in the *Wall Street Journal*, July 15, 1991, p. 1.

43. See Rocard's November 1991 Leffingwell Lectures to the Council on Foreign Relations in New York, published as Michel Rocard, *Europe and the United States*, Critical Issues no. 2 (New York: Council on Foreign Relations Press, 1992), p. 14.

44. See "Les déclarations du président de la République," *Le Monde*, October 23, 1991, p. 10.

45. See Nicole Gnesotto, "France and the New Europe," in David P. Calleo and Philip H. Gordon, eds., *From the Atlantic to the Urals: National Perspectives on the New Europe* (Washington, D.C.: Seven Locks' Press, 1992), p. 135.

46. See Dumas cited in French Embassy, *News from France*, Vol. 91.08, May 2, 1991, p. 1.

47. See Mitterrand at the Forum de l'Ecole de guerre, "La défense de l'Europe de l'Ouest ne peut se concevoir que dans le respect de l'alliance atlantique," *Le Monde*, April 13, 1991, p. 5. For Dumas, see Claire Tréan, "Défense: Les divergences entre Paris et Washington," in *Le Monde*, June 8, 1991.

48. See Joxe's declaration, "La constitution d'une véritable identité européenne en matière de défense prendra du temps," *Le Monde*, March 24–25, 1991.

49. Elysée spokesman Hubert Védrine's reference to the "synergy" and "proximity" between the French and American positions is cited in Claire Tréan, "Bush et Mitterrand célèbrent l'entente," *Le Monde*, March 15, 1991; On Chevènement's resignation, see Ian Davidson, "French Defence Minister Quits over Gulf Policies," *Financial Times*, January 30, 1991.

50. On France joining the NATO strategy review, see Theresa Hitchens, "French Turnabout May Lead to Compromise on NATO Dispute," *Defense News*, March 18, 1991, p. 16. On the excellent relations between Mitterrand and Bush after the Gulf War, see Claire Tréan, "MM. Bush et Mitterrand célèbrent l'entente franco-américaine," *Le Monde*, March 15, 1991, p. 1; and William Drozdiak, "French-U.S. Relations Blossom Amid Desert Storm, *Washington Post*, February 26, 1991.

51. See Claire Tréan, "MM. Bush et Mitterrand célèbrent l'entente franco-américaine," *Le Monde*, March, 15, 1991, p. 1.

52. See "Un entretien avec M. Roland Dumas," *Le Monde*, March 12, 1991.

53. See Claire Tréan, "Le refus de Bagdad de rencontrer les Douze est un camouflet pour l'Europe," *Le Monde*, January 8, 1991.

54. For Vauzelle's comment, see "M. Michel Vauzelle et Yalta," *Le Monde*, February 10–11, 1991. For Chevènement, see "M. Chevènement craint que M. Mitterrand ne renonce au 'rôle moteur' de la France en Europe," *Le Monde*, April, 29, 1991.

55. See Jean-Marie Colombani, "Le 'rang' de la France," *Le Monde*, March 5, 1991; and André Fontaine, "Retrouver l'Europe," *Le Monde*, March 8, 1991.

56. IFOP poll of February 1991.

57. France's transport capability was also hindered by the fact that although all of its aircraft were capable of in-flight refueling, it had only eleven aging C-135 tankers with which to service them. Figures on airlift missions provided by Pierre Joxe in his June 6, 1991, speech to the National Assembly; text provided by SIRPA, p. 4. For a more thorough assessment of France's airlift and sealift capabilities, see Diego A. Ruiz-Palmer, *French Strategic Options in the 1990s*, Adelphi Paper 260, (London: IISS, Summer 1991), pp. 65–71.

58. The French navy is the last in the world to fly the 1950s-vintage Crusaders, the Philippine navy having replaced its Crusaders in 1988. In late 1989, French navy leaders recommended that France buy or lease U.S. F-18s until the maritime version of the French-made Rafale is deployed (around 1997), but then Defense Minister Chevènement chose to extend the life of the Crusader instead, citing

"industrial" criteria for his decision. For a contemporaneous report on the Crusader decision, see Edward Cody, "French Turn Down U.S. F-18s," *Washington Post*, December 23, 1989.

59. The Mirage 2000 N can be adapted for use in conventional missions within two weeks using what is called a "Kit K2," and it is not yet clear why this was not done. Explanations range from the delays involved in conversion, to the need to maintain the nuclear deterrent for the national sanctuary, to the air force chief of staff's unwillingness to risk his best planes in a conflict with Iraq. For some hypotheses, see Elie Marcuse and James Sarazin, "Une armée à réformer," *L'Express*, March 29, 1991, pp. 11–13; and Ian Davidson, "Paris 'Holding Back Mirage 2000N'," *Financial Times*, January 26–27, 1991, p. 3.

60. On the percentages of various French forces that are professional, see Ewen Faudon (pseudonym for a French official), "La guerre avec l'Irak et la programmation militaire française," *Libération*, February 27, 1991; Jean Guisnel, "Le dispositif français mal adapté au conflit," *Libération*, February 1, 1991, pp. 7–8; and Pascal Vennesson, "Une année charnière pour les forces armées," in Dominique Chagnollaud, ed., *Etat politique de la France, année 1991* (Paris: Quai Voltaire, 1992), pp. 147–48.

61. See the November 1991 announcement by Army Chief of Staff Amédée Monchal in Jacques Isnard, "L'armée de terre perdra le cinquième de ses effectifs," *Le Monde*, November 14, 1991, p. 1.

62. These decisions are discussed in Jacques Isnard, "Moratoire sur les essais nucléaires: La dissuasion n'a plus la même priorité," *Le Monde*, April 10, 1992, p. 11. For Bérégovoy, see his first speech to the National Assembly, "Je chercherai, non par la démagogie mais par l'action à restaurer la confiance et renouer avec l'espérance," *Le Monde*, April 10, 1992, p. 8. On reductions in the nuclear share in the French defense budget, for the first time in more than thirty years, see Jacques Isnard, "La France réduira ses investissements nucléaires," *Le Monde*, October 30, 1991, p. 11.

63. See Joxe cited in *Le Monde*, April 12, 1991; and Joxe's May 6, 1991 speech to the IHEDN, "Défense et renseignement," *Défense nationale* 47 (July 1991): 13–15. Other French officials also believe that satellite capabilities will be to the twenty-first century what nuclear weapons were to the second half of the twentieth and emphasize the similarities between the present situation and that of the early 1960s. "Then," according to one interview source, "the Americans wrongly told us that nuclear weapons cost too much, were technically too complex for France, and would be redundant in an alliance context. This is exactly what the Americans are saying about satellites today."

64. An unnamed participant in meetings on the subject at the prime minister's office, cited in Jean Guisnel, "La France cherche son salut dans l'espace," *Libération*, April 4, 1991.

65. See Roger Jolly, "Renseignement: La grande misère," *Le Point*, March 18–24, 1991, p. 16.

66. See Pierre Servent, "Le gouvernement et les députés tirent les enseignements de la guerre du Golfe," *Le Monde*, June 6, 1991, p. 9; and Joxe's June 4, 1991, speech to the WEU Assembly, cited in Giovanni de Briganti, "France Offers Helios Data to Allies," *Defense News*, June 10, 1991. See also Jacques Isnard,

"M. Joxe veut privilégier le renseignement spatial," *Le Monde*, February 13, 1992, pp. 1, 11.

67. For the IHEDN speech, see Joxe, "Défense et renseignement," pp. 9–22. For spending on space programs, see the report for the Finance Commission of the National Assembly by Alain Richard and François Hollande, Assemblée Nationale, *Rapport fait au nom de la Commission des Finances de l'Economie Générale et du Plan sur le projet de loi de finances pour 1992*, no. 2255, October 9, 1991, p. 75.

68. See Edouard Balladur, "Pour une nouvelle politique de défense," *Le Monde*, March 6, 1991, pp. 1–2. The "Gaullist" wing of the RPR takes a similar view: See Philippe Séguin, "La nouvelle armée française," *Le Monde*, June 6, 1991.

69. On Hélios participation, see Assemblée Nationale, Richard and Hollande, *Rapport* no. 2255, October 9, 1991, p. 75. On the European satellite system, see Giovanni de Briganti, "Five European Nations to Study Military Satellite Network," *Defense News*, December 9, 1991, p. 40. For the WEU satellite information center, see the communiqué of the WEU Council of Ministers, June 27, 1991, Vianden, Luxembourg, p. 6.

70. Joxe's declaration to the National Assembly during the 1992 defense budget debates, cited in Jean-Louis Saux, "Les incertitudes internationales 'interdisent d'amputer notre dispositif de défense,' déclare M. Joxe," *Le Monde*, November 15, 1991, p. 10.

71. Not surprisingly, only 29 percent of the Americans and 25 percent of the British agreed that France was a great power. See "La France est-elle encore une grande puissance?" *L'Express*, March 1, 1991, pp. 28–33.

Chapter 8
Epilogue

1. See Charles de Gaulle, *Mémoires de guerre*, vol. 3, *Le salut, 1944–1946* (Paris: Plon, 1959), p. 47.

2. See the June 20 and June 30, 1966, speeches in de Gaulle, *Discours et messages* 5:43, 55.

3. See the speech in Moscow of June 20, 1966 in de Gaulle, *Discours et messages* 5:177.

4. See Stanley Hoffmann, "De Gaulle's Foreign Policy: The Stage and the Play, the Power and the Glory," in *Decline or Renewal?*, p. 294.

5. The first comment is from a radio-TV broadcast of November 4, 1960, the second from a press conference of July 29, 1963. See de Gaulle, *Discours et messages* 3:260; and 4:122.

6. See Hoffmann, *Decline or Renewal?* p. 294.

7. See the July 23, 1964, press conference in de Gaulle, *Discours et messages* 4:227.

8. See the statement of May 1965 in de Gaulle, *Lettres, notes et carnets* (Paris: Plon, 1986), 10:165; and the speech of December 31, 1966 in de Gaulle, *Discours et messages* 5:129.

9. This, after all, would not have been the first time the General acted to pre-

vent history from passing him by. When the French people failed to call him back to power soon after his January 1946 resignation, de Gaulle created a political movement (the RPF) to provoke the change of regime he had thought would come more naturally. Again in 1958, with the Fourth Republic bogged down in Algeria and, apparently, with no way out, de Gaulle encouraged (or at least did not discourage) the opposition that was pressing that regime to call him back to power. De Gaulle the "man of action" was not one to sit passively by while history leisurely took its time.

10. "Communism will pass. But France will not pass." See de Gaulle, Mémoires de guerre, vol. 1, L'appel, 1940–1942 (Paris: Plon, 1954), p. 232.

11. See Historical Statistics, OECD Economic Outlook (Paris: OECD, 1990), p. 48.

12. For GDP and population comparisons, see European Economy, no. 50 (December 1991): 40, 218; and OECD Main Economic Indicators (Paris: OECD, April 1992), pp. 174, 180.

13. From a September 5, 1960, Elysée press conference, see de Gaulle, Discours et messages 3:246.

14. See de Gaulle's May 15, 1962, press conference in de Gaulle, Discours et messages 3:406.

15. See de Gaulle's somewhat presumptuous declaration of August 17, 1950, cited in Roger Massip, De Gaulle et l'Europe (Paris: Flammarion, 1963), p. 151.

16. See Alfred Grosser, Affaires extérieures, p. 193.

Glossary of French Terms Used

Alternance — Changeover. Transfer of power from one political party to another.

Armes préstratégiques — Prestrategic weapons. Used since 1984 to designate tactical nuclear weapons in French nuclear doctrine.

Bombinette — "Little bomb." Mocking reference to French nuclear weapons in early 1960s.

Bonapartiste — Bonapartist. See *Orléaniste*.

Une certaine idée de la France — A certain idea of France. From the first sentence of de Gaulle's war memoirs, "*Toute ma vie, je me suis fait une certaine idée de la France*" (All my life, I have thought of France in a certain way).

Domaine privilégié — Privileged domain. Most often used to refer to the special authority of a French president in defense and foreign policy.

Domaine réservé — Reserved domain. See *domaine privilégié*.

Demandeur — Petitioner. Usually the weaker party in a relationship, as was France when dependent on a U.S. security guarantee.

Du faible au fort — From the weak to the strong. Theory of French nuclear deterrence policy vis-à-vis the Soviet Union.

Ennemi héréditaire — Hereditary enemy.

Esprit de défense — Defensive spirit, willingness to defend one's country.

L'Europe des Six — Europe of the Six. Reference to the first six members of the Common Market: France, West Germany, Italy, Belgium, the Netherlands and Luxembourg.

Europe Tricolore — Tricolor Europe. Jean Lacouture's description of de Gaulle's Europe, one tinted with the three-color symbol of the French flag.

Force de frappe — Nuclear striking force. Term used by Gaullists in the 1960s to denote the French nuclear force.

Force de dissuasion — Deterrent force.

Glacis — Glacis. Literally, a slope that runs downward from a fortification. Term sometimes used to refer to German territory in French military strategy.

La Grande Muette — The Silent One. Historic nickname for the French army, which is supposed to refrain from comment on political affairs.

Les grands — The great powers.

Guerre révolutionnaire — Revolutionary war. French term for colonial wars of the 1950s.

l'Hexagone — The Hexagon. Based on the geographic shape of the country; refers to continental France.

Metropole — Metropolis, home country. Like *Hexagone*, it refers to continental France as opposed to colonial territories.

Mission civilizatrice — Civilizing mission. French belief that France's imperial role was a mission to civilize colonial peoples.

Nation-phare — Lighthouse nation. Nation that leads others by its virtue and example.

Offensive à outrance — Full-force military offensive. Used by both France and Germany during World War I.

Orléaniste — Orleanist. In classic distinction of French Right by René Rémond in *Les droites en France*, Orléaniste is bourgeois, liberal wing, as opposed to Bonapartiste (populist, authoritative) and Legitimiste (conservative).

Patrie — Native country, homeland.

Rang — Rank, status.

Rayonnement — Radiance. Usually used in the sense of the radiance of French cultural influence in the world.

Redressement — Recovery, renewal.

Réflexe communautaire — Community reflex. Habit of doing things within the framework of the European Community.

Rigueur — Rigor, or austerity. Refers to the French economic austerity plan begun in late 1982.

Sanctuaire national — National sanctuary. Refers to the protected national homeland in French nuclear doctrine.

Sanctuarisation élargie — Enlarged sanctuarization. French notion of extended nuclear deterrence broached in 1976.

Tous azimuts — All azimuths, or all directions. French nuclear doctrine broached in 1968 that suggested French nuclear force should have global scope.

Les trente glorieuses — The thirty glorious years. Reference to nearly three decades of rapid French economic growth from 1945 to 1974 in the title of a book by Jean Fourastié.

Vastes entreprises — Great undertakings. Considered necessary by de Gaulle (as stated in the opening passage of his *Mémoires de guerre*) to keep contentious French from fighting among themselves and for France to "be herself."

Documents

David, Dominique, ed. *La politique de défense de la France: Textes et documents.* Paris: Fondation pour les Etudes de Défense Nationale, 1989.

Europe. Agence Internationale d'Information pour la Presse. *Europe Documents* series. Brussels: Agence Internationale d'Information pour la Presse.

France. Ambassade de France. *The First Five Years of the Fifth Republic in France, January 1959–January 1964.* New York: Service de Presse et d'Information, 1964.

————. *French Foreign Policy* (series). New York: Service de Presse et d'Information.

France. Assemblée Nationale. *Avis présenté au nom de la commission de la défense nationale et des forces armées sur le projet de loi de programme relative à certains équipements militaires.* No. 1155. Paris: Imprimerie Nationale, 1964.

————. *Journal officiel de la République française: Débats parlementaires.* Paris: Imprimerie de l'Assemblée Nationale.

————. *Loi de programme No. 70–1058 du 19 novembre 1970 relative aux équipements militaires de la période 1971–1975.* Paris: Imprimerie de l'Assemblée Nationale.

————. "Loi No. 76-531 du 19 juin 1976 portant approbation de la programmation militaire pour les années 1977–1982." Paris: Imprimerie de l'Assemblée Nationale, 1976.

————. "Loi No. 83-606 du 8 juillet 1983 portant approbation de la programmation militaire pour les années 1984–1988." Paris: Imprimerie de l'Assemblée Nationale. July 9, 1983.

————. "Projet de loi portant approbation de la programmation militaire pour les années 1984–1988." No. 1452. Paris: Imprimerie Nationale, 1983.

————. "Projet de loi de programme relative à certains équipements militaires." No. 784. Paris: Imprimerie Nationale, 1960.

————. *Rapport d'information.* Raymond Tourrain, rapporteur. No. 1730, May 22, 1980.

————. *Rapport du gouvernement sur le programme d'équipement militaire.* Paris: Imprimerie Nationale, 1964.

————. *Rapport fait au nom de la Commission de la Défense Nationale et des Forces Armées sur le projet de loi de programme (No. 432) relatif à l'équipement militaire pour les années 1987–1991.* François Fillon, rapporteur, No. 622. Paris: Imprimerie Nationale, 1987.

————. *Rapport fait au nom de la Commission des Finances, de l'Economie Générale et du Plan sur le projet de loi de finances pour 1992.* Alain Richard and François Hollande, rapporteurs. No. 2255. Paris: Imprimerie Nationale, 1991.

France. Ministère de la Défense. *Le budget de la défense* (series). Paris: Service d'Information et de Relations Publiques des Armées.

———. *Débats parlementaires* (series). Paris: Service d'Information et de Relations Publiques des Armées.

———. *Une politique de défense pour la France: 1974–1981*. Paris: Actualités Documents.

———. *Propos sur la défense* (series). Paris: Service d'Information et de Relations Publiques des Armées.

———. *La programmation militaire: 1984–1988*. Dossier d'information no. 72. Paris: Service d'Information et de Relations Publiques des Armées.

———. *Regards sur la défense: 1981–1986*. Paris: 1986.

———. *Livre blanc sur la défense nationale*. Vol. 1. Paris: 1972.

France. Ministère des Relations Extérieures. *Bulletin d'information* series. Paris: Ministère des Relations Extérieures.

———. *La politique étrangère de la France: Textes et documents* series. Paris: La Documentation Française.

France. *Rapport sur la programmation des dépenses militaires et des équipements des forces armées pour la période 1977–1982*. Paris: Service d'Information et de Diffusion du Premier Ministre, 1976.

North Atlantic Treaty Organization. *NATO: Facts and Figures* (series) 1971, 1989. Brussels: NATO Information Service.

United States Arms Control and Disarmament Agency (ACDA). *World Military Expenditures and Arms Transfers: 1986*. Washington, D.C.: ACDA, 1987.

United States. Department of Defense. *Report on Allied Contributions to the Common Defense*. Washington, D.C.: Department of Defense, 1985.

United States. *Economic Report of the President: 1981*. Washington, D.C.: U.S. Government Printing Office, January 1981.

Books and Reports

Ailleret, Charles. *L'aventure atomique française*. Paris: Grasset, 1968.

Aron, Raymond. *Le grand débat* (Paris: Calmann-Lévy, 1963). Published in English as *The Great Debate: Theories of Nuclear Strategy*. Garden City, N.Y.: Doubleday, 1965.

———. *Mémoires: 50 ans de réflexion politique*. Paris: Julliard, 1983.

———. *Paix et guerre entre les nations*. Paris: Calmann-Lévy, 1962.

———. *Penser la guerre: Clausewitz*. 2 vols. Paris: Gallimard, 1976.

Aron, Robert. *An Explanation of de Gaulle*. New York: Harper and Row, 1966.

Auriol, Vincent. *Mon septennat: 1947–1954*. Journal entries selected by Pierre Nora and Jacques Ozouf. Paris: Gallimard, 1970.

Beaufre, André. *Deterrence and Strategy*. Trans. Major General R. H. Bary. New York: Frederick A. Praeger, 1965.

———. *Introduction to Strategy*. New York: Frederick A. Praeger, 1965.

———. *NATO and Europe*. Translated by Joseph Green. New York: Alfred A. Knopf, 1966.

Beuve-Méry, Hubert. *Onze ans de règne: 1958–1969*. Paris: Flammarion, 1974.

Boltho, Andrea. *The European Economy: Growth and Crisis*. London: Oxford University Press, 1982.

Boniface, Pascal, and François Heisbourg. *La puce, les hommes et la bombe*. Paris: Hachette, 1986.

Bourges, Yvon. *Notre politique de défense*. Paris: Ministère de la Défense, 1976.

Bozo, Frédéric. *La France et l'OTAN: De la guerre froide au nouvel ordre européen*. Paris: Masson, 1991.

Burin des Roziers, Etienne. *Retour aux sources: 1962, l'année décisive*. Paris: Plon, 1986.

Calleo, David P. *The Atlantic Fantasy: The U.S., NATO, and Europe*. Baltimore, Md.: Johns Hopkins University Press, 1970.

————. *Beyond American Hegemony: The Future of the Western Alliance*. New York: Basic Books, 1987.

————. *Europe's Future: The Grand Alternatives*. New York: Horizon Press, 1965.

————. *The Imperious Economy*. Cambridge, Mass.: Harvard University Press, 1982.

Calleo, David P., and Claudia Morgenstern, eds. *Recasting Europe's Economies: National Strategies in the 1980s*. Lanham, Md.: University Press of America, 1990.

Carr, Edward Hallett. *Nationalism and After*. London: Macmillan, 1965.

Chagnollaud, Dominique, ed. *Etat politique de la France, année 1991*. Paris: Quai Voltaire, 1992.

Cohen, Samy. *La monarchie nucléaire*. Paris: Fayard, 1986.

Cohen, Samy, and Marie-Claude Smouts, eds. *La politique extérieure de Valéry Giscard d'Estaing*. Paris: Presses de la Fondation Nationale des Sciences Politiques, 1985.

Cole, Allan B. *Conflict in Indochina and International Repercussions*. Ithaca, N.Y.: Cornell University Press, 1956.

Convention des Institutions Républicaines, *Un socialisme du possible*. Paris: Editions du Seuil, 1970.

Costigliola, Frank. *France and the United States: The Cold Alliance since World War II*. New York: Twayne Publishers, 1992.

Couve de Murville, Maurice. *Une politique étrangère, 1958–1969*. Paris: Librairie Plon, 1971.

Debré, Michel. *Au service de la nation: Essai d'un programme politique*. Paris: Editions Stock, 1963.

de Carmoy, Guy. *The Foreign Policies of France: 1944–1968*. Chicago: University of Chicago Press, 1970.

de Gaulle, Charles. *La discorde chez l'ennemi*. Paris: Librairie Berger-Levrault, 1924.

————. *Discours et messages*. 5 vols. Paris: Plon, 1970.

————. *Le fil de l'épée*. Paris: Librairie Berger-Levrault, 1932.

————. *La France et son armée*. Paris: Librairie Plon, 1938.

————. *Lettres, notes et carnets*. 9 vols. Paris: Plon, 1980–86.

————. *Mémoires de guerre*. 3 vols. Paris: Plon, 1954–1958.

————. *Mémoires d'espoir*. vol. 1, *Le renouveau, 1958–1962*. Paris: Plon, 1970.

de Gaulle, Charles. *Vers l'armée de métier*. Paris: Librairie Berger-Levrault, 1934.

de Rose, François. *Contre la stratégie des curiaces*. Paris: Julliard, 1983.

———. *Défendre la défense*. Paris: Julliard, 1989.

———. *La France et la défense de l'Europe*. Paris: Editions du Seuil, 1976.

Ely, Paul. *L'armée dans la nation*. Paris: Arthème Fayard, 1961.

Favier, Pierre, and Michel Martin-Roland. *La décennie Mitterrand*. Vol. 1, *Les Ruptures (1981–1984)*. Vol. 2, *Les Epreuves (1984–1988)*. Paris: Editions du Seuil, 1990, 1991.

Fourastié, Jean. *Les trente glorieuses ou la révolution invisible de 1946 à 1975*. Paris: Fayard, 1979.

François Mitterrand, l'homme, les idées. Paris: Flammarion, 1974.

Freedman, Lawrence. *The Evolution of Nuclear Strategy*. 2d ed. New York: St. Martin's Press, 1989.

Friend, Julius W. *Seven Years in France: François Mitterrand and the Unintended Revolution, 1981–1988*. Boulder, Colo.: Westview Press, 1989.

Furniss, Edgar S., Jr. *De Gaulle and the French Army: A Crisis in Civil-Military Relations*. New York: Twentieth Century Fund, 1964.

Gaddis, John Lewis. *Strategies of Containment: A Critical Appraisal of Postwar American Security Policy*. New York: Oxford University Press, 1982.

Gallois, Pierre. *The Balance of Terror: Strategy for the Nuclear Age*. Trans. Richard Howard. Boston: Houghton Mifflin, 1961.

———. *Le renoncement: De la France défendue à l'Europe protégée*. Paris: Plon, 1977.

Garntham, David. *The Politics of European Defense Cooperation: Germany, France, Britain, and America*. Cambridge, Mass.: Ballinger Publishing, 1988.

Girardet, Raoul. *L'histoire de l'idée coloniale en France de 1871 à 1962*. Paris: Fayard, 1972.

———. *Le nationalisme français*. Paris: Editions du Seuil, 1983.

———. *Problèmes militaires et stratégiques contemporains*. Paris: Dallioz, 1989.

———, ed. *La défense de l'Europe*. Brussels: Editions Complexe, 1988.

Giscard d'Estaing, Valéry. *Le pouvoir et la vie*. Vol. 1. Paris: Compagnie 12, 1988.

———. *Le pouvoir et la vie*. Vol. 2, *L'affrontement*. Paris: Compagnie 12, 1991.

Gordon, Philip H. "French Security Policy after the Cold War: Continuity, Change and Implications for the United States." R-4229-A. (Santa Monica, Calif.: RAND Corporation, 1992).

Grosser, Alfred. *Affaires extérieures: La politique de la France, 1944–1984*. Paris: Flammarion, 1984.

———. *La IVe République et sa politique extérieure*. Paris: Librairie Armand Colin, 2d ed., [1961] 1972.

———. *La politique extérieure de la Ve République*. Paris: Editions du Seuil, 1965.

———. *The Western Alliance: European-American Relations since 1945*. London: Macmillan, 1980.

Guisnel, Jean. *Les généraux: Enquête sur le pouvoir militaire en France*. Paris: Editions la Découverte, 1990.

Guyard, Jacques. *Le miracle français*. Paris: Editions du Seuil, 1965.

Haas, Ernst B. *Beyond the Nation State*. Stanford, Calif.: Stanford University Press, 1964.

Hall, Peter. *Governing the Economy: The Politics of State Intervention in Britain and France*. Oxford: Oxford University Press, 1986.

Harrison, Michael M. *The Reluctant Ally: France and Atlantic Security*. Baltimore, Md.: Johns Hopkins University Press, 1981.

Hernu, Charles. *Soldat citoyen: Essai sur la défense et la sécurité*. Paris: Flammarion, 1975.

Hoffmann, Stanley. *Decline or Renewal? France since the 1930s*. New York: Viking Press, 1974.

Hoffmann, Stanley, Charles P. Kindelberger, Lawrence Wiley, Jesse R. Pitts, Jean-Baptiste Duroselle, and François Goguel. *In Search of France: The Economy, Society, and Political System in the Twentieth Century*. New York: Harper and Row, 1963.

Hunt, Kenneth. *NATO without France: The Military Implications*. Adelphi Paper, no. 32, London: International Institute for Strategic Studies, 1966.

International Institute for Strategic Studies. *The Military Balance* (annual series). London: International Institute for Strategic Studies.

————. *Strategic Survey* (annual series). London: Author.

Kaiser, Karl, and Pierre Lellouche, eds. *Le couple franco-allemand et la défense de l'Europe*. Paris: Institut Français de Relations Internationales, 1986.

Kennedy, Paul. *The Rise and Fall of the Great Powers: Economic Change and Military Conflict from 1500 to 2000*. New York: Random House, 1987.

Kissinger, Henry A. *The Troubled Partnership: A Re-appraisal of the Atlantic Alliance*. New York: Anchor Books, 1966.

Kohl, Wilfred L. *French Nuclear Diplomacy*. Princeton, N.J.: Princeton University Press, 1971.

Kolodziej, Edward A. *French International Policy under de Gaulle and Pompidou*. Ithaca, N.Y.: Cornell University Press, 1974.

————. *Making and Marketing Arms: The French Experience and Its Implications for the International System*. Princeton, N.J.: Princeton University Press, 1987.

Krauss, Melvyn. *How NATO Weakens the West*. New York: Simon and Schuster, 1986.

Krop, Pascal. *Les socialistes et l'armée*. Paris: Presses Universitaires de France, 1983.

Lacouture, Jean. *De Gaulle*. 3 vols. Paris: Editions du Seuil, 1984–1986.

Lacouture, Jean, and Roland Mehl, eds. *De Gaulle ou l'éternel défi*. Paris: Editions du Seuil, 1988.

La Gorce, Paul-Marie de. *The French Army: A Military-Political History*. Trans. by Kenneth Douglas. New York: Georges Braziller, 1963.

Laird, Robbin F. *France, the Soviet Union, and the Nuclear Weapons Issue*. Boulder, Colo.: Westview Press, 1985.

————, ed. *French Security Policy: From Independence to Interdependence*. Boulder, Colo.: Westview Press, 1986.

Lauber, Volkmar. *The Political Economy of France: From Pompidou to Mitterrand*. New York: Frederick A. Praeger, 1983.

Lellouche, Pierre. *L'avenir de la guerre*. Paris: Mazarine, 1985.

Luttwak, Edward. *The Strategic Balance: 1972.* Washington Papers, no. 3. New York: Library Press, 1972.

McCarthy, Patrick, ed. *The French Socialists in Power, 1981–1986.* New York: Greenwood Press, 1987.

Maillard, Pierre. *De Gaulle et l'Allemagne: Le rêve inachevé.* Paris: Plon, 1990.

Marcus, John T. *Neutralism and Nationalism in France: A Case Study.* New York: Bookman Associates, 1958.

Martin, Michel. *From Warriors to Managers: The French Military Establishment since 1945.* Chapel Hill: University of North Carolina Press, 1981.

Massip, Roger. *De Gaulle et l'Europe.* Paris: Flammarion, 1963.

Mendl, Wolf. *Deterrence and Persuasion: French Nuclear Armament in the Context of National Policy, 1945–1969.* (London: Faber and Faber, 1970).

Mitterrand, François. *Le coup d'état permanent.* Paris: Plon, 1965.

———. *Ici et maintenant.* Paris: Fayard, 1980.

———. *Lettre à tous les Français.* Document distributed as supplement to many French newspapers, April 7, 1988.

———. *Reflexions sur la politique extérieure: Introduction à vingt-cinq discours (1981–1985).* Paris: Fayard, 1986.

Morse, Edward L. *Foreign Policy and Interdependence in Gaullist France.* Princeton, N.J.: Princeton University Press, 1972.

Nay, Catherine. *Le noir et le rouge.* Paris: Grasset, 1984.

———. *Les sept Mitterrand ou les métamorphoses d'un septennat.* Paris: Grasset, 1988.

Newhouse, John. *De Gaulle and the Anglo-Saxons.* New York: Viking Press, 1970.

North Atlantic Treaty Organization. *NATO and the Warsaw Pact: Force Comparisons.* Brussels: NATO Information Service, 1984.

Parti Socialiste. *Changer la vie: Programme de gouvernement du parti socialiste.* Paris: Flammarion, 1972.

———. *Pour la France de années 80.* Paris: Club Socialiste du Livre, 1980.

———. *La sécurité et l'Europe.* Paris: Parti Socialiste, June 1985.

Parti Socialiste, Parti Communiste, Mouvement des Radicaux de Gauche. *Programme commun de gouvernement.* Paris: Flammarion, 1973.

Passeron, André. *De Gaulle parle.* Vol. 1, *Des institutions, de l'Algérie, de l'armée, des affaires étrangères, de la communauté, de l'économie et des questions sociales.* Paris: Plon, 1962.

———. *De Gaulle parle.* Vol. 2. Paris: Plon, 1967.

Pognon, Edmond. *De Gaulle et l'histoire de France.* Paris: Albin Michel, 1970.

Poirier, Lucien. *Des stratégies nucléaires.* Paris: Hachette, 1977.

———. *Essais de stratégie théorique.* Paris: Fondation Pour les Etudes de Défense Nationale, 1982.

Posner, Theodore Robert. *Current French Security Policy: The Gaullist Legacy.* Westport, Conn.: Greenwood, 1991.

Rassemblement pour la République. *La défense de la France: 4 ans de gestion socialiste. Propositions pour le renouveau.* Paris: RPR, 1985.

———. *Réflexions sur la défense.* Presented by Michel Aurillac. Paris: RPR, 1980.

Rémond, René. *Les droites en France.* Paris: Aubier, 1982.

———. *Notre siècle: 1918–1988.* Paris: Fayard, 1988.

Révél, Jean-François. *Le style du général: Précédé de la légende vivante au mythe posthume.* Paris: Editions Complexe, 1988.

Rioux, Jean-Pierre. *La France de la Quatrième République.* 2 vols. Paris: Editions du Seuil, 1980.

Rocard, Michel. *Europe and the United States.* Critical Issues no. 2. Leffingwell Lecture Series at the Council on Foreign Relations in New York. New York: Council on Foreign Relations Press, 1992.

Rosecrance, Richard, ed. *America as an Ordinary Country.* Ithaca, N.Y.: Cornell University Press, 1976.

Ross, George, Stanley Hoffmann, and Sylvia Malzacher, eds. *The Mitterrand Experiment: Continuity and Change in Modern France.* New York: Oxford University Press, 1987.

Rudelle, Odile. *Mai 1958: La République.* Paris: Institut Charles de Gaulle, 1988.

Ruehl, Lothar. *La politique militaire de la Ve République.* Paris: Presses de la Fondation Nationale des Sciences Politiques, 1976.

Ruiz-Palmer, Diego A. *French Strategic Options in the 1990s.* Adelphi Paper no. 260 (Summer 1991). London: International Institute for Strategic Studies.

Sanguinetti, Alexandre. *La France et l'arme atomique.* Paris: René Julliard, 1964.

Schuman, Robert. *Pour l'Europe.* Paris: Editions Nagel, 1964.

Schwartz, David N. *NATO's Nuclear Dilemmas.* Washington, D.C.: Brookings Institution, 1983.

Snyder, Glenn. *Deterrence and Defense.* Princeton, N.J.: Princeton University Press, 1961.

Solzhenitsyn, Alexander. *The Gulag Archipelago* (New York: Harper and Row, 1974).

Touchard, Jean. *Le gaullisme: 1940–1969.* Paris: Editions du Seuil, 1978.

Tourrain, Raymond. *De la défense de la France à la défense de l'Europe.* Paris: 1987.

Toynbee, Arnold, J. *A Study of History.* London: Oxford University Press, 1940.

Ullman, Richard H. *Securing Europe.* Princeton, N.J.: Princeton University Press, 1991.

Union pour la Démocratie Française. *Une doctrine de défense pour la France.* Presented by Jean-Marie Daillet. Paris: UDF, 1980.

———. *Redresser la défense de la France.* Paris: UDF, 1985.

Université de Franche-Comté and Institut Charles de Gaulle. *L'aventure de la bombe: De Gaulle et la dissuasion nucléaire, 1958–1969.* Paris: Plon, 1985.

Valentin, François. *Une politique de défense pour la France.* Paris: Calmann-Lévy, 1980.

Viansson-Ponté, Pierre. *Histoire de la République gaullienne: Mai 1958–avril 1969.* Paris: Robert Laffont, 1984 (first published in 1971).

Werth, Alexander. *De Gaulle.* Baltimore, Md.: Penguin Books, 1967.

Willis, F. Roy. *France, Germany and the New Europe, 1945–1967.* Rev. ed. New York: Oxford University Press, 1968.

Yost, David S. *France and Conventional Defense in Central Europe.* Boulder, Colo.: Westview Press, 1985.

Yost, David S. *France's Deterrent Posture and Security in Europe*. Adelphi Papers no. 194, 195. London: International Institute for Strategic Studies, 1984.

Articles, Papers, and Speeches

Adrets, André [pseud.]. "Les relations franco-allemands et le fait nucléaire dans une Europe divisée." *Politique étrangère*, no. 3 (Fall 1984): 649–64.

Ailleret, General Charles. "'Défense dirigée' ou défense tous 'azimuts.' " *Revue de défense nationale* 23 (December 1967): 1,923–27.

―――. "Defense in All Directions." *Atlantic Community Quarterly* (Spring 1968): 17–25.

―――. "Evolution nécessaire de nos structures militaires." *Revue de défense nationale* 21 (June 1965): 947–55.

―――. "Opinion sur la théorie stratégique de la 'flexible response'." *Revue de défense nationale* 20 (August 1964): 1,323–40.

Armes, Keith. "France: The Defense Debate." *Atlantic Community Quarterly* 24, no. 4 (Winter 1986–1987): 278–85.

Aron, Raymond. "French Public Opinion and the Atlantic Treaty." *International Affairs* no. 1 (January 1952): 1–8.

Bairoch, Paul. "Europe's Gross National Product: 1800–1975." *Journal of European Economic History* 5 (1976): 273–340.

Barre, Raymond. "Foundations for European Security and Co-operation." *Survival* (July–August 1987): 291–301.

―――. "La politique de défense de la France." Discours de M. Raymond Barre, premier ministre, à la séance inaugurale de la 33ᵉ session nationale de l'Institut des Hautes Etudes de Défense Nationale, Paris, le 11 septembre 1980. *Défense nationale* 36 (October 1980): 9–19.

―――. "Speech by Prime Minister Barre." *Survival* (September–October 1977): 225–28.

Beaufre, André. "Le problème du partage des responsibilities nucléaires." *Stratégie* no. 5 (July–September 1965): 7–20.

―――. "The Sharing of Nuclear Responsibilities: A Problem in Need of a Solution." *International Affairs* 31, no. 3 (July 1965): 416.

―――. "Stratégie de dissuasion et stratégie de guerre." *Revue de défense nationale* 18 (May 1962): 761–68.

Bourges, Yvon. "Speech by Yvon Bourges." *Survival* 22, no. 1 (January–February 1980): 39–40.

Bozo, Frédéric. "La France et l'Otan: Vers une nouvelle alliance." *Défense nationale* 47 (January 1991): 19–34.

―――. "Paradigm Lost: The French Experience with Détente." In Richard Davy, ed., *European Détente: A Reappraisal*. London: Royal Institute of International Affairs (1991).

Bundy McGeorge, George F. Kennan, Robert S. McNamara, and Gerard Smith. "Nuclear Weapons and the Atlantic Alliance." *Foreign Affairs* 60, no. 4 (Spring 1982): 753–68.

Capillon, Bernard. "L'armée de l'air d'hier à aujourd'hui: Le fait aérien, une nouvelle dimension de la défense." *Défense nationale* 41 (June 1985): 23–30.

Chevènement, Jean-Pierre. "La France et la sécurité de l'Europe."*Politique étrangère* (Fall 1990): 525–32.

Chirac, Jacques. "Au sujet des armes nucléaires tactiques françaises." *Défense nationale* 31 (May 1975): 11–15.

———. "La France et les enjeux de la sécurité européenne." Allocution du Premier Ministre le 12 décembre 1987, devant les auditeurs de l'Institut des Hautes Etudes de Défense nationale. *Défense nationale* 44 (February 1988): 9–18.

———. "La politique de défense de la France." Allocution du premier ministre le 12 septembre 1986, lors de la séance d'ouverture de la 39ᵉ session de l'Institut des Hautes Etudes de Défense Nationale. *Défense nationale* 42 (November 1986): 7–17.

———. "Pour une nouvelle loi de programmation militaire, *Lettre de Matignon* no. 196 (Paris: Service d'Information et de Diffusion, August 4, 1986): 2–4.

———. "Principes et moyens de la politique de défense de la France." Allocution de M. Jacques Chirac à l'Institut des Hautes Etudes de Défense Nationale. *Défense nationale* 31 (November 1975): 7–26.

Conseils-Sondages-Analyses. "Les Français et les dépenses militaires," sondage des 22 et 23 novembre 1988." Paris: CSA, November 1988.

Debré, Michel. "La France et sa défense." *Revue de défense nationale* 28, no. 1 (January 1972): 5–21.

———. "France's Global Strategy." *Foreign Affairs* 49, no. 3 (April 1971): 395–406.

———. "La politique nationale de défense." *Revue de défense nationale* 26, no. 12 (December 1970): 1,767–84.

DePorte, Anton W. "De Gaulle's Europe: Playing the Russian Card." *French Politics and Society* (Fall 1990): 25–40.

———. "France's New Realism." *Foreign Affairs* 63, no. 1 (Fall 1984): 144–65.

de Rose, François. "La crise des stratégies." *Défense nationale* 46, no. 5 (May 1990): 61–71.

———. "La défense de la France et la défense de l'Europe." *Défense nationale* 38 (December 1982): 71–79.

———. "Inflexible Response." *Foreign Affairs* 61, no. 1 (Fall 1982): 136–50.

———. "La politique de défense du Président Giscard d'Estaing." In Samy Cohen and Marie-Claude Smouts, eds., *La politique extérieure de Valéry Giscard d'Estaing*. Paris: Presses de la Fondation Nationale des Sciences Politiques, 1985.

Dumoulin, André. "Les forces multinationales." *Défense nationale* 47 (August–September 1991): 67–85.

Duroselle, Jean-Baptiste. "The Crisis in French Foreign Policy."*Review of Politics* 16, no. 4 (October 1954): 412–37.

Fillon, François. "Défense européenne: La coopération politique." *Défense nationale* 45 (May 1989): 11–22.

———. "D'un anniversaire à l'autre." *Politique étrangère*, no. 4 (1988): 831–39.

———. "Sécurité et défense: Quel avenir pour la France et l'Europe? *Relations internationales et stratégiques* no. 3 (1991): 21–32.

Forget, Michel. "Le changement dans la troisième dimension." *Défense nationale* 41 (June 1985): 31–40.

Fourquet, General Michel. "Emploi des différents systèmes de forces dans le cadre de la stratégie de dissuasion." *Revue de défense nationale* 25 (May 1969): 757–67.

———. "The Role of the Forces." *Survival* 11, no. 7 (July 1969): 206–11.

Fricaud-Chagnaud, Georges. "L'armée de terre face à ses missions en Europe." *Défense nationale* 39 (May 1983): 35–44.

Fritsch-Bournazel, Renata. "France: Attachment to a Nonbinding Relationship." In Gregory Flynn and Hans Rattinger, eds., *The Public and Atlantic Defense*. London: Croom Helm, 1985.

Gallois, Pierre. "Les conséquences stratégiques et politiques des armes nouvelles." *Politique étrangère*, no. 2 (1958): 1667–80.

———. "French Defense Planning: The Future in the Past." *International Security* 1, no. 2 (Fall 1976): 16–31.

———. "The Raison d'Etre of French Defense Policy."*International Affairs* (October 1963): 497–510.

———. "U.S. Strategy and the Defense of Europe." *Orbis* 8 (Summer 1963): 226–49.

Giraud, André. "Construction européenne et défense." *Politique étrangère* 3 (Fall 1990): 513–24.

———. "La défense de la France et la sécurité européenne."*Défense nationale* 44 (May 1988): 11–19.

———. "Donner à la France une défense forte." Discours de Monsieur André Giraud, Ministre de la Défense, à l'Assemblée Nationale le 12 Novembre 1986 à l'occasion de la présentation du budget de la défense pour 1987. *Défense nationale* 43 (January 1987): 11–25.

Giscard d'Estaing, Valéry. "Allocution de M. Valéry Giscard d'Estaing, Président de la République, à l'occasion de sa visite à l'Institut des Hautes Etudes de Défense Nationale." (Paris, June 1, 1975) *Défense nationale* 32 (July 1976): 5–20.

Gnesotto, Nicole. "France and the New Europe." In David P. Calleo and Philip H. Gordon, eds. *From the Atlantic to the Urals: National Perspectives on the New Europe* (Washington, D.C.: Seven Locks' Press, 1992), pp. 127–40.

Godard, Jean. "L'Aide américaine à la France." *Revue de science financière* 17, no. 3 (July–September 1956).

Gombin, Richard. "Le Parti socialiste et la politique étrangère." *Politique étrangère*, no. 2 (1977): 835–48.

Gordon, Philip H. "Charles de Gaulle and the Nuclear Revolution." Paper presented to Nuclear History Program Conference "Nuclear Weapons and Cold War Statesmen," Athens, Ohio, September 19, 1991 (forthcoming).

———. "France and European Security After the INF Treaty." *SAIS Review* 8, no. 2 (Summer–Fall 1988): 191–209.

Harrison, Michael M. "Foreign and Security Policy." In Patrick McCarthy, ed., *The French Socialists in Power, 1981–1986*, New York: Greenwood Press, 1987, pp. 45–60.

———. "Mitterrand's France in the Atlantic System." *Political Science Quarterly* 99, no. 2 (Summer 1984): 219–46.

———. "A Socialist Foreign Policy for France?" *Orbis* 21, no. 4 (Winter 1976): 1,471–98.

Hassner, Pierre. "Un chef d'oeuvre en péril: Le consensus français sur la défense." *Esprit* (March–April 1988): 71–82.

———. "France and the Soviet Union." In Michael Mandelbaum, ed., *Western Approaches to the Soviet Union*, New York: Council on Foreign Relations, 1988, pp. 25–49.

———. "Vers l'Est du nouveau?" *Esprit* (March–April 1989): 108–16.

Heisbourg, François. "Défense française: L'impossible status quo." *Politique internationale* 36 (Summer 1987): 137–53.

———. "Défense française: La quadrature du cercle." *Politique internationale* 53 (Fall 1991): 257–74.

Herz, John H. "The Rise and Demise of the Territorial State."*World Politics* 9 (July 1957): 473–94.

Hoffmann, Stanley. "De Gaulle, Europe, and the Atlantic Alliance." *International Organization* 18 (Winter 1964): 1–28.

———. "The European Community and 1992." *Foreign Affairs* 68, no. 4 (Fall 1989): 27–47.

———. "La France dans le nouvel ordre européen." *Politique étrangère* (Fall 1990): 503–12.

———. "Mitterrand's Foreign Policy, or Gaullism by any Other Name." In George Ross, Stanley Hoffmann and Sylvia Malzacher, eds., *The Mitterrand Experiment: Continuity and Change in Modern France*. New York: Oxford University Press, 1987.

Howorth, Jolyon. "Consensus of Silence: The French Socialist Party and Defense under François Mitterrand." *International Affairs* 60, no. 4 (Autumn 1984): 579–600.

Jones, Erik. "French Defense since Cohabitation: Consensus and Military Planning for 1990–1993." Topical Papers no. 2, Université Libre de Bruxelles (July 1989).

Joxe, Pierre. "Défense et Renseignement." Discours de Monsieur Pierre Joxe, ministre de la défense, le 6 mai 1991, devant les auditeurs de l'Institut des Hautes Etudes de Défense Nationale. *Défense nationale* 47 (July 1991): 9–21.

Kaiser, Karl, Georg Leber, Alois Mertes, and Franz-Josef Schulze. "Nuclear Weapons and the Preservation of Peace." *Foreign Affairs* 60, no. 5 (Summer 1982): 1,157–70.

Klein, Jean. "France, NATO and European Security." *International Security* (Winter 1977): 21–41.

Klein, Jean, and Jacques Vernant. "Indépendance nationale et défense." *Paradoxes*, no. 39 (April–May 1980).

Kolodziej, Edward A. "French Security Policy: Decisions and Dilemmas." *Armed Forces and Society* 8 (Winter 1982): 185–221.

Komer, Robert W. "Is Conventional Defense of Europe Feasible?" *Naval War College Review* 35 (September–October, 1982): 80–91.

Lacaze, Jeannou. "L'avenir de la défense française." Conférence du chef d'etat-major des armées à l'Institut des Hautes Etudes de Défense Nationale le 11 mai 1985. *Défense nationale* 41 (July 1985): 15–33.

———. "Politique de défense et stratégie militaire de la France." Exposé du chef d'etat-major des armées devant l'Institut des Hautes Etudes de la Défense Nationale, le 3 mai 1983. *Défense nationale* 39 (June 1983): 11–28.

Lacaze, Jeannou. "La politique militaire." Exposé du chef d'etat-major des armées au Centre des Hautes Etudes de l'Armement, le mardi 29 septembre 1981. *Défense nationale* 37 (November 1981): 7–26.

Laird, Robbin F. "France Nuclear Forces in the 1980s and 1990s." *Comparative Strategy* 4, no. 4 (1984): 387–412.

Leenhart, Admiral Yves. "Réflexions pour une stratégie navale d'avenir." *Défense nationale* 41 (August–September, 1985): 11–34.

Lellouche, Pierre. "L'après-Washington." *Politique étrangère*, no. 1 (1988): 153–67.

———. "France and the Euromissiles: The Limits of Immunity." *Foreign Affairs* 62, no. 2 (Winter 1983–1984): 318–34.

"Loi de programme d'équipement militaire 1987–1991." *Armées d'aujourd'hui*, no. 116 (December 1986–January 1987): 12–15.

McCarthy, Patrick. "France Faces Reality: *Rigueur* and the Germans." In David P. Calleo and Claudia Morgenstern, eds. *Recasting Europe's Economies: National Strategies in the 1980s.* (Lanham, Md.: University Press of America, 1990), pp. 25–78.

McNamara, Robert S. "Statement," in United States Department of Defense, *The Fiscal Year 1969–73 Defense Program and the 1969 Defense Budget.* Washington D.C.: U.S. Government Printing Office, 1968.

Maurin, General François. "L'originalité française et le commandement." *Défense nationale* 45 (July 1989): 45–57.

Mauroy, Pierre. "Vers un nouveau modèle d'armée." *Défense nationale* 38 (November 1982): 9–28.

Méry, Guy. "Comments by General Guy Méry, March 15, 1976." *Survival* 18, no. 5 (September–October): 226–30.

———."Défense de la France et Défense de l'Europe." *Défense nationale* 39 (January 1983): 7–25.

———. "Réflexion sur le concept d'emploi des forces." *Défense nationale* 31 (November 1975): 15–26.

———. "Une armée pour quoi faire et comment?" *Défense nationale* 32 (June 1976): 11–24.

Mesmin, Georges. "1986: L'année des choix décisifs pour la défense." *Défense nationale* 42 (April 1986): 49–65.

Messmer, Pierre. "L'armée de demain." *Revue des deux mondes* (February 1962): 481–93.

———. "The Atom, Cause and Means of an Autonomous Military Policy." *Atlantic Community Quarterly* 4, no. 2 (Summer 1968): 270–77.

———. "Notre politique militaire." *Revue de défense nationale* 19 (May 1963): 745–61.

Moïsi, Dominique. "French Foreign Policy: The Challenge of Adaptation." *Foreign Affairs* 67, no. 1 (Fall 1988): 151–64.

Pierre, Andrew, J. "Enhancing Conventional Defenses: A Question of Priorities." In Andrew J. Pierre, ed., *The Conventional Defense of Western Europe: New*

Technologies and New Strategies. New York: Council on Foreign Relations, 1986.

Planchais, Jean. "Le tournant de 1958." *Pouvoirs* no. 38 (1986): 5–12.

Poirier, Lucien. "Dissuasion et puissance moyenne." *Revue de défense nationale* 28 (March 1972): 356–81.

———. "La greffe." *Défense nationale* 39 (April 1983): 5–32.

———. "Quelques problèmes actuels de la stratégie nucléaire française." *Défense nationale* 35 (December 1979): 43–62.

Renouveau Défense. "Le défi du double zéro." *Défense nationale* 44 (February 1988): 19–37.

Rocard, Michel. Allocution de M. Michel Rocard, premier ministre à la première session européenne de l'Institut des Hautes Etudes de Défense Nationale, le 15 novembre 1988. *Défense nationale* 45 (January 1989): 13–25.

———. "La France et l'ordre international." Discours de Monsieur Michel Rocard, Premier Ministre, le 22 Octobre 1990, Devant les Auditeurs de l'Institut des Hautes Etudes de Défense Nationale. *Défense nationale* 46 (December 1990): 9–21.

Rogers, General Bernard. "The Atlantic Alliance: Prescriptions for a Difficult Decade," *Foreign Affairs* 60, no. 5 (Summer 1982): 1,145–56.

Rudney, Robert. "Mitterrand's New Atlanticism: Evolving French Attitudes toward NATO." *Orbis* 28, no. 1 (Spring 1984): 83–101.

Ruiz-Palmer, Diego. "Between the Rhine and the Elbe: France and the Conventional Defense of Central Europe." *Comparative Strategy* 6, no. 4 (1987): 471–512.

Société Française d'Enquêtes et de Sondages. "Les Français et les problèmes de la politique extérieure." Paris: SOFRES, April 1987.

Tiberghien, Frédéric. "L'effort de défense depuis 1981." *Défense nationale* 41 (November 1985): 31–70.

Ullman, Richard H. "The Covert French Connection." *Foreign Policy*, no. 75 (Summer 1989): 3–33.

Vaillant, Gérard. "Défense en France." *Défense nationale* 32 (July 1976): 146–48.

Valentin, General François. "L'arête étroite." *Défense nationale* 39 (May 1983): 45–56.

———. "Quelle défense pour quelle Europe?" *Politique étrangère* (Fall 1990): 533–42.

Vennesson, Pascal. "Une année charnière pour les forces armées," in Dominique Chagnollaud, ed., *Etat politique de la France, année 1991*. Paris: Quai Voltaire, 1992, pp. 147–53.

Wells, Samuel Jr. "Mitterrand's International Policies." *The Washington Quarterly* 11, no. 3 (Summer 1988): 59–75.

Yost, David S. "France and West European Defence Identity." *Survival* 33, no. 4 (July–August 1991): 327–51.

———. "France in the New Europe." *Foreign Affairs* 69, no. 5 (Winter 1990–1991): 107–28.

———. "Franco-German Defense Cooperation." *Washington Quarterly* 11, no. 2 (Spring 1988): 173–95.

Yost, David S. "French Defense Budgeting: Executive Dominance and Resource Constraints." *Orbis* 23, no. 3 (Fall 1979): 579–608.

———. "The French Defense Debate." *Survival* 23 (January–February 1981): 19–27.

———. "Radical Change in French Defense Policy?" *Survival* (January–February 1986): 53–68.

———. "The Reykjavik Summit and European Security." *SAIS Review* 7, no. 2 (Summer–Fall 1987): 1–22.

Index